FROM THIS DAY FORWARD

ALSO BY COKIE ROBERTS

We Are Our Mothers' Daughters

ALSO BY STEVEN V. ROBERTS

Eureka!

FROM THIS DAY FORWARD

COKIE *and* STEVE

ROBERTS

Perennial
An Imprint of HarperCollins*Publishers*

A hardcover edition of this book was published in 2000 by William Morrow and Company.

FROM THIS DAY FORWARD. Copyright © 2000, 2001 by Cokie and Steven V. Roberts. All rights reserved. Printed in the United States of America. No part of this book may be used or reproduced in any manner whatsoever without written permission except in the case of brief quotations embodied in critical articles and reviews. For information address HarperCollins Publishers Inc., 10 East 53rd Street, New York, NY 10022.

HarperCollins books may be purchased for educational, business, or sales promotional use. For information please write: Special Markets Department, HarperCollins Publishers Inc., 10 East 53rd Street, New York, NY 10022.

First Perennial edition published 2001.

Designed by Debbie Glasserman

Library of Congress Cataloging-in-Publication Data is available.

ISBN 0-06-095954-1

01 02 03 04 05   ❖/RRD   10 9 8 7 6 5 4 3 2 1

TO OUR PARENTS
Lindy and Hale Boggs
Dorothy and Will Roberts

AND OUR CHILDREN
Liza and Lee Roberts
Rebecca Roberts and Dan Hartman

Acknowledgments

———∞∞∞———

When we sat down to write a whole book together about marriage, it was with some trepidation. We'd written together for years, but never undertaken a project this big or this personal. So only half-jokingly we agreed that we would give back the publisher's advance if the book started to endanger the relationship. In reality, it was surprisingly smooth sailing, mainly because we had a lot of help along the way. Some wonderful people aided us in the actual writing of the book—our editor, Claire Wachtel, came up with the idea of a joint effort and guided us through it, nobly assisted by the industrious and delightful Jennifer Pooley. Ann Charnley, a friend of many decades, provided invaluable historical research; Colleen Connors, a former student of Steve's, shepherded us through the telling of our own story and brought her estimable daughter, Molly Rose Opinsky, along to entertain us; Jan Vulevich, who keeps track of our lives, transcribed and transmitted all of this material, while giving us a running review. Mike Silverstein at ABC Radio first told us the story of Lilly Friedman, and Suzy Snyder at the Holocaust Museum filled in some details. Jane Friedman and Cathy Hemming welcomed us warmly to HarperCollins, and Laura Leonard's telling the world about this book, along with our colleague Su Lin Nichols at ABC News.

Taking on a project like this meant that we had to ask our friends at work for consideration and understanding, and they provided both in abundance. Robin Sproul, the bureau chief, and everyone else at ABC News in Washington, especially the folks who work with Cokie at *This Week* and with Steve at ABC Radio, have been cheerleaders and handholders. We'd also like to thank Steve's colleagues at George Washington University, particularly Jean Folkerts, director of the School of Media and Public Affairs, and his producers at CNN's *Late Edition,* PBS's *Washington Week in Review,* and NPR's *The Diane Rehm Show.* Cokie's colleagues at National Public Radio, especially Ellen McDonnell, executive producer of *Morning Edition,* have been thoughtful and supportive as always. In our joint enterprises, Bob Laird, op-ed-page editor at the New York *Daily News,* Marcia Bullard, publisher of *USA Weekend,* and the people at United Media encouraged us along the way. Our dear friend Bob Barnett, lawyer extraordinaire, can always be counted on for good advice, and Kim Roellig keeps body and soul together for us on the homefront. We'd also like to say thanks to the Workman family of Charlotte, North Carolina. Their house at Pawleys Island, South Carolina, has been a place of renewal and refreshment for more than twenty years and it's where we started writing this book. A final word of gratitude to all the "old marrieds"—particularly our moviegoing and beach-walking buddies, Linda and Fred Wertheimer—who continue to inspire us with their devotion to each other.

Contents

Introduction

———— ∞∞∞ ————

This is a book of stories about marriage, not sermons or sociology. We deliberately focus on American marriages, our own and others', because marriage in this country is a rather peculiar institution. You might even say it's un-American. After all, the Founding Fathers made it clear that individuals—not couples or groups or communities—have an "inalienable right to life, liberty and the pursuit of happiness." But by definition, marriage is a partnership, not an individual enterprise. Married couples have to pursue happiness together, not as separate entities. And the essence of any successful marriage is self-sacrifice, not self-absorption. A friend recently told us about a twenty-fifth-anniversary party where the husband gave a toast and said, "The key to our success is very simple. Within minutes after every fight, one of us says, 'I'm sorry, Sally.' " Good line, but it's also true that what you don't say in a marriage can be as important as what you do say. We often joke that the success of a marriage can be measured by the number of teeth marks in your tongue. Keeping quiet in the first place means you don't have to say "I'm sorry" quite so often.

Since America is a nation that constantly reinvents itself, the institution of marriage is always changing and adapting as well. We write about John and Abigail Adams, keeping their union together over long periods of separation and anxiety; slaves who defied the indignity of bondage to dignify their own vows to each other; immigrants and pioneers who had to live by new rules in new places with new partners. In our own lives, we were children of the fifties, coming of age in the sixties, and living through a series of cultural aftershocks, from birth control and the Beatles to the rise of feminism and the decline of civility. As a result, concludes the National Marriage Project at Rutgers University, when young couples marry today, "they are entering a union that looks very different from the one that their parents or grandparents entered." True enough, and here are some of the reasons:

- Divorce is much more common. If current trends hold steady, almost half of all contemporary marriages will not survive. And the "divorce revolution," which picked up steam in the early sixties and reached a peak around 1980, is now into its second generation. Young people today are much more likely to be the products of a failed marriage than their parents or grandparents ever were.

- Marriage is no longer a rite of passage for most Americans, the moment when they leave home and become adults. The mean age at marriage has jumped sharply since 1960—from twenty to twenty-five for women and from twenty-three to twenty-seven for men—so most newlyweds have been out working and supporting themselves for some time. They are also having sex earlier—more than half of all women lose their virginity by age seventeen—so the average bride has been sexually active for seven or eight years before her first marriage. Indeed, notes the National Marriage Project, the term "premarital sex" has lost its meaning, because sexual activity is no longer tied in most cases to the "promise or expectation of marriage."

• The sexual revolution has helped fuel a 1,000 percent increase since 1960 in the number of unmarried couples living together. By one estimate, about one out of four single women between the ages of twenty-five and thirty-nine is now living with a partner, and about half have done so at some point. But to call these living arrangements a "trial marriage" strikes us as profoundly wrong. The whole point about marriage is making a permanent commitment to each other, and any relationship lacking that commitment is not a marriage, trial or otherwise. In fact, researchers for the National Marriage Project found some evidence that couples who live together before marriage are slightly *more* likely to get divorced than those who don't cohabit.

• Americans will spend a smaller portion of their adult lives being married. Later marriages, longer life spans, and more common cohabitation all play a part. So does the easy availability of sex outside of marriage. The current college culture has spawned the term "friends with privileges," which basically means, "we sleep together but aren't really a couple." Add in another important trend: more people are remaining single permanently. Going back to the mid-1800s, well over 90 percent of American women married by age forty-five. If current rates continue, that figure could drop below 85 percent.

• Mobility has always been a fact of American life and marriage, but it's getting more pronounced. Steve grew up in Bayonne, New Jersey, with one grandfather in the house and two other grandparents a few blocks away. Cokie's grandmother lived with her family a good part of the time and the Boggs house in New Orleans was next door to a great-aunt.

Today our own children live in San Francisco and London, and most of our adult nieces and nephews don't live anywhere near their parents. Young marrieds are often far from home, and while we know the advantages of that experience, we also know how painful it can be. And when a marriage hits a rough patch, the absence of a supportive community can be devastating. A friend of ours, reflecting on his grandparents' sixty-five-year marriage said, "When they got married it was a package deal. You bought into the whole family network. Divorce was inconceivable, because you had to divorce *all* of those people."

• Feminism has had an enormous impact on marriage. Women are far less dependent on a husband for financial support or sexual gratification. Moreover, adds the Marriage Project, women have "higher expectations for emotional intimacy in marriage and more exacting standards for a husband's participation in child rearing and the overall work of the household." Thus a paradox: women have less need of marriage just as they expect more from the relationship. But just because women *need* marriage less does not mean they *want* it less. Many of our single female friends, all accomplished and independent women, would still prefer the support and companionship of a committed mate.

• Marriage has been devalued and even defamed by the popular culture, according to some scholars in the field. One of them, Professor Leon R. Kass of the University of Chicago, argues that most young people today "lack a cultural script whose denouement is marriage." As a result, "for the great majority, the way to the altar is uncharted territory. It's every couple on its own bottom, without a compass, often without a goal. Those who reach the altar seem to have stumbled on it by accident."

But we do not despair about the future of marriage. Our parents were married for a combined total of more than ninety years, and we see strong unions of old friends all around us. Our children seem to attend a wedding every few weeks. We are also heartened by the number of young people who come to us for conversation and counsel, wanting eagerly to make their relationships work. One of them, an Italian-Catholic woman, wrote recently to announce she was marrying her Jewish boyfriend. It took them three years and a lot of heartache. They didn't "stumble" on the altar "by accident"; they made it there because marriage meant so much to them.

For all of its many problems, marriage is also showing other signs of health. While the divorce rate is still at historically high levels, it's leveled off in recent years and even seems to be declining a bit. Moreover, a wide variety of forces are mobilizing to bolster the institution. A group of therapists and counselors has started a movement devoted to teaching couples the practical skills that seem to be present in most enduring matches. One of the founders, Diane Sollee, voices the hope "that in the near future, couples will come to accept that the most romantic thing they can do is walk hand in hand into a course on making marriages work." A similar effort, Marriage Savers, urges pastors to require several months of counseling for any young couple wanting to get married. And after the ceremony, older couples in the congregation are assigned as sort of marriage mentors to the newlyweds. In one widely watched experiment, Florida has become the first state to mandate marriage education courses as a high-school graduation requirement. Louisiana has passed a law enabling couples to enter a "covenant" marriage, which makes divorce a lot harder.

We do have a prejudice. We're big fans of marriage and don't apologize for that. We have always agreed with the author Judith Viorst, who once wrote a book called *Married*

Is Better. Not better for everyone, to be sure, but for most people. And we believe strongly that a devoted marriage can be reconciled with individual growth and development. Marriage has enlarged our lives, not encircled them; it has opened new doors, not closed them. We are better people together than we are separately.

But let's be honest. We quote a young woman in this book as saying marriage "just scares me," and she has a right to feel that way. Marriage is serious business and hard work. It's not just becoming roommates, it's becoming soul mates; it's not just signing a license, it's sharing a life. That explains our title. The words in the marriage ceremony "from this day forward" *are* scary. At the moment a couple exchange those vows, they can never know what they really mean, what hills and valleys stretch out in front of them in the years ahead. But if you take the words seriously, there's no going back. There's only the future, unlimited and unknowable, and the promise to make the journey together.

FROM THIS DAY FORWARD

Chapter One

OUR LIVES

EARLY DAYS

COURTSHIP

We are often asked how we met, usually by young people who are still wondering about this marriage thing. When do you know you've found the right person? How can you tell? The problem is summed up by Steve's twin brother, Marc, who likes to put it this way: Choosing a mate is like being told to walk through a forest and pick up the biggest stick you can find. But you only get to pick up one stick and you never know when the forest will end. In our case it was even more complicated. Since Cokie is Catholic and Steve is Jewish, the *kind* of stick each of us chose was also an issue—to ourselves and to our families. But in another sense we were following a familiar pattern, meeting and marrying young. We both have brothers who married at twenty. Like us, Cokie's parents, Hale and Lindy Boggs, met in college, where they worked on the student newspaper together. Steve's father, Will, met his bride, Dorothy, on her seventeenth birthday. And he used to look around at gatherings of his children and grandchildren, when the tribe had reached eighteen, and say with considerable pride, "See what happens when you walk a girl home from a birthday party?" Our story is not quite so romantic, but typical of our life—public and private threads woven together. Steve was nineteen, Cokie eighteen. It was the summer of 1962, between our sophomore and junior years in college, and we both were attending a student political conference at Ohio State.

CR: I saw Steven across the yard and he looked familiar to me because I knew his twin brother. And I kept thinking, Is that Marc Roberts? He doesn't quite look like Marc Roberts, but he looks a whole lot like Marc Roberts. And then I got up close to him and he had a name tag, so I said, "Are you Marc Roberts's brother?" And he said, "Yes, are you Barbara Boggs's sister?" And that's how we met.

SR: I had actually heard of Cokie all that summer. I had been recruited by one of my Harvard professors, Paul Sigmund, who was looking for student journalists to put out a newspaper at the World Youth Festival in Helsinki, Finland. I didn't know that our trip was financed by the CIA, or that Paul would later marry Cokie's sister, making us brothers-in-law as well as co-conspirators. Another recruit was Bob Kaiser, then at Yale, an old friend of the Boggs family, and in Helsinki he kept telling me about this girl he knew at Wellesley, Cokie Boggs. But Bob made a critical mistake: he stayed in Europe. I went home early for the political meeting, and since I'd heard about her from Bob, I knew who she was when I met her.

CR: But he has this picture in his mind that I was wearing a pair of charcoal-gray Bermuda shorts and I have never in my life owned a pair of charcoal-gray Bermuda shorts. It was 1962. It might have been 1932 in terms of men and women. The fact that I actually spoke at this meeting was highly unusual.

SR: But I also found that intriguing. I think from the very beginning, the fact that Cokie was so independent-minded and so forceful appealed to me. I mean, she was not the secretary sitting at the back of the room taking notes.

CR: Although really, I took quite a few.

SR: We started flirting, writing notes to each other during these endless meetings, and Cokie has actually saved some of them all these years. On a long list of people who had been nominated for national office, I scribbled on the side, "You're so efficient it hurts." She wrote back, "I'm the youngest child of an insane family—somebody had to be efficient, otherwise we'd starve!" I answered, "Be efficient, but Jeezus—don't ever get comfortable. It's such a deadly disease!" That statement probably defines the word "sophomoric," but it also shows how little I knew about myself. I was actually looking for comfort and I think she might have known that. Her final word on the "deadly disease" question was, "Would that I could ever have the opportunity to catch it!"

CR: And then we went back to school. Our dorms were only twelve and a half miles apart, we later learned, but at first he didn't call me. So I think I called him and invited him to the Junior Show. Is that what happened?

SR: That would be typical. I remember sitting in the audience, watching her sing—a symbolic way to spend our first date. I remember afterward she was wearing a bright green dress, and we went to the Howard Johnson's down in the village for something to eat.

CR: And then I came home and I'd had such a good time, such a good time, I went dancing up the stairs singing "I Feel Pretty." And then he never called.

SR: I didn't call because I was petrified. I had this rule that I didn't call a girl more than twice. I really liked her and I enjoyed the show, but I was unnerved. I was a typical guy. I was nineteen. But there were other guys from Harvard who went out to Wellesley regularly and I would hear from them, "Cokie Boggs asked after you." So we had this long-distance communication. I knew where she was. I knew where to find her.

CR: And then in March of '63 my sister was putting on a big conference in Washington on creating a domestic peace corps. Most of the schools paid for their students to stay in hotels, but Harvard didn't, so Barbara had arranged for people to stay at our parents' house if they wanted to. We were expecting a whole crowd, but in the end, it was just me and Steven.

SR: We drove down to Washington together. I remember walking up to the car in Cambridge and seeing Cokie in the backseat of the car and saying to myself, "You made a mistake by not calling her." Even before I got in the car, I knew there was something there. And the whole way down to Washington, we talked even though others were in the car.

CR: When we arrived at the house late that night, Steve had a terrible cold; he was coughing and hacking all through the night.

SR: I was staying in Cokie's girlhood room—later our daughter's room—and at some point I heard a knock on the door. Since this was 1963, I pretty much figured it wasn't Cokie. The door opened and there stood my future mother-in-law dressed in this flowing peach negligee—clouds of peach. I sat up in bed and my mouth just dropped to the floor. I had never met a woman like this in Bayonne, New Jersey. And she whispered, "Now, darling, you sound terrible, drink this." She didn't have to say "Open your mouth" because my mouth was already open! And it was some home brew, probably three-quarters bourbon, but it did the trick. The family joke is that I fell in love with my mother-in-law first and then got around to Cokie! And there's some truth to that.

We went to the conference the next day and a party that night. Bob Kaiser was there, and he was angling to take Cokie home, but since I was staying there, I had the inside track. We stayed up half the night talking in the den, and at some point Cokie made us scrambled eggs. In many ways we've been together since that night. It was clearly a turning point in terms of starting to feel connected to each other.

CR: Also during that trip, we went to visit my brother Tommy and sister-in-law Barbara's house. They were only twenty-two and twenty-three but they already had two children. Elizabeth was six months old and Hale was one and a half. We walked in and I said, "Hale, this is my friend Steve." Hale immediately started chanting, "Bite, dump, bite, dump." Steve was totally mystified and somewhat miffed because he didn't understand why everyone was laughing. Well, Hale had a Little Golden Book called *Steve the Steam Shovel*, and the steam shovel spent all day going, "Bite, dump, bite, dump." You learned quickly that if you were going to have a relationship with me, you were going to have a relationship with all these other people.

SR: That's true. That first weekend certainly set a tone— meeting Cokie's mother, meeting Barbara and Tommy and those tykes who are now the parents of our grand-nieces and -nephews. And that was very much the way life was and continued to be; family always comes first.

CR: Then we drove home and we smooched all the way back even though there were other people in the car—but that part was embarrassing.

SR: That *was* embarrassing. But fun.

CR: So we had had this whole long night of talking, we had our embarrassing ride home, then we went out on a date and had a good time. Then you didn't call again.

SR: True enough—it took some sherry to push me over the edge. I lived in Eliot House, and our master, John Finley, regularly invited interesting people over for dinner. The guest one evening was a visiting professor of English named Mark Van Doren, and since I was taking his wonderful course that spring, I was the first one to sign up. Those dinners were among the few times that serving alcohol was officially sanctioned—we always heard that some rich alum had given a grant to supply the house with sherry. I had several drinks and was getting a buzz going and Van Doren was a marvelous speaker and the whole evening was just terrific. And I had to talk to somebody about it. I went back to my dorm room and I was bouncing off the walls and I called Cokie and started babbling.

Luckily I was supposed to speak on a panel at Radcliffe the next weekend. Harvard was a very sexist place—Master Finley used to say that his job was to keep his young men thinking about women 60 percent of the time instead of 80 percent—and girls were thought of as weekend dates, period. This never struck me as right, and I had been writing some articles in the *Crimson,* the student newspaper, about how women were not taken seriously enough in the community. Mary Bunting, the president of Radcliffe, was thrilled to discover this odd Harvard man who actually thought that women had brains. So she would trot me out at various events, and in my inebriated excitement, I told Cokie about my speech. And she said, "Well gee, I'd like to come hear it."

CR: No dummy I!

SR: I started to say, "Great, come to the speech Saturday afternoon and we'll go out that night." Somewhere in my deepest male soul I knew that I was crossing a line that I had never crossed before. This was breaking my rule of only dating a girl twice. It was so traumatic.

CR: Terrifying.

SR: So terrifying that I choked on the words. I actually had trouble getting them out, but eventually did. So she came to that event and we did go out that night.

CR: And then we went out all that spring. It was one of those years where the weather was gorgeous during the week and poured every weekend and our dating was pretty much confined to weekends because there were all these college rules. I had to be in the dorm at ten o'clock on a weeknight. Despite the rain, we had a very nice spring. We knew our religious differences could block any long-term relationship, so we kept saying, "Well, this is just because it's spring."

SR: It later became something of a joke, as the seasons changed and we were still together, so we engraved "forever spring" into our wedding rings. But that spring did have a magic quality to it. I had always been uncomfortable and uptight on dates, but at some point I realized I could be at ease with this girl. That I could be myself with this girl. That I didn't have to worry about going to exactly the right restaurant or making sure we had the right movie tickets. If one thing didn't work out, something else would. It was the first time in my life I felt that way in the presence of a girl.

CR: On spring break we went to New York for the weekend. Steve was staying at home in New Jersey and I was staying at a friend's apartment in Manhattan. We went for a walk through Central Park, then to a movie, then to the Russian Tea Room. We had apricots and plums and Steve said he liked those colors together, and from there on out I kept desperately trying to find apricot-and-plum combinations.

SR: I still plant flowerpots with those colors.

CR: And then we went back to my friend's and sat up all night talking and reading poetry, if you can believe it! Early Sunday morning I went to church and Steve got on a bus and went back to Bayonne.

SR: I walked into the house and my grandfather, who lived with us, was up already. He looked at me sternly because I had been out all night. He didn't say anything; he was a rather mild-mannered man. But I remember thinking, "Pop, if you knew the half of it. The girl I just left went straight to Mass."

CR: We still told each other it was just a spring romance. And I certainly thought that was the safest thing to say. Anything more would have scared him off. But we were very happy and clearly in love. Then came summer and I went home to work for the government and Steve stayed in Cambridge to edit the student newspaper. But we did spend a few weekends in Washington together, and I went to visit Steve's parents in Bayonne for the first time.

SR: That was important because my parents were very uneasy about this relationship and we knew instinctively that the best way to deal with it was for them to get to know Cokie in a way that the Boggses were getting to know me. As a real person, not just a stereotype.

CR: But that summer Steve dated somebody else, which I found out about and didn't like a bit.

SR: I was still struggling with the whole commitment thing, and there were a lot of girls around who thought that the editors of the *Harvard Crimson* were pretty neat. At the end of that summer we went to another student political meeting in Bloomington, Indiana. I was flat-out mean to Cokie; that's the closest we ever came to breaking up.

CR: When we went back to school, it was tense.

SR: Slowly we started seeing each other again and we rediscovered there was something special between us. But it took a while to get over the resentments of the summer, and at one point she agreed to go to the Harvard–Yale game with somebody else.

CR: But I broke that date, and then the day before the game Jack Kennedy was killed. Steve and I decided to go away for that weekend because I was too upset to stay in the dorm with everybody watching TV and crying. We stayed at a friend's house in New Hampshire and I remember driving to church that Sunday. By this time Steve's parents had given him a car for senior year, so that made a big difference, but it was a miserable car which did not have a heater. This was Boston. Trying to get to church that Sunday was terrifying because the weather was bad and the car didn't have a defroster. This little tiny church in this little town in New Hampshire had a catafalque in the middle of the aisle to represent Kennedy. It was so strange.

SR: But that was an important weekend. We decided that we wanted to be together. Our college careers were defined by Kennedy's presidency—he was elected in the fall of our freshman year—and killed in the fall of our senior year. He gave young people a sense that we could participate and make a difference, and we fully shared that belief. It was one of the things that attracted us to each other.

CR: In some ways we missed a huge American pageant that weekend because we didn't have a TV. All of America was experiencing the same thing and we weren't.

SR: We were learning a lot about each other. But I was starting to write a senior thesis and working very hard and continuing to act out these silly male attitudes toward dates.

CR: He would call me on Saturday morning and break a date for that night, saying he had to work too hard. So I finally caught on and started going in to Cambridge early on Saturdays and studying in the stacks at the Harvard library so he couldn't reach me to break the date. I would just show up at the appointed hour.

SR: Many of our dates followed the same pattern. I was working for *The New York Times* as their campus correspondent. It was a great job because I got a chance to write stories for the paper and establish a relationship with them and make a few dollars as well. My typical Saturday assignment was to cover some Harvard sporting event, like a track meet, then write a brief story. I would have to send it to New York and I had two choices. One was a really old-fashioned Western Union office, where I would peck out a cable on a totally dilapidated typewriter. Or I would call a recording room at the *Times* and dictate the story and spell all the names, to make sure there were no mistakes. To this day Cokie remembers the spelling of the star sprinter, Chris Ohiri, who was Nigerian. I repeated his name so often because I was convinced the desk would put in an apostrophe and try to make him Irish. I would make a swift $5.00 for this effort, but there was a restaurant in Harvard Square named Cronin's that had a dinner special for $1.98, so the $5.00 covered dinner for two, plus tip. After dinner, Cokie often sang with her a cappella group, the Wellesley Widows. On many Saturday evenings they would perform around Boston, at different clubs or events, and I would sit in the audience with the other groupies. As the head of the group, Cokie was the emcee, so not only did I learn the words to every one of their songs, I heard her jokes over and over again. I guess not much has changed.

CR: Then your thesis was done. It was spring break and you decided to break up with me.

SR: I did? What happened?

CR: I went to Jamaica to sing and I came back really tan, which was a good thing because you met me at the airport determined to break up with me. But I looked great. Thank goodness I wasn't worried about skin cancer and wrinkles in those days. You had been home seeing your parents and they were quizzing you because we were getting close to graduation and the real world was about to happen. You had essentially said to them, "Not to worry, this relationship is not going anywhere." And then you met the tan me and we went to Princeton to see my sister, Barbara, and her husband, Paul, and had a really nice time. So you went back home the next day and said, "Well, actually, maybe it is going somewhere." And that was the beginning of the conversations with your folks and what it meant for the future.

SR: They were very uneasy. Bayonne was a strange place; the Jewish community was completely self-contained. I had friends outside of the Jewish community because I played sports around town. And occasionally there were non-Jewish girls in my high-school class who I got to know. I went to a sweet-sixteen party at a Polish-American home and it was like going to another country, because hardly any Jews dated non-Jews. Also many of the brightest Catholic kids went to Catholic high schools, so I had had a very unfortunate experience in high school—I knew relatively few smart Catholic kids. It was easy to absorb the prejudice that most smart people were Jewish. In Bayonne, the first question anyone asked was "What's your religion?" At Harvard it was the fifth or sixth question. It was a thoroughly different environment. But my parents still lived in a world where it was the first question you asked. I remember my father saying, "If you marry this girl, we'll be strangers in your house, and we won't know our grandchildren." That understandably frightened him terribly. But that's why the time we spent getting to know each other's parents was very well invested. At some point my father admitted to me, "Well, it would be a lot easier to oppose this match if it weren't so obvious that she's the perfect girl for you." When I counsel young people these days who are in a mixed religious relationship, I always tell them, the more time you spend with each other's families, the better.

CR: My mother actually thought I might be taking up with Steven in order to show the world that my parents weren't prejudiced. My sister, Barbara, had been engaged to Allard Lowenstein and my parents opposed the match. Barbara and I believed they objected because Al was Jewish, and we were hurt and upset because we thought they had raised us not to have any prejudices at all, except, as Barbara used to say, against "Republicans and senators." This was flying in the face of everything they had taught us, and I told Daddy that when he was driving me to work one day. He said, "Cokie, I've gone around and around in my own mind about this and I swear to you that is not it." If it were Hermie Kohlmeyer, he insisted, the son of a Jewish friend in New Orleans, he would be giving his blessing. But Al scared him. "I just don't think this guy will ever be there for her," he said, which was fair enough. He had really thought about it a long time, grappled with it in his own mind, and that conversation convinced me that it was not prejudice that caused their opposition. But a lot of other people thought it was.

SR: I think it made a big difference that Cokie's parents had fought through this issue before I came along and had confronted their own feelings. It also helped that many of Hale and Lindy's strongest political supporters and good friends in New Orleans were Jewish, so they had had a different life experience from my parents.

CR: But none of this was easy. We graduated from college in an era when everyone got married right out of college. We were going to a wedding a week. So that began a period of angst, not knowing if we could ever work it out.

SR: One of Cokie's roommates got married in the summer after junior year and moved to California, taking her wardrobe with her. Suddenly many of Cokie's best outfits disappeared. There was one in particular, a beige corduroy number, that I missed for years.

CR: So while many of our friends were getting married, we were still dating. But we both ended up in Washington after graduation, so that meant we continued to see each other often. I got a job through the college placement office, of all things, working for a television production company here.

SR: During the fall of senior year I had heard about an internship offered by James Reston, the Washington bureau chief of *The New York Times,* and after I wrote to him, he invited me to Washington for an interview. I came down on November 1, 1963—I remember the date because it was the day the Diem government fell in Vietnam, a huge news story.

Still, Reston spent hours with me. Then of course the Kennedy assassination happened three weeks later, and yet, when I was home for Christmas, Reston sent me a handwritten letter saying, "Here's another Christmas present, you have the job!"

CR: My mother wrote you a letter of recommendation.

SR: Is that right? I had forgotten that.

CR: He said you were recommended by everybody but Charles de Gaulle.

SR: It was a very good thing that I came to Washington. Cokie was living at home and I was living downtown, but I was at the Boggs house—now our house—all the time. I even got used to Tabasco sauce on my eggs and chicory in the coffee, a New Orleans specialty that is definitely not for everybody. The other thing that really made a difference that year was the example of Scotty Reston. When I worked for him he was the most influential person in American journalism. His column set the tone and rhythm of the city. Yet he cared very much about helping me and developing my writing and he always made time to answer questions. But he was even more important as a personal role model. He had a long wonderful marriage to his college sweetheart, Sally—"my gal Sal," he called her—and his wife and three sons were absolutely central to his life. Just by living that way and setting those priorities, he communicated to me that being married and having a family were completely compatible with reaching the top of your profession. In addition, he was a relentless advocate for marriage. He knew Cokie. He liked Cokie. He knew her parents. He would storm into my office, trailing pipe ashes, and say, "When are you going to marry that girl?" It made a big difference.

CR: But they were agonizing years, they really were. Oh, I don't mean we didn't have fun. Of course we did, a lot of fun. I particularly loved a trip to Coney Island where you won a stuffed animal for me by shooting basketballs, and then I made you go on the parachute jump. After showing off with the baskets, you were so terrified on the parachute ride—I can still see that look of sheer horror on your face.

SR: I've never quite forgiven you for that.

CR: Too late for that. It was because we liked being together so much that we agonized. There were times when we absolutely thought that this was not going to work, because of religion. I remember at some point that you thought your parents would cut you off if we got married, and I thought that we could not live like that. Your family meant much too much to you. I was traveling a lot, producing TV shows in different cities, and I remember miserable phone conversations late at night in hotel rooms.

SR: In one sense caring so much about family and tradition made it all harder. We could not ignore who we were or what we'd been taught. Converting was never a possibility for either one of us and abandoning religion was also out of the question. But gradually we came to realize how much we shared. The labels were different but the values were the same. And since then, we've often reflected that Catholics and Jews make good matches. We're both really good at loyalty and guilt.

CR: My reaction to all this was to be inclusive, to try to learn as much about Judaism as possible. I was in Cincinnati over Rosh Hashanah and one of the oldest temples in Reform Judaism, the Plum Street Temple, is there. I had no idea that tickets were required for services, so I went up to the door and the usher asked, "What do you want?" I said, "I want to come in. I want to go to services." They guy said okay and he walked me down the aisle and said in this huge stage whisper so the entire congregation could hear, "Here's one that came without her boyfriend." It was not a good moment.

SR: We both understood that if this was going to work, we had to be supportive of each other and had to learn about each other's background. During college Cokie once took me to visit the nuns at Newton College outside of Boston. They were from the same Sacred Heart order that taught her in grade school and high school, and seeing Cokie's love and loyalty toward these women made a big impact on me. One of the things that I always tell people is that it can't be one way. It has to be two ways. Often I find that Jewish partners in a mixed marriage think that the Christian should learn about the Jewish part but don't necessarily understand that the Jew has to learn about the Christian part. It's got to be mutual. And by going to temple—even without me there—Cokie was making an important gesture of respect that helped convince me this could work. Today everyone says that Cokie is the best Jew in the family, and it's true. Not long ago our daughter had to bring a special dish, called *haroset*, to a Passover Seder, and she called her Catholic mother for the recipe. Eventually I came to realize that if you're serious about one religion, you're serious about all of them. The real question is whether you care about faith and ritual or not. And Cokie certainly proves that.

CR: One year when I was dragging Steve off to temple on Rosh Hashanah, he joked, "My mother was right. I should have married a Jewish girl; she wouldn't have made me go to services."

SR: Even though we were working this through, and even though Scotty was on my case, none of that could get me to pop the question. After my year in Washington, the *Times* moved me to New York, and we were separated again.

CR: And I decided I was wasting the best years of my life. I was twenty-two and I was about to be an old maid! Steven began to get a sense of how fed up I was one day when we stopped at a rest stop on the Jersey Turnpike and decided to share a Danish pastry. I was raised to believe a woman always gave a man the best piece of everything, and Steven was raised to expect that. That day, when I ate the center out of the Danish and left him the crust, he knew I was truly ticked. I finally said, "I'm not doing this anymore, I'm going to California." And I really meant it. To me it seemed more painful to stay together, not knowing if we would ever be married, than to just end it and hope to meet somebody else.

SR: She did force me to make a decision. I knew that it was the right girl and the wrong time. But when I contemplated her actually leaving—that I couldn't imagine. If it was a choice, which it clearly was, then I knew what I had to do. The joke in the family is that the way I proposed was to say, "Oh, all right, Cokie!" There's more than a little truth to that.

CR: I said this is the only time. If you want this girl, *this* is the time.

SR: I was a little resentful, but she was right. Remember this was 1966, and we were really shaped more by the late fifties than the late sixties. Getting married was the thing to do. I've looked up the statistics, and that year the average age for a man to get married was 22.8 years, and I was already older than that. For women it was 20.5 years, so Cokie was right, she was well on her way to spinsterhood. Of my nine roommates who lived together senior year, seven were already married. It was almost like playing musical chairs. The music stopped on the day you graduated, and you married the person you were dating at the time. That was true for most of our friends.

CR: We kidded that girls' schools advertised, "A ring by spring or your money back." I think for a lot of girls there was also an expectation that we would not have a career, even though we had equally fine educations as the men. We expected to work for a couple of years and have kids and then do something good in the community. To succeed as a young woman meant finding the right guy. Marriage became very, very important because that was pretty much it. That was your goal in life. The man you married not only determined your well-being and sense of happiness, he also determined your status. Was the person you married good enough for you? I remember my sister saying once when she was about twenty-three, "I don't even want to be married now. I just wish I knew who I was going to marry so I could be relaxed about it." It was such a different era. I was reading a letter recently from my roommate who moved to California, and she was writing about the Berkeley campus in October of 1963 and saying it was so intimidating, all the sorority girls were so well dressed, everybody wore pearls to class every day. A year or two later that campus was in flames. The world changed in so many ways overnight.

SR: So Cokie reflected the era when she insisted that it was now or never if I wanted to marry her. When I finally realized that was my choice, we planned this romantic moment— we would take a carriage ride around Central Park and I would ask her to marry me. But the words snagged in my throat, just like they had three years before when I finally broke the two-date rule. The ride was practically over before I got them out, and Cokie was not pleased! Then she announced that I had to come to Washington to ask her father for her hand before the engagement could be official. She also insisted that before I came, I had to tell my parents what was going on. True to my form, I put it off and put it off. Finally, ten minutes before the plane took off, I called my mother from the airport. "Hi, how are you?" she asked, and I blurted into the phone, "Well, actually, I'm going to Washington this week and Cokie and I are getting engaged." Mom burst into tears and I hung up the phone. The morning it came time to talk to Cokie's dad, he had escaped to the tomato patch and I had to be pushed out the door. My future father-in-law was so nervous he handed me a watering can, and I was so nervous I started watering my shoes. I told him that Cokie and I wanted to get married and he said, "Fine." But I didn't take yes for an answer. I plunged ahead; I said, "Well, sir, I do know that you think Cokie and I will have problems because of religion, but we do think that we can work them out." And he answered, "Yes, I do think you'll have problems, but not half as many problems as I'll have if I try to tell Cokie who to marry."

CR: So you came back in. We opened some champagne. Your twin brother, Marc, was here for a friend's wedding and he said a very smart thing, which was, "Come on. Let's get in the car and drive up and see our folks."

SR: Through this period my brother had played a very important role. Our parents had focused on their own fears, which was fair enough, but they were not focused on the implications of their attitude. My brother went to our parents and said, "Look, Steve and Cokie are going to get married, and if there is any sort of a breach, any sort of a problem, it's going to be your fault. All they want is your blessing." That shocked my parents and forced them to rethink their feelings. My father said to me later that he felt an obligation to urge caution and raise questions while it was still up in the air. But once it was settled, then it was their role to become more supportive. And that's what happened. But my father never did get used to chicory in his coffee.

So now we were engaged, with a wedding to plan—lots of possible potholes along that road! Under the best of circumstances, weddings can drive perfectly loving caring families to the edge of violence. For us, the way we decided some aspects of the ceremony carried the weight of how we would make religious decisions for the rest of our lives. Over the years we've watched couples of different faiths work out their marriages and seen three essential models. In many cases, one partner converts, or steps back from any religious input, and the family practices a single faith. For other couples, religion is not important, and simply fades out of their lives. Neither of these options made sense for us. We were too rooted in our own traditions, and too respectful of each other's, to consider anything but the third version: running our family, and raising our children, with both religions as integral parts of our lives. Easy to say, not so easy to do, and our wedding became the first serious test of our theory. Could we really be both, Catholic and Jewish? Could our relations with our parents, and each other, survive the stress? The whole process, painful as it was at times, taught us a great deal about solving problems, showing patience, focusing on what was truly important. And looking back, it's clear the wedding became a metaphor for how we would live our lives together. Or at least try.

CR: Only a few days after that eventful carriage ride, I made an appointment with a priest in a nearby parish because I didn't want to waste any time on my way to the aisle. My question for the priest: what was the current state of play in the Church about marrying a non-Catholic, particularly a nonbaptized person? I was twenty-two and I was pretty brave about doing this on my own, but I wanted to have all my facts down before I talked to my parents about what I wanted, which was to get married at home. The garden of our house had always been a very special place to me, and I knew it would be much easier for Steve's family if they didn't have to actually go into a church, even though it was extremely important to me that it be a Catholic wedding. For years the Church had been, to put it mildly, unwelcoming to non-Catholics, insisting that they marry at home or in the rectory of the church. Then they were allowed inside but on the side altar, then on the main altar but with no nuptial Mass. But, the priest told me, the Second Vatican Council, in a gesture toward other religions, had just recently changed all that—a full nuptial Mass could now be said in a mixed marriage. When I told him that not only did I not want a Mass, but that I wanted to be married at home, he said, "That's going to be a bit of a public relations problem for us." He knew that my father's position as Majority Whip of the House of Representatives would mean the wedding would be in news-papers all over the country and the priest worried that people would think we weren't allowed to marry in a church. And I remember saying, "I'm afraid that's your problem, not mine. My problem is that my husband's grandparents had to escape Europe, their families suffered through horrible pogroms, don't you think it's pretty harsh to insist that they walk into a Catholic church?" To his credit, the priest totally got it and received permission from the bishop for me to marry at home. But when I told my mother that's what I wanted to do, she was distressed. She said to me, "That's not a wedding, that's a party." She wanted the solemnity of a sanctuary. Then I said to her, "Mamma, think of it from the perspective of Grandpa Abe, Steve's grandfather." Given her truly kind na-ture, she instantly understood. So from there on out it was a question of trying to make it as comfortable for everybody as humanly possible. We had the ceremony after sundown on Saturday, so it wouldn't be on a Sabbath day. We had a *chuppah*, which is a Jewish wedding canopy. My father's brother was a priest and he would officiate, and we tried to convince a rabbi to come as well, but that was not easy.

SR: I asked the rabbi from my old temple in Bayonne. No luck. My parents had moved to Lakewood, New Jersey, but their new rabbi wouldn't come either. After a while it got demeaning. There was this odd underground of people who had rabbis' names who would whisper to you, "Hey, I know one who does them. . . ."

CR: We were given the name of one guy who was known for performing mixed marriages. He actually had another job, working at the White House. But when I called him there and addressed him as "Rabbi" as opposed to "Mr.," he said quickly, "I'll call you back from a pay phone." When he called me back he asked me all these questions about things like "vicarious atonement" and I had no idea what he was talking about. I kept saying, "Why don't you talk to my fiancé about all of this?" Finally he agreed to marry us but he wouldn't share the platform with a priest. So we were still left with no rabbi.

SR: It was frustrating because both of us were trying to be attentive to everybody's feelings. Cokie's uncle didn't have much choice about being part of the ceremony; he had learned that weddings of his nieces and nephews came with the territory of priesthood. I was faced with the question of having a priest sign the marriage certificate. In the end I thought, no, that didn't bother me, that was not important. But it *was* important to me to have some Jewish element in the ceremony. I understand why most rabbis will not participate in mixed marriages. Their fear that Judaism will be diluted is very real. But in the end I think their stand can be counterproductive. They will not stop most mixed couples from getting married, but they will deprive those couples of a Jewish presence, and a Jewish blessing, at their wedding and in their home. If rabbis were more welcoming to mixed couples, I think they would actually strengthen Judaism, but I know most of them disagree with me.

CR: Just that spring, the Catholic Church had officially given its blessing to a cleric of another faith joining a priest for the ceremony. In fact, the doctrine is very clear. The ministers of the sacrament of matrimony are the couple themselves. All those other people up there are merely witnessing.

SR: It was important to Cokie to be married by a priest, and I had come to accept and respect her Catholicism. In fact, I had come to realize that many of the qualities I loved most about her came directly from her training by the nuns—her sense of charity, her consideration for others. So how could I object to a priest's name on our marriage certificate? Too bad we couldn't have a nun do it! But I did draw a line at signing a promise to the Church that I would raise the children Catholic. My view was, and still is, that I would promise Cokie anything, but I didn't want any outside clergyman—Jewish or Catholic—telling us what to do. So when we decided to raise the children in both religions, we agreed that we would train them ourselves. I knew I could live with Cokie's version of Catholicism, but I wasn't sure I could accept what some priest I didn't know told my children. On the promise issue, I had balked at signing something because the Catholic Church required it. But that spring, Pope Paul VI changed the rules so that only the Catholic partner was required to sign a pledge to raise the children in the faith, not the non-Catholic. Cokie teased me then that the pope had taken away my last excuse for not marrying her. It was the Jewish side that was much more difficult.

CR: Well, it was easy for the Catholic side to be cooperative; there was never any question in my mind about having a fully church-sanctioned wedding. That's why I felt an obligation to find a rabbi, so I made most of the phone calls looking for one. I must say I hated that. In the end it was Steve's mother who finally said it was getting a little much. When she and Steve's father came to meet my parents toward the end of August, she came up with the answer.

SR: Whenever the Boggses socialized with Jewish friends, which was often, I'd make sure to tell my parents, just to reassure them that these were not strangers. And it happened that my future in-laws were friends with Arthur and Dorothy Goldberg. He had been a justice of the Supreme Court and had just left to become the UN ambassador. That spring Hale and Lindy went to the Goldbergs for their Seder, which was a famous Passover tradition in Washington. Goldberg came out of the labor movement, he had been counsel to the AFL-CIO before he was secretary of labor, and they would sing old labor organizing songs. So we eagerly told my parents about this event.

CR: Also, at Luci Johnson's wedding, on the sixth of August, my father had read one of the lessons, and that gave Steve's mother the idea. It didn't have to be a cleric up on the altar. Finally, she said to me, "You know, Cokie, in Jewish tradition a rabbi is a learned man, an elder of the tribe, and all of this search for a rabbi is humiliating. So why don't you consider a learned man like, say, Arthur Goldberg?" We asked him and thankfully he agreed.

SR: It was funny, though. He was already contemplating a political career in New York—eventually he did run for governor—so his first reaction was to say, "Great, I'd be happy to do it." Then he started consulting with rabbis in New York because he was a little concerned about his political base and he came back to us and said, "I can't pretend in any way to be a rabbi." The rabbis' "union" made it clear he had to play a different role, and Arthur Goldberg never bucked a union.

CR: Actually he tried to back out with, "Can't I just give a toast?" We said no.

SR: In the end he hit exactly the right note—a short talk on the Jewish view of marriage, a few Hebrew prayers, the traditional breaking of the glass. And that fulfilled our main goal, making my parents and their friends feel recognized and respected. But Goldberg's presence was important for me, too, a way of saying, very publicly, this is who I am, this is my tribe and my tradition, and that tradition will always be part of our family.

But the other big question was who to invite. Hale was the whip of the House, the Democrats were in the White House, and this wedding was going to have a political dimension to it. So my mother-in-law kept bugging my father-in-law, "Who should we invite from the Congress?" And finally, in exasperation, he said to her, "All the Democrats from the House."

CR: This was after the '64 landslide.

SR: There were over three hundred Democrats in the House of Representatives. And a good many of them came. Years later, when we reported on the House in the eighties, people would come up to us all the time and say, "I came to your wedding!" And we had no idea who they were.

CR: We have more presents with the seal of the House of Representatives engraved on them!

SR: In fact, many look like they were stolen because they just say U.S. Representative "X" on them. One of our favorites, a great conversation stopper in New York in the sixties, was a cake server signed by Senator Strom Thurmond. Cokie's mother was incredibly well organized, every present got a number so we could tell who gave it to us, and all these years later we still find little numbered stickers on the back of a tray or dish we don't use very often. But Lindy left some of the organization to Cokie, and she managed to fall down on one key issue.

CR: Here I was, frantically making notes about everything that had to get done—apartments, china, priests, all that. My boss at the TV production company where I was working, Sophie Altman, gave us a party on the Wednesday before the Saturday wedding, and when Steve flew in from New York, I immediately asked, "Did you pick up the wedding rings?" With some irritation, he answered, "Yes, yes, I picked up the wedding rings." I said, "Good, that's it, that means we're set. I've picked up the dress, we've got the rings, Uncle Robbie and Arthur Goldberg are set, and so the one other thing is . . . marriage license!" I had completely and totally forgotten about the marriage license. So the next morning at the crack of dawn we went out to Rockville, the county seat, now something of a suburban horror, but then a beautiful little town with a pre–Civil War courthouse. Sitting there was what was surely a pre–Civil War clerk in a pre–Civil War gray sweater. We told her we needed to apply for our marriage license and she informed us of a forty-eight-hour waiting period. "Okay," we said, "we'll pick it up on Saturday." "Closed on Saturday," came the oh-so-self-satisfied response. Steven kept trying to argue with her, "But—but—but we're having fifteen hundred people at the wedding on Saturday!" She was really loving this now: "Sorry, you'll just have to get married on Monday." Poor Steven was practically in tears:

"But the president's coming!" None of this impressed her one bit. I was asking more practical questions like, "What's the fine for getting married without a license?" Which tells you a lot about our subsequent life—I was always the one more willing to break the rules, or at least bend them. Then we had to call my parents for help—not exactly an easy call to make—and my father dispatched my brother, who was licensed to practice law in the state of Maryland. It doesn't get more humiliating than that—my big brother to the rescue! When he found a judge to waive the forty-eight-hour waiting period, the judge told Tommy, "You're lucky you caught me now because I have a full docket today and a full docket tomorrow and there is no way I would've seen you." We got in just under the wire with the marriage license, and my father's press secretary thought this was such a funny story he released it to the news wires. So it was in newspapers all over the country that I had forgotten to get our marriage license. It was unbelievably embarrassing. That Saturday night my uncle Robert, the priest, asked from the altar, "Has somebody got the marriage license?" Which I've never heard before or since at any wedding. He wanted to make sure it was legal.

SR: Of course it wasn't your normal wedding, with the president coming, and I think that was the first day I got a taste of life in the public eye.

CR: It wasn't normal in a lot of ways. My grandmother wouldn't let me into the bathroom to get dressed. I stood in the hall outside the door, begging, "Coco, I really need to get in there, I'm getting married!" And she kept saying, "Darling, just another minute, just another minute. If you give me a whole minute, I'll let you borrow my eye shadow." (My thrice-widowed grandmother had an interesting perspective on the institution of marriage. "All of life is one long date," she used to tell my sister and me. "When you're married, you have to date the man you're married to, but before and after him, you can date whomever you please.") When I finally did get in the bathroom, my father started banging on the door shouting, "Cokie, you've got to come out of there. The president's here." And I blew up: "Well, the bride's not!"

Then I hustled and bustled to get ready, run downstairs, and rush outside to get married because the president was there! The wedding party lined up outside, including my not-quite-five-year-old nephew Hale, who was the ring bearer. We have pictures of his mother carefully tying the rings onto the little satin pillow he carried. But just as the trumpet started Purcell's "Voluntary," Hale turned to my father and said, "Pawpaw, I lost the ring." We have a picture of that moment, too! We all started scrambling around looking for the ring, with my father pulling on my arm, insisting, "Come on, Cokie, we've got to do this now. We've got to do this wedding!" Wedding guests handed me their rings. We didn't know which one was lost, so I had about a half-dozen men's and women's rings on my fingers, but I protested, "No, I'm not going to do it. I'm not going on without the ring." My sister, the matron of honor, kept trying not to laugh as I stamped my foot, pouting: "Daddy, the symbolism of this is just all wrong." And he said, "Cokie, don't you think there's enough symbolism going on here for one night?"

He persuaded me to go down the aisle, but I was all teary. There's nothing worse than teary brides; they always make you wonder if they should be doing this. Fortunately, my niece, who was not quite four, saved me. She was the flower girl, and at the rehearsal the night before, my mother kept repeating, "Strew the petals, Elizabeth, strew the petals." Instead she took clumps of petals and dumped them out of her little basket, making everyone laugh, including me. Then of course she ran out of flowers halfway down the aisle, so she had to retreat and collect a bunch to refill her basket. It was so funny that I cracked up and from there on out I had a good time. When I got under the *chuppah*, I learned it was Steve's ring that was missing. It landed in the bushes where the doctor who always travels with the president found it with his little ear light before the ceremony was over.

SR: Remember, this was 1966, I was twenty-three, the Vietnam War was heating up. The president was not all that popular with people our age and my ushers had threatened, only half-jokingly, to march down the aisle chanting, "End the war in Vietnam." Not such a great idea. But my ushers did perform one important job. There were only two or three rows of chairs, reserved for elderly aunts and cabinet officers. Everyone else had to stand. At one point a tall man with a crew cut in a red dinner jacket, a brusque, aggressive fellow, pushed his way to the front.

CR: It was a black-tie wedding.

SR: Following instructions, one of my ushers asked him, "Excuse me, sir, these seats are reserved, so could you please tell me who you are?" At that point he drew himself up to his full height and said, "I am the head of Steven's draft board." Which he was. His name was Harold Tucker, an old friend of my father's. They had run many losing political campaigns together—being a reform Democrat in Hudson County, New Jersey, was not a promising career. But they had actually won once, helping elect a high-school drafting teacher as mayor of Bayonne. And as the payoff for that one victory, this man had become the postmaster, and in that job he was head of the draft board, a rather important man in my life. So we kicked someone out, I think it was Justice Tom Clark, and Harold got his seat!

One of the most memorable parts of the ceremony was Arthur Goldberg's talk. He turned to Cokie and said, "In my tradition a home has rarely been a castle; throughout the ages it is something far higher, a sanctuary." He was right about that—eleven years later we moved back into that same house where we were married and it has been a sanctuary for us ever since. Then he said to me, "Be careful not to cause a woman to weep, for God counts her tears." He got that one right, too.

CR: I don't much remember what happened after that. It was a beautiful night. There were lots and lots of people. We were in the receiving line forever and ever. Gene McCarthy kept bringing us champagne because we were stuck in the receiving line for so long.

SR: My new mother-in-law, who had been slaving for weeks cooking for this extravaganza, looked like she didn't have a care in the world as she greeted almost every one of the fifteen hundred guests by name. The ones she didn't know she simply called "Darlin', " her all-purpose form of address. My brother later said that watching Lindy perform that night was like watching Heifetz play the violin or DiMaggio play baseball—nobody did it better. I don't think we ever got off the receiving line.

CR: No, we did. There are pictures of us dancing. We definitely danced. It was a truly special wedding; my mother had done a fabulous job. A big tent covered the side yard, and white flowers, including my favorite, lilies of the valley, decorated the whole thing; the *chuppah* was covered with flowers as well. Mamma remembered an outdoor wedding from her youth where the bridesmaids, instead of marching all the way forward, unwound a ribbon and formed the aisle. So we did the same thing. The bridesmaids carried baskets of multicolored flowers and each one wore any long white dress she wanted to wear. But my sister and my best friend and Steve's sister did process down the aisle, and they wore these awful

1966 dresses I chose for them, olive green with cotton lace flounces. Horrible. When our daughter Becca and I went dress shopping for her wedding, we carried around one of my wedding pictures, because she was trying to decide whether to wear the same veil that I wore. The picture included my sister in that dreadful dress. The wedding-dress saleswomen took one look and laughed: "Sixty-five, sixty-six, right?"

SR: Our parents had started married life in such a different way, at such a different time—right in the middle of the Depression. They all told stories about how they didn't have any money. Hale helped work his way through college giving out gum samples to other students and writing for a New Orleans newspaper. He and Lindy used to talk about sharing one po'boy sandwich for dinner. My folks would return used soda bottles to scrape up enough change to afford the movies, and lunch was often a ketchup sandwich.

CR: There's a very funny story about my parents' first date. My mother claims they originally met her freshman year of college at a dance when Daddy said to her, "Lindy Claiborne, I'm going to marry you someday." He denied that mightily, but at some point they did go out and his car, an old Model A Ford, broke down. They had to keep stopping and filling it with water from the ditch next to the road. They got home very, very late. Mamma lived with her grandmother Morrison, her mother's mother, who ran a boardinghouse in New Orleans. Daddy kept saying to her, "Don't you think we ought to call your grandmother and let her know why we're so late?" Mamma said, "She absolutely never wakes up. We would just be bothering her." When they got home, every light was on. My great-grandmother was up and pacing, furious. My father was abashed beyond belief and not too pleased with my mother. Her grandfather Claiborne had died that night and they had been trying to reach her to tell her.

Which was the only reason her grandmother was up. Then Daddy went to his house, he was living at home of course, and his mother was also pacing the floor, also furious at the hour. She demanded, "What kind of girl would keep you out until all hours of the night like that?" And he said, "A wonderful girl that you'd be lucky if you ever got to meet." But their serious dating didn't start until later, when Mamma had graduated from college and was teaching school.

SR: After my parents met, on Mom's seventeenth birthday, they never dated anyone else, but they got married secretly, at City Hall in New York. Which is maybe the exact opposite of having fifteen hundred people at your wedding. They didn't have enough money to set up housekeeping, but they wanted to be married, so they went to City Hall on their lunch hour with a couple of friends. My father had been saving money for a wedding lunch, that was about all he could afford, and as he told the story, he was carrying this coin bank with him. It was a metal bank, and he dropped it, right in the middle of the ceremony. Fortunately, it didn't break, but it made a horrendous crash. After the wedding they didn't tell anyone. They were both still living at home, with their own parents, only a few blocks apart. My mother's older sister was also married and was living with her husband in the family house. A few months later my aunt and uncle got enough money together to rent their own place, and the day they moved out my father and mother announced that they had in fact been married for three months. And my father moved in the same day.

CR: And he lived in that house until you were what? Ten years old?

SR: Thirteen. Half a house really, because we only lived on one of the two floors.

CR: Well, my parents had a real wedding. It was in New Roads, Louisiana, the country town where Mamma had grown up. Daddy must have graduated from law school in June and they got married in January, when she was twenty-one and he was twenty-three. Mamma's saved the accounts from the local newspaper which describe old St. Mary's Church, which was filled with camellias from her neighbors' gardens, and the reception at her uncle's house. Her father died when she was only two, and when this uncle told her that her daddy was dead, she told him he would have to be her Uncle Daddy. And that's what we all called him. It was a big family wedding in the country, and when the newly-weds returned from their honeymoon ten days later, they found many of the houseguests still there, having a wonderful time.

SR: After our wedding we were going to spend the night downtown . . .

CR: . . . at the Hay Adams Hotel . . .

SR: . . . and fly off to Puerto Rico the next day. But because we were in the receiving line the whole time, neither one of us had anything much to eat. When we were driving downtown Cokie insisted we go to . . .

CR: Eddie Leonard's Sandwich Shop, which was a real dive but it was the only thing open at that time of the night. I was starving and he wouldn't take me to the Eddie Leonard's Sandwich Shop. I thought this was a terrible failing as a husband.

SR: Something I've always regretted. It would have been a cool thing to do. But I wasn't exactly a cool kind of guy.

CR: Then we got to the Hay Adams and I had told them that it was our wedding night, which I thought merited at least a bottle of champagne in the room. But no! Then the next morning, after we flew to Puerto Rico, my mother told me that the weather turned terrible, just absolutely terrifying. Hurricanelike weather. No tent on earth would have protected the wedding against that weather.

SR: Over the years since our own wedding, lots of other Jewish-Christian couples have talked to us and some have asked our advice about how to handle the actual ceremony. We're careful to stress we have no formulas that work for everybody. But I do think we learned several things from that process, and one was inclusion. Every effort that makes people feel wanted or respected is worth doing. We have young friends, a Catholic-Jewish couple, who got married under a *chuppah*, but the canopy was draped with an Irish lace table-cloth. In another case the bride's elderly father insisted on bringing his homemade chopped liver to the reception—that was his way of contributing. Each couple works out the details for itself, but the basic idea of inclusion is very important. The other thing I've always believed is that the wedding itself becomes a metaphor for how you solve problems in a relation-ship. Part of that is tolerance. Part of that is realizing that when one partner feels really strongly about something, they get a little more weight. Part of that is figuring out what is really important, just listening to the other person.

CR: And listening to yourself as well. Saying to yourself, "Hold on here, does this really matter to me?" There are so many times when I automatically react: "That's the way I thought it would be or that was my image of it." And then, at least on my better days, I say to myself, "Why? Does it really matter?" Actually, I found myself going through that with Becca's wedding, too. She would say to me, "I don't want a white bouquet, I want a multicolored bouquet of bright flowers." My first reaction was, "That's wrong, brides don't do that." Then I thought, "Why not? What's wrong with that?" I think that's a very good jumping-off point for a marriage, to say to yourself, "Hold on here, is this really important to me or is this just some notion that I have?"

SR: Marriage is not only a ceremony between two people. It is a communal event, symbolizing a relationship between families and friends and relatives. That's one of the reasons we never listened to my parents when they only half-jokingly suggested we elope so they wouldn't have to deal with what could have been an uncomfortable ordeal. We worked hard to make it comfortable for them, and that told them something about how we would try to always make them comfortable. Cokie had wanted to be a bride ever since she was a little girl; she wanted a wedding. But more than that, even at that young age we somehow understood that the guests serve as witnesses, people who promise to support this young couple. That's a real job. That's a real responsibility. Healthy marriages need those kinds of relationships and connections— as role models and advice givers and shoulders to cry on—as we've learned over and over through the years. Marriage is hard enough, and doing it in isolation without those support systems makes it much more difficult. So if we had been faced with any sort of a breach with our families, it would have been devastating. From the beginning part of what we saw in each other was a shared value about family. So for us, there was only one possibility and that was to do both, to embrace both traditions. In some ways it was easier because there was an equality about the whole situation. We each care about our own traditions and our own families. We could see why the other did and we could respect that strength of commitment and not expect the other to compromise too much because each of us knew we wouldn't. In a curious way, that was a source of strength. It was never a puzzlement to me why Cokie was devoted to her family and her faith. I never for one second expected her to become more like me or accept my faith. I give our parents credit. They did come to understand what we had been trying to tell them. That the labels were less important than the core values and the individuals involved. In an ideal world, they would have preferred some things to be different. But they did come to see what we were trying to tell them, and have been wonderful about it ever since.

CR: They also came to love us, and better yet, like us.

Chapter Two

OTHER LIVES

EARLY AMERICA

COMPANIONATE MARRIAGE

Women were in short supply in the early years of New World settlement, which gave them a certain advantage when it came to marriage. Lonely men would pay for single women to cross the treacherous Atlantic, plus give the brave maidens a sizable sum in tobacco leaf as a payment to persuade them to become their brides. It put women in a better position than they would have held in the old countries, where the weight of hundreds or thousands of years of tradition governed the rules of marriage. Here, though men certainly headed the household, they depended on women to work alongside them carving civilization out of the wilderness. And early colonists trying to impose English laws governing property rights and inheritance soon found that European laws differed, often giving women a greater share and a greater say than the English, and women from the Continent were not willing to submit to the English strictures. So, from the beginning, the institution of marriage in this country was shaped by forces different from the ones left behind. Women acted as partners, junior partners to be sure, but still partners, in these colonial marriages. Then, with the coming of the American Revolution and the absence of many men from home, women managed the farms and businesses. Not only did the war have a practical effect on marriages, it had a philosophical one as well. As the colonists threw over the king, and the voices of enlightenment filled the land, women questioned the authority of their husbands. It would be a couple of hundred years before the laws caught up with the egalitarian sentiments of some of the women of Revolutionary times, but their own marriages reflected their sense of partnership. Lucky for us, we have first-person accounts of one of the most remarkable of those unions—that of the nation's second president, John Adams, and his wife, Abigail.

Abigail and John Adams: Friends of the Heart

When John Adams met Abigail Smith in 1759, she was a lively fifteen-year-old minister's daughter in Weymouth, Massachusetts, he was a somewhat stuffy twenty-three-year-old Harvard graduate, studying law. It was not love at first sight; Adams thought the three Smith sisters a little too sharp-tongued for his taste. But a couple of years later he changed his mind, and started calling at the Smith household regularly. It didn't take long for him to fall completely in love, and for Abigail to passionately respond. How do we know? They've told us so. They wrote hundreds of letters over the years and many of those extraordinary missives were preserved. What they tell is a fascinating story—a story of the American colonies on the road to revolution, then war, then the struggles of a new nation. Abigail paints vivid pictures of eighteenth-century life in Massachusetts, detailing the everyday activities of a wife and mother, and the extraordinary anxieties of a woman alone in tumultuous times. John gives us a behind-the-scenes look at the events leading up to the

Declaration of Independence, and of diplomatic life in Europe. They exchange political information and express political views. Abigail's most famous admonition to her husband as he helped form a new government, that he and his colleagues "remember the ladies," is but one of many of her strong statements on affairs of state. But, above all, the Adams letters tell the story of a marriage, a marriage of genuine partnership for more than fifty years. Because the couple were separated by momentous events, their letters give us a close view throughout a ten-year window in their marriage when the only way they could communicate was through the primitive post. From the time of their courtship in the early 1760s until Abigail joined John in Europe in 1784, we can see the relationship evolve and mature through the letters. Even today, it's rare to find a union like the one we learn about from this couple's own words; think how unusual it must have been in the late eighteenth century!

John Adams doesn't seem to have been a very fun-loving person—except with Abigail. In their courtship, he addressed her as "Miss Adorable," and ordered her, at age seventeen, to give him "many kisses . . . I presume I have good right to draw upon you for the kisses as I have given two or three millions at least." When he went to Boston for a lengthy and dangerous inoculation procedure against smallpox, it wasn't the treatment he was worried about, it was his six-week separation from his lady love. Once he went home to Braintree, a town not far from Boston to the south, he couldn't wait to see her: "I am, until then, and forever after will be your admirer and friend, and lover." Even as he proclaims his love, though, the always priggish Adams tells Abigail he will write her a list of her faults: "You'll be surprised, when you come to find the number of them." From the tone of her next letter, she was understandably miffed and curious, and demanded the accounting: "There can be no time more proper than the present, it will be harder to erase them when habit has strengthened and confirmed them." But then, a couple of weeks later, she beat him to it, letting him know she'd heard from her friends that he had a few failings of his own—his haughtiness and unsociability: "I expect you to clear up these matters, without being in the least saucy." That got a quick response, with him telling her that she neglects some social skills such as cardplaying and singing, that she lacks a certain bashfulness, that she walks funny, hangs her head oddly, and crosses her legs. Her retort? "A gentleman has no business to concern himself about the legs of a lady." John Adams certainly knew he wasn't taking up with a shy violet when he finally married Abigail in 1764.

He set up law practice and she set about having babies. Abigail, John Quincy, Susanna, who died before she was two, Charles, and Thomas had all been born by the time Abigail went to visit her parents in 1773 and had occasion to write John at home: "The roads at present are impassible with any carriage. . . . My daily thoughts and nightly slumbers visit thee, and thine." John traveled the court circuit and wrote home regularly urging his wife to watch her spending, and giving her various instructions for managing the farm and bringing up the children in his absence. One letter from this venerated founder, dated July 1, 1774, two years almost to the day before he would help lead the revolution for independence, sounds like one of those consumer groups' warnings to modern parents. He recounts that some facts came out in a trial about the effects of loud noises on children: "A gun was fired near a child . . . the child fell immediately into fits, which impaired his reason, and is still a living idiot. Another child was sitting on a chamber floor. A man rapped suddenly and violently on the boards which made the floor under the child tremble. The child was so startled, and frightened, that it fell into fits, which never were cured. This may suggest a caution to keep children from sudden frights and surprises."

The next year John went off to the Continental Congress

in Philadelphia, writing letters to Abigail filled with news of deliberations "grave and serious indeed," but also loaded with lessons on how to run the farm and raise the children: "Frugality must be our support. Our expenses in this journey will be very great. . . . The education of our children is never out of my mind. Train them to virtue, habituate them to industry, activity and spirit. . . . It is time, my dear, for you to teach them French." Still, important matters like whether to move the law office to Braintree from Boston, he leaves to her judgment of whether the problems with the British are becoming threatening. She provides him with regular accounts of the preparations for war, including "mounting cannon upon Beacon Hill, digging entrenchments upon the Neck, placing cannon there, encamping a regiment there, throwing up breast works, etc., etc." He tells her, in case of real danger, to "fly to the woods with our children." How abandoned she must have felt! And how lonely.

"I dare not express to you at 300 miles distance how ardently I long for your return." She couldn't wait to see him: "The idea plays about my heart, unnerves my hand whilst I write, awakens all the tender sentiments that years have increased and matured, and which when with me were every day dispensing to you." And she hoped he couldn't wait to see her: "May the like sensations enter thy breast, and (in spite of all the weighty cares of state) mingle themselves with those I wish to communicate."

When the fighting started, she described their house as a scene of confusion: "Soldiers coming in for lodging . . . sometimes refugees from Boston tired and fatigued seek an asylum for a day or night, a week—you can hardly imagine how we live." Then, a few weeks later: "Courage I know we have in abundance, conduct I hope we shall not want, but powder—where shall we get a sufficient supply?" With a house full of babies, she was worried about the soldiers' lack of ammunition. But then, even as battles raged around her,

Abigail gives news of the farm: "The English grass will not yield half so great a crop as last year. Fruit promises well, but the caterpillars have been innumerable." And, ever practical despite the turmoil of war, she asks John to buy her some pins: "The cry for pins is so great that what we used to buy for 7.6 are now 20 shillings and not to be had for that." He, for once, was duly impressed: "It gives me more pleasure than I can express to learn that you sustain with so much fortitude, the shocks and terrors of the times. You are really brave, my dear, you are an heroine." But she is a heroine with a complaint: "All the letters I receive from you seem to be written in so much haste, that they scarcely leave room for a social feeling . . . I want some sentimental effusions of the heart. I am sure you are not destitute of them or are they all absorbed in the great public?" It was a complaint she would have cause to repeat in the years ahead.

As Abigail struggled with managing the farm, tending to her own and the children's illnesses and her mother's death, she also thought a good deal about John's endeavor. When he first arrived in Philadelphia, he was almost in awe of the men in the Congress, but soon he wrote, "I am wearied to death with the life I lead. The business of the Congress is tedious, beyond expression. This assembly is like no other that ever existed. Every man in it is a great man—an orator, a critic, a statesman, and therefore every man upon every question must show his oratory, his criticism and his political abilities." They might be remembered now as larger-than-life "Founding Fathers," but they took forever to do anything. In Abigail's mind, the mission of the Congress was clear—to declare independence from Britain in short order, but she wondered what would come after that: "If a form of government is to be established here what one will be assumed? . . . If we separate from Britain what Code of Laws will be established? How shall we be governed so as to retain our liberties?" Months later, in March of 1776, she's still worrying the question: "I long to hear that you have declared an independency—and by the way in the new Code of Laws which I suppose it will be necessary for you to make I desire you would remember the ladies, and be more generous and favorable to them than your ancestors. Do not put such unlimited power into the hands of the husbands. Remember all men would be tyrants if they could. If particular care and attention is not paid to the ladies we are determined to foment a rebellion, and will not hold ourselves bound by any laws in which we have no voice, or representation."

It was truly a shocking concept, and John rudely rejected it. "As to your extraordinary Code of Laws, I cannot but laugh. . . . We know better than to repeal our masculine systems. Although they are in full force, you know they are little more than theory. We dare not exert our power in its full latitude. We are obliged to go fair, and softly, and in practice you know we are the subjects. We have only the name of masters, and rather than give up this, which would completely subject us to the despotism of the petticoat, I hope General Washington and all our brave heroes would fight." So much for the ladies. But John was not entirely heartless; he missed her and wanted some form of communication other than letters: "I want to hear you think, or to see your thoughts. The conclusion of your letter makes my heart throb, more than a cannonade would." Abigail tried to suffer her solitude in silence, telling John that "all domestic pleasures and enjoyments are absorbed in the great important duty you owe your country. . . . Thus do I suppress every wish, and silence every murmur, acquiescing in a painful separation from the companion of my youth, and the friend of my heart." But she still wanted to have a say in his work: "I can not say that I think you very generous to the ladies, for whilst you are proclaiming peace and good will to men, emancipating all nations, you insist upon retaining an absolute power over wives. But you must remember that arbitrary power is like most other things which are very hard, very liable to be broken—and not withstanding all your wise laws and maxims we have it in our power not only to free ourselves but to subdue our masters." Not so much has changed in the "power play" of marriage as we might think.

John must have decided that silence was the better part of wisdom, because he didn't address the matter again, but he was willing to give Abigail her due. As the Continental Congress came closer to declaring independence, he took time to congratulate her on her management of the farm: "I begin to be jealous that our neighbors will think affairs more discreetly conducted in my absence than at any other time. . . . I think you shine as a stateswoman, as well as a farmeress. Pray where do you get your maxims of state, they are very apropos." Then, after the praise, he told her the disappointing news that he wouldn't be coming home anytime soon: "The affairs of America, are in so critical a state, such great events are struggling for birth, that I must not quit this station at this time. . . . I am, with constant wishes and prayers for your health and prosperity, forever yours." It was indeed a critical time. it was May 27, 1776. Two weeks later the Congress appointed Adams to a committee of five to draft a statement of independence from Britain.

Finally, on July 3, John delivered the news Abigail had been waiting to read: "Yesterday the greatest question was decided, which ever was debated in America, and a greater perhaps, never was or will be decided among men." The Declaration of Independence had been approved. But John's rejoicing soon gave way to fear about his family. He heard through the grapevine that Abigail had taken herself and the children off for the dangerous smallpox inoculations without asking or telling him. He frantically wondered why no one reported to him on their condition: "Do my friends think that I have been a politician so long as to have lost all feeling? Do they suppose I have forgotten my wife and children?" He assured Abigail that he didn't expect her to be in touch:

"Don't mistake me, I don't blame you. Your time and thoughts must have been wholly taken up, with your own and your family's situation and necessities. But twenty other persons might have informed me." Abigail couldn't be kept down by the weakness caused by the inoculation. She rallied and sent off a stirring description of the reading of the Declaration from the statehouse in Boston: "the cry from the balcony was God Save our American States and then 3 cheers which rended the air, the bells rang, the privateers fired, the forts and batteries, the cannon were discharged, the platoons followed and every face appeared joyful." While she stayed in Boston for the duration of the antismallpox regimen, Abigail attended public worship regularly: "I rejoice in a preacher who has some warmth, some energy, some feeling. Deliver me from your cold phlegmatic preachers, politicians, friends, lovers and husbands. I thank heaven I am not so constituted myself and so connected." Ahem.

Independence had been declared; now what? "We daily see the necessity of a regular government," Abigail fretted in August; particularly galling her was the neglect of education. Then she added another one of her shockers: "If you complain of neglect of education in sons, what shall I say with regard to daughters who every day experience the want of it? . . . If we mean to raise heroes, statesmen and philosophers, we should have learned women. The world perhaps would laugh at me, and accuse me of vanity, but you I know have a mind too enlarged and liberal to disregard the sentiment." Abigail herself had no formal education; she acquired her extensive literary and historical knowledge at home, where various friends of her father guided her reading and conversation. She was so determined that young girls not be deprived of schooling that she returned to the subject whenever she saw an opening.

It was late summer 1776, John Adams had spent most of

two years away from home, and Abigail missed him terribly. Now that independence had been declared, she was more than ready for him to return: "with the purest affection I have held you to my bosom till my whole soul has dissolved in tenderness and my pen fallen from my hand." She tells him she knows he feels the same way and says of such pleasures, "tell me they are not inconsistent with the stern virtue of a senator and a patriot." The senator and patriot was taking his time coming home, and by September, Abigail had had it: "I cannot consent to your tarrying much longer . . . whilst you are engaged in the senate your own domestic affairs require your presence at home . . . your wife and children are in danger of wanting bread. . . . I know the weight of public cares lie so heavy upon you that I have been loath to mention your private ones." It was one thing to found a nation, but what about the family? Finally, in October, Adams left Philadelphia and headed home. But not for long. After only a couple of months, it was back to Congress. John's brief sojourn in Braintree made its mark, however: Abigail was pregnant.

Returning to an assembly of revolutionaries meant a perilous journey for Adams as he skirted British-occupied territory and made his way to Baltimore, where Congress had convened. He was not a happy man: "When I reflect upon the prospect before me of so long an absence from all that I hold dear in this world, I mean all that contributes to my private personal happiness, it makes me melancholy. When I think on your circumstances I am more so, and yet I rejoice at them in spite of all this melancholy." Not only were Abigail's personal "circumstances" of pregnancy difficult, the political circumstances made for hazardous conditions everywhere. British ships blockaded New England, creating a flour shortage. Here's Abigail in March 1777: "There is such a cry for bread in the town of Boston as I suppose was never before heard, and the bakers deal out but a loaf a day to the largest families." When a friend of hers died in childbirth in April,

Abigail grew apprehensive about her own condition: "Every thing of this kind naturally shocks a person in similar circumstances. How great the mind that can overcome the fear of death!" John, too, regretted his plight. Worried that the war was going badly and frustrated by Congress, he lamented, "Posterity! You will never know how much it cost the present generation to preserve your freedom! I hope you will make a good use of it. If you do not, I shall repent in heaven that I ever took half the pains to preserve it." What would he think about posterity now?

Despite her discomfort, Abigail showed glimpses of her usual feistiness when describing how the currency had become so worthless that only by bartering could she supply the household, telling her lawmaker husband that the government should stop printing money; "I hope in favor you will not emit any more paper, till what we have at least becomes more valuable." But she had trouble summoning her spirit: "I want a companion at nights, many of them are wakeful and lonesome. . . . Do you sigh for home? And would you willingly share with me what I have to pass through? . . . I wish the day past, yet dread its arrival." Abigail's foreboding about the day of childbirth only grew worse. In July, when she sat down to write, she thought it might be for the last time: "I was last night taken with a shaking fit, and am very apprehensive that a life was lost. As I have no reason today to think otherways, what may be the consequences to me, heaven only knows." John, too, was worried sick: "Oh that I could be near, to say a few kind words, or show a few kind looks, or do a few kind actions. Oh that I could take from my dearest a share of her distress, or relieve her of the whole. Before this shall reach you I hope you will be happy in the embraces of a daughter as fair, and good, and wise, and virtuous as the mother, or if it is a son I hope it will still resemble the mother in person, mind and heart."

Remarkably, though she was certain she was carrying a

dead baby, Abigail managed to get off a newsy, chatty letter, apologizing for the somber one of the day before. But the next day, as she suspected, a baby girl was stillborn. A friend sent the news to John Adams. A few days later, Abigail took up her pen, thankful that she was still alive: "Join with me my dearest friend in gratitude to heaven, that a life I know you value, has been spared and carried through distress and danger although the dear infant is numbered with its ancestors. . . . My heart was much set upon a daughter. . . . [I] feel myself weakened by this exertion, yet I could not refrain from the temptation of writing with my own hand to you." John was deeply moved: "Never in my whole life was my heart affected with such emotions and sensations. . . . Devoutly do I return thanks to God, whose kind Providence has preserved to me a life that is dearer to me than all other blessings in this world." Still, even in his relief that Abigail had made it through, he grieved for the baby daughter he would never know: "Is it not unaccountable that one should feel so strong an affection for an infant that one has never seen, nor shall see? Yet I must confess to you, the loss of this sweet little girl has most tenderly and sensibly affected me."

Soon Abigail was her old self, trying to manage with few farmhands as more men were called to fight, leaving her with little help. "We can scarcely get a day's work done for money and if money is paid 'tis at such a rate that 'tis almost impossible to live. I live as I never did before, but I am not going to complain. Heaven has blessed us with fine crops." She goes on to tell him about everything she's done on the farm, including paying off debts and setting up a cider press: "I should do exceeding well if we could but keep the money good, but at the rate we go on I know not what will become of us." Or what would become of John, who, with the other instigators of independence, was a marked man. British troops moved on Philadelphia, the members of Congress scattered, eventually reconvening in York, Pennsylvania. Abigail kept him apprised of the situation at home. The women of Boston suspected certain merchants of hoarding sugar and coffee to jack up the price. One wealthy-bachelor coffee supplier was particularly suspect. "A number of females, some say a hundred, some say more, assembled with a cart and trucks, marched down to the warehouse and demanded the keys, which he refused to deliver, upon which one of them seized him by his neck and tossed him into the cart. Upon his finding no quarter he delivered the keys, when they tipped up the cart and discharged him, then opened the warehouse, hoisted out the coffee themselves, put it into the trucks and drove off." Score one for the ladies! And for the American troops, who were defeating the British in battle after battle. On their thirteenth wedding anniversary, October 25, 1777, Abigail was convinced it was the last they would spend apart, that the British would soon lose the war and John would be back in his law practice. She couldn't have been more wrong.

Adams did return home that fall, but only a month after he went back on the court circuit, a letter arrived from James Lovell, a fellow Massachusetts delegate to Congress. It was to inform John Adams of his election as a commissioner to France, where he would join Benjamin Franklin and Arthur Lee. It was important to keep France on the side of the United States during the Revolutionary War, and to make sure key diplomats were there negotiating all eventualities. With her husband off arguing a court case, Abigail received the letter and took it upon herself to fire off an answer. "O Sir, you who are possessed of sensibility, and a tender heart, how could you contrive to rob me of all my happiness?" she challenged Lovell. "My life will be one continued scene of anxiety and apprehension, and must I cheerfully comply with the demand of my country?" Try to imagine a political wife writing a letter like that today! It must have been infinitely more shocking then. If John was to go, Abigail wanted to take the children and go with him. She was soon persuaded that this would be a hazardous course, with the British gunning for her husband, and she relented. In February 1778, judging that a stay in Europe would provide an invaluable education for their son, John took the ten-year-old John Quincy and sailed to Paris for what was to be the most trying period of his and Abigail's marriage.

Adams was quite taken with the French, "stern and haughty Republican as I am," and he made the mistake of writing his long-suffering wife: "To tell you the truth, I admire the ladies here. Don't be jealous. They are handsome, and very well educated. Their accomplishments are exceedingly brilliant." What was he thinking? Well, no one ever claimed John Adams was a good politician. Abigail used his reveries about Frenchwomen to push home one of her pet points: "I regret the trifling narrow contracted education of females of my own country. . . . You need not be told how much female education is neglected, nor how fashionable it has been to ridicule female learning." She kept complaining about the lack of education for women for the rest of her days.

But Abigail's much more serious complaint was John's neglect. She scolds him that she hasn't heard much from him, that his letters are short and cold. So what, she asks, if the enemy intercepts them? "Friendship and affection will suggest a thousand things to say to an intimate friend which if ridiculed by an enemy will only be another proof among the thousands we already have of savage barbarity." John's reaction was one of exasperation, claiming to have written her many more letters than he actually had. (He kept a ledger with copies of all his letters to her, so they were well documented.) Abigail was truly distraught: "I have scarcely ever taken my pen to write but the tears have flowed faster than the ink." Soon she moves, however, from sorrow to anger. Another "very short letter" from John brings on her fury: "By heaven if you could you have changed hearts with some frozen Laplander or made a voyage to a region that has chilled every drop of your blood. But I will restrain a pen already I fear too rash, nor shall it tell you how much I have suffered from this appearance of—inattention."

He would not be moved, closing one letter, "It is not possible for me to express more tenderness and affection to you than will be suggested by the name of . . . John Adams." Some of the letters did get lost at sea, and it took months for the others to arrive. After John had been gone nine months and Abigail had received only three short letters, her pen was white-hot: "I have never let an opportunity slip without writing to you since we parted, though you make no mention of having received a line from me; if they are become of so little importance as not to be worth noticing with your own hand, be so kind as to direct your secretary." She immediately regretted those words: "I will not finish the sentence, my heart denies the justice of the accusation, nor does it believe your affection in the least diminished by distance or absence." Still, she wanted desperately to hear it from him: "The affection I feel for my friend is of the tenderest kind, matured by years, sanctified by choice and approved by heaven. Angels can witness to its purity, what care I then for the ridicule of Britains should this testimony of it fall into their hands." The message was clear: he had more to fear from her than the British.

If she hoped for an outpouring of apologies and testaments of undying affection, Abigail must have been sorely disappointed. John's first, somewhat tepid, response: "For heaven's sake, my dear don't indulge a thought that it is possible for me to neglect, or forget all that I hold dear to me in this world." And then, a couple of weeks later, after another letter from her had made its way across the Atlantic: "This is the third letter I have received in this complaining style. . . . If you write me in this style I shall leave off writing entirely, it kills me. . . . What course shall I take to convince you that my heart is warm? You doubt, it seems—shall I declare it? Shall I swear to it? . . . I beg you would never more write to me in such a strain for it really makes me unhappy." He sternly adds, "I write to you so often as my duty will permit." And then, in the face of ever-more-complicated relations with France, a few months later: "The character and situation in which I am here, and the situation of public affairs absolutely forbid my writing freely."

In February 1779, after a year abroad, Adams briefly thought he would be going home. He informed Abigail in a short noncommunicative letter, "I must not write a word to you about politics because you are a woman. What an offense have I committed?—a woman! I shall soon make it up. I think women better than men in general and I know that you can keep a secret as well as any man whatever. But the world doesn't know this. Therefore if I were to write any secrets to you and the letter should be caught, and hitched into a newspaper, the world would say I was not to be trusted with a secret." She was right all along, he *was* worried about someone reading his mail. In the next letter he's even more explicit: "Let me entreat you to consider, if some of your letters had by any accident been taken, what a figure would they have made in a newspaper to be read by the whole world. Some of them it is true would have done honor to the most virtuous and most accomplished Roman matron, but others of them would have made you and me very ridiculous." And today's public figures think it's new to report on private lives! Abigail's agonies finally came to an end when, with the war winding down, and her husband somewhat confused about his instructions from Congress, in June of 1779 John Adams went home.

Again, it was for a short but productive stay, since Adams took the time to write the constitution for the Commonwealth of Massachusetts. In November, Congress sent him back to Europe, this time as the sole minister responsible for negotiating peace and commerce with Great Britain. Nine-year-old Charles went with his father to Paris this time, along with twelve-year-old John Quincy. And, though Abigail made it clear that she missed both him and the boys, the tone of her letters was much cheerier than that of the earlier ones to Europe. John must have done some fast talking while he was home.

To help make ends meet, he would send her European goods, which she would then sell in Massachusetts. Abigail would tell him in a no-nonsense way what sold and what didn't (the market was glutted with Barcelona handkerchiefs) and she casually mentioned her plans to buy property; she didn't ask him about it, she told him about it. What Adams really wanted was political news and Abigail was happy to oblige. She, correctly as it turned out, predicted that the man they wanted for governor of Massachusetts would lose the election to "the tinkling cymbal," John Hancock: "What a politician you have made me. If I cannot be a voter upon this occasion, I will be a writer of votes." She never let up on her lobbying for the ladies.

Instead of complaining about her abandoned state, this time Abigail used humor to get her point across. The wife of one of John's aides visited her and they talked of their "dear absents," agreeing that the men were "so entirely satisfied with their American dames that we had not an apprehension of their roving. We mean not however to defy the charms of the Parisian ladies, but to admire the constancy and fidelity with which they are resisted—but enough of romance." Then she told him she heard he was getting very fat. When, after he had been gone about a year, John wrote telling her that her letters were a great delight when they did not censure or complain, she took umbrage: "I am wholly unconscious of giving you pain in this way since your late absence." Giving a hint of what must have been said while John was home, Abigail continued, "Did we not balance accounts though the sum was rather in your favor? . . . In the most intimate of friendships there must not be any recrimination. If I complained, it was from the ardor of affection which could not endure the least apprehension of neglect." She then reminds her husband that it all turned out all right: "We no sooner understood each other properly, but as the poet says, 'The falling out of lovers is the renewal of love.' " She insists that "not a syllable of complaint has ever stained my paper" since he left this time, and continues, "You well know I never doubted your honor. Virtue and principle confirm the indissoluble bond which affection first began and my security depends not upon your passion, which other objects might more easily excite, but upon the sober and settled dictates of religion and honor. It is these that cement, at the same time that they ensure the affections." How's that for a definition of long marriage?

Adams started running into problems with the French in the spring of 1781, when they objected to his assumption that the two nations should form an alliance of equals. The French minister in Philadelphia persuaded Congress to name other peace ministers to join Adams, depriving him of his exclusive role. Because the nascent nation could not afford to alienate its most important ally, the American delegation was directed to govern itself according to the advice and opinion of the French court. When Abigail heard the news, she was furious, and let her member of Congress know it. She tore off a letter to Elbridge Gerry excoriating Benjamin Franklin, who had led the plot to undo Adams, and imploring Gerry, "Will you suffer female influence so far to operate upon you as to step forth and lend your aid to rescue your country and your friend?" She then told John, "I will not comment upon this low, this dirty, this infamous, this diabolical piece of envy and malice as I have already done it where I thought I might be of service—to your two friends Lovell and Gerry." So much for the myth that political wives didn't interfere in their husbands' careers until modern times.

John was pleased to have Abigail intervene for him, and he used her as his informant on what Congress had in store. Though, on the subject of his enemies, he assures her, "they will never hurt your husband whose character is fortified with a shield of innocence and honor ten thousandfold stronger than brass or iron," Adams in fact worried constantly that his honor was being besmirched. He had also decided it was foolish to try to take care of his little son Charles in Europe and sent the eleven-year-old home with a tutor, on what turned out to be a harrowing trip. Most of all, John was beginning to miss Abigail terribly: "what a fine affair it would be if we could flit across the Atlantic as they say the angels do from planet to planet. I would dart to Pens Hill and bring you over on my wings. . . . But one thing I am determined on. If God should please to restore me once more to your fireside, I will never again leave it without your ladyship's company." With that encouragement, Abigail started figuring out how to join her husband in Europe.

By then he had been gone more than two years, and she ached for him: "the age of romance has long ago past, but the affection of almost infant years has matured and strengthened until it has become a vital principle, nor has the world any thing to bestow which could in the smallest degree compensate for the loss." John, too, was more than ready for the years apart to end: "I must go to you or you must come to me," he wrote. "I cannot live in this horrid solitude which it is to me amidst courts, camps and crowds." Adams was ready to go home, but his mission was incomplete and he was concerned about what a return would mean for his career. He left France for the Netherlands, determined to show the Congress his value. There he negotiated a successful trade agreement and bought what amounted to the first American embassy in Europe. But he was worried about the homefront, particularly about his own children.

Soon John had reason to worry about his daughter; seventeen-year-old "Nabby" was being courted by a suitor he found unacceptable. Abigail's description didn't help: "Losing his father young and having a very pretty patrimony left him, possessing a sprightly fancy, a warm imagination and an agreeable person, he was rather negligent in pursuing his business in the way of his profession, and dissipated two or three years of his life and too much of his fortune for to reflect upon with pleasure, all of which he now laments but cannot recall." Even so, Abigail clearly likes him and thinks he's good for Nabby. The mother paints a remarkably clear-eyed picture of her daughter: "She is handsome, but not beautiful. No air of levity ever accompanies either her words or actions. Should she be caught by a tender passion, sufficient to remove a little of her natural reserve and soften her form and manners, she will be a still more pleasing character." Her father was appalled. "My child is a model, as you represent her and as I know her, and is not to be the prize, I hope of any even reformed rake. . . . A youth who has been giddy enough to spend his fortune or even half his fortune in gaieties is not the youth for me." He chastises his wife for her assessment of Nabby: "In the name of all that is tender don't criticize your daughter for those qualities which are her greatest glory, her reserve and her prudence which I am amazed to hear you call want of sensibility. The more silent she is in company the better for me in exact proportion and I would have this observed as a rule by the mother as well as the daughter." It wasn't only Abigail who got off a shot across the bow from time to time.

John's mood was not improved by his work. He was in the midst of extremely delicate negotiations with the British about a final peace treaty, and the French were causing all kinds of trouble. As Adams and his fellow diplomats waited for word on treaty ratification from Congress in the early months of 1783, the proper Bostonian father continued his tirades against his daughter's suitor, telling his wife, "I am so uneasy about this subject that I would come instantly home, if I could with decency. But my Dutch Treaty is not yet exchanged. . . . There are other subjects too about which I am not on a bed of roses." Congress had revoked his commission to make a commercial treaty with Britain without saying why: "therefore I will come home, whether my resignation is accepted or not, unless my honor is restored." Only a renewal of his commission could restore his honor— but that, of course, would mean yet more time abroad. If so, he finally tells the eager Abigail, "come to me, with your daughter if she is not too much engaged, and master Tommy." He charges her with finding out what Congress is up to.

That turned out to be a tough assignment, as the end of the war brought chaos in the former colonies, and uncertainty about what powers Congress actually possessed. It seemed that John Adams would, in fact, finally go home. Abigail had managed to break up the romance between Nabby and her young man to please her father, though the mother still found the suitor a fine fellow. The breakup should make John even more ready to come home, in Abigail's view. "I do not wish you to accept an embassy to England, should you be appointed. This little cottage has more heartfelt satisfaction for you than the most brilliant court can afford, the pure and undiminished tenderness of wedded love, the filial affection of a daughter who will never act contrary to the advice of a father or give pain to the maternal heart." In July, Adams's fate was still uncertain. Congress did not want to accept his resignation until the peace treaties were finalized, but he desperately wanted to return. "I cannot live much longer without my wife and daughter and I will not," he insisted, but he was having second thoughts about them joining him abroad.

"If you and your daughter come to Europe you will get into your female imaginations fantastical ideas that will never wear out and will spoil you both. . . . The question is whether it is possible for a lady to be once accustomed to the dress, show, etc. of Europe, without having her head turned by it? This is an awful problem." This from the man who had been urging frugality all those years, to a woman who had bravely been making ends meet.

The question seemed settled when Adams was appointed to a commission to negotiate trade relations with Britain, a job that might only last a few months: "I am so unhappy without you that I wish you would come at all events. . . . I must however leave it with your judgment, you know better than I the real intentions of Philadelphia." One of the major players in government conceded that his wife knew more about Congress than he did: "You gave me more public intelligence than anybody. The only hint in Europe of this commission was from you." By October, when Adams had been gone from home almost exactly four years, his tone grew more urgent: "I have only to repeat my earnest request that you and our daughter would come to me as soon as possible."

But Abigail started to get cold feet; she wanted him to turn down the job; she also warned her husband that though Nabby's romance had broken off, she could tell the couple were still enamored of each other. By the time John received the letter, in January of 1784, he was so desperate to see Abigail that he was ready to say yes to Nabby's young man. "I must entreat you to come to me, for I assure you, my happiness depends so much upon it that I am determined if you decline coming to me, to come to you. If Miss Nabby is attached to Braintree and you think, upon advising with your friends, her object worthy, marry her if you will and leave her with her companion in your own house, office, furniture, farm and all."

Poor Abigail was torn: "You invite me to you, you call me

to follow you, the most earnest wish of my soul is to be with you—but you can scarcely form an idea of the conflict of my mind." She didn't want to leave her children and friends without her husband to console her: "But on the other hand I console myself with the idea of being joyfully and tenderly received by the best of husbands and friends, and of meeting a dear and long absent son. But the difference is my fears and anxieties are present, my hopes and expectations distant." How's that for self-awareness, late-eighteenth-century style?

Not surprisingly, her hopes, and John's wishes, won out and Abigail set off for Europe with Nabby in June 1784, "without any male friend, connection or acquaintance." As it happened, Thomas Jefferson, another member of the commission, tried to accompany her across the Atlantic but missed her by a day. She had already left when he arrived in Boston. The sometimes rough trip took exactly a month, Abigail's ship landing on the British coast on July 20. It took another three days for the women to reach London, where they hoped to be met by their husband and father. But, much to his dismay, Adams was in The Hague conducting business—"I am twenty years younger than I was yesterday," he wrote when he learned the women had arrived safely—so he sent John Quincy to greet his mother and sister. John dispatched a letter via his son, explaining that John Quincy would purchase a coach for travel to Paris, and that the ladies should buy clothes, "let the expense be what it will." "The happiest man on earth," signed off, "Yours with more ardor than ever."

Mother and daughter amused themselves in London, writing wonderfully descriptive letters home, but by July 30, Abigail was getting anxious. Finally, almost five years after he had last seen his wife, John Adams arrived in London on August 7. For all their letter and diary writing over the years, neither one described the moment of reunion at the Adelphi Hotel. Abigail knew her sisters would be dying to know how it went, but she wrote to one of them, "poets and painters wisely draw a veil over those scenes which surpass the pen of one and the pencil of the other."

Abigail and John spent four years together in Europe, where she developed a close friendship with Thomas Jefferson, returning to Braintree in 1788 when it was clear Adams would become the first vice-president of the United States of America under the just-adopted Constitution. Though the couple was sometimes separated when Adams traveled to Philadelphia, Abigail often accompanied John, so their continual correspondence about their feelings and frustrations as a couple ended at their meeting in the Adelphi Hotel.

In the periods when they were apart, mainly because her health kept her home in Massachusetts, she sent him letters full of political advice, and he sent her congratulatory notes on her handling of the farm, along with secrets of state. They both wrote frankly about deteriorating relations with France, a nation they knew well and did not trust. After George Washington's two terms as president, Adams wanted to succeed him, but feared he would lose to Jefferson and be once again elected vice-president. Not if Abigail had anything to do with it: "Resign, retire. I would be second unto no man but Washington." She had her own concerns about him running for president; she was afraid her outspokenness would get him in trouble. He replied, "A woman *can* be silent, when she will." Once John won the election, she vowed to try: "I hope to acquire every requisite degree of taciturnity which my station calls for," but she knew, "it will be putting a force upon nature." In the end, it was a force she wasn't willing to exert.

Abigail missed John's inauguration. Her health didn't allow her to travel to Philadelphia for the event, but he couldn't be president without her: "I never wanted your advice and assistance more in my life." Then, two weeks later: "I must have you here." Her mother-in-law and niece were dying; she first tended to them, then arranged for the management

of their property, and then she joined him. It was a tumultuous presidency, with her smack in the middle of the con-
troversies—the XYZ affair, possible war with France, and the
Alien and Sedition Acts. Taciturnity had long since gone out
the window, and Abigail was every bit as controversial in her
day as Eleanor Roosevelt and Hillary Clinton have been in
ours. While she was lobbying to declare war on France, Abigail also planned a surprise for her husband: she built an extensive addition to their home without telling him. When a
friend accidentally spilled the beans, the president was thoroughly delighted and sorry her secret was spoiled; the house
was comfortable and pleasant. Not so the new president's
house in the not-yet-finished District of Columbia. When
John and Abigail moved there in November 1800, it was an
unfinished disaster, where she famously hung the family laundry in the East Room. But they didn't have to stay in the
White House long; John was defeated for reelection by their
old friend Thomas Jefferson.

Abigail had a harder time dealing with John's loss than he
did; she was hurt by Jefferson's opposition and convinced the
country would go to rack and ruin. Her husband would remain "the President" in her view, and Abigail referred to John
that way for the rest of her life. But the couple lived in mostly
contented retirement for another seventeen years, constantly
surrounded by children, grandchildren, nieces, and nephews,
and treated as dignitaries by the community. The death of
their son Charles did not come as a surprise; he had become
a miserable alcoholic, cut off by his father but still mourned
by his mother. Abigail was also deeply touched when Jefferson's daughter Polly died, remembering her as a little girl in
London. The former first lady took the occasion to renew
their old friendship with Jefferson by starting a correspondence with him. John left the management of their properties
to his wife; she had gotten good at it over the years. He started
reading romance novels in his old age, enjoying them like "a

girl in her teens," wrote the amazed Abigail. She kept up her campaign for women's education as long as she breathed. The great blot on their later years was the death of their daughter Nabby, who had married someone other than the "rake" her father opposed; still, she hadn't made much of a match. The great success among their children, John Quincy, served in Congress but spent most of his life as a diplomat, having been raised in the courts of Europe, then as secretary of state. His mother did not live to see him become president, but his father did, though John Adams died before seeing his son defeated after one term, just as he had been.

When the Adamses celebrated their golden anniversary, Abigail told the gathering that her only unhappiness in her time with John came from the long separation during the Revolutionary years. But what a window on a marriage that separation provided the generations following them. As much as all their other contributions to this nation's institutions, John and Abigail Adams gave us a picture of a partnership in the much older institution of marriage.

NOTE: Most of the Adams letters quoted in this chapter come from *The Book of Abigail and John,* edited by L. H. Butterfield, Marc Friedlaender, and Mary-Jo Kline (Cambridge, MA: Harvard University Press, 1975). Spelling and punctuation have been modernized and corrected.

The very words "slave marriage" can start an argument. Since slaves had no legal rights, no rights to form contracts, they could not really get married in the eyes of the law. Masters could sanction or veto a union of slaves; owners could at any time sell a husband away from his wife, children away from their parents. None of the promises or protections that human beings in most societies expect from marriage applied to slaves. Still, the written records as well as the recorded memories of the centuries-long period of slaveholding in this country make it clear that marriage played a major role in slave society. Couples struggling to cleave together often risked great harm in order to hold on to their mates, to keep their families united. Some of those stories have been handed down in the narratives written by former slaves and in letters collected by later historians.

The ability of the human spirit to survive and even thrive in horrendous circumstances comes through strikingly in tales of slave marriages. Not only was the fundamental fact of existence—human bondage—one of constant humiliation and physical danger, every aspect of that life could be disrupted and degraded by a mean-spirited master. Slave men could not protect their wives from sexual abuse and beatings by their owners, slave women were forced to witness the emasculating brutality toward their husbands, slave parents knew that their hard labor would never lead to better lives for their children. Still, men and women fell in love and found ways to dignify their feelings for each other through ritual. In some areas of the country, the masters presided over the ceremony; in some areas, clergy pronounced the vows; in some areas, it was an elder in the slave community. The old stories of jumping over a broomstick turn out to be true, though the custom varied in different places. Carolina Johnson Harrison, a slave in Virginia, gave this account of her own wedding: "Just go to Aunt Sue and tell her you want to get mated. She told us to think about it hard for two days because marrying is sacred in the eyes of Jesus. After two days, Mose and I went back and said we thought about it and still want to get married. Then she called all the slaves after tasks to pray for the union that God was going to make. Pray we stay together and have lots of children and none of them get sold away from the parents. Then she lays a broomstick across the sill of the house we're going to live in and joins our hands together. Before we step over it, she asks us once more if we were sure we wanted to get married. Of course we say yes. Then she says, 'In the eyes of Jesus, step into the holy land of matrimony.' When we stepped across the broomstick, we were married."

Often, particularly in the Chesapeake region, where there were fewer slaves per tobacco farm than on the large cotton, rice, and sugar plantations of the Deep South, men married women on another plantation. Husbands could only visit these "abroad" or "broad" wives over Saturday night, with a pass from the master. And some masters only grudgingly allowed that. Peter Smith, a runaway Tennessee slave interviewed by a newspaper in 1845, told of his master's decree that if he returned late from seeing his wife, he would receive one hundred lashes and be forbidden to visit her. When Smith realized he was late one morning, he ran away rather than face that punishment; he had nothing to lose, since he could never see his wife again. Breakup of marriage and family concerns inspired runaways, as men escaped to follow their wives who had been sold, or women fled to raise their children in freedom. Because they wanted to discourage bolting and encourage breeding, many slave owners promoted marriage and childbearing, particularly after the importation of slaves was prohibited in 1807. On large plantations where slaves lived in their own area, or "quarters," there was some small modicum of privacy that allowed for a semblance of "normal" family life.

But nothing could be truly normal for a human being who was not considered a human being. That's abundantly clear in the accounts that have come to be called "slave narratives," the most famous written by former slaves in the period shortly before the Civil War. Intended to stir up abolitionist sentiments by revealing the evils of the institution of slavery, the narratives also reveal a good deal about their authors' experiences with marriage.

Henry Bibb: Family Versus Freedom

When Henry Bibb told his life story, a group of Detroit abolitionists formed a truth commission to check out his hairraising history. Buttressed by letters from his former owner, and a slave trader who hated him, as well as friends and protectors along the way, the Detroit Liberty Association endorsed Bibb's harrowing account, which was published in 1849.

Born in Kentucky in 1815, Bibb learned from his mother, who was a slave, that his father was a white man named James Bibb. Though he was put to work at a young age, Henry never accepted his treatment, and started his long career as a runaway at about age twenty. He actually succeeded several times in making it to the North, where he could enjoy his freedom, but he repeatedly went back home to Kentucky to try to rescue his wife and child. As he told the story years later, it was with some degree of irony: "To think that after I had determined to carry out the great idea which is so universally and practically acknowledged among all the civilized nations of the earth, that I would be free or die, I suffered myself to be turned aside by the fascinating charms of a female, who gradually won my attention from an object so high as that of liberty."

When he was eighteen, Bibb met a girl named Malinda who lived about four miles away. He started visiting her, with no intention of marrying her, because he knew marriage would hinder his quest for freedom, "but in spite of myself, before I was aware of it, I was deeply in love." He proposed to Malinda on the condition that she understand two things: he was deeply religious and determined to be free. She was sympathetic on both counts and, after a couple of weeks' reflection, accepted his proposal. They decided they would marry a year later if they hadn't changed their minds and that they would run away to Canada as soon as they could. Everyone was against the marriage—his mother thought he was too young, her mother thought she could do better, his master worried that he would steal food from the farm for Malinda. But in the end the owner gave his consent and the couple had a "jolly time" at their wedding party, held over the Christmas holidays: "Notwithstanding our marriage was without license or sanction of law, we believed it to be honorable before God."

Bibb's owner moved away and eventually Henry was sold to Malinda's master, a situation not at all to his liking, "to live where I must be eye witness to her insults, scourgings and abuses . . . was more than I could bear." When a daughter, Mary Frances, was born, Bibb became even more restive. While her mother and father worked in the field, the baby stayed with the owner's wife, who treated her roughly. It was too much for Bibb—to see his family abused and to be powerless to do anything about it; he decided he must break free. First he would go, then he would find a way to rescue his wife and child. Lucky for him, the Ohio River wasn't far from home. He was able to accumulate a little money by doing some work on the side, and he hopped a steamship and counted on his almost white skin to camouflage him through the night until landing the next morning in Cincinnati. Though Ohio was a free state, the fear of slave hunters was real, so Bibb moved carefully until he found a black man who hooked him up with the Underground Railroad. Moving to a safer spot north, Bibb spent the spring working in Perrysburg, Ohio, then, against the advice of his protectors, went back to Kentucky to collect his family. Think of it: he was free and could have lived out the rest of his life in freedom, but the matrimonial ties pulled him back to the dangers of a slave state.

Wearing a disguise, Bibb crept back into Kentucky, gave his wife money, and quickly stole away again, telling her to meet him in Cincinnati the next Sunday. Once again he successfully made his way to Ohio, but this time he was tricked by some slave catchers, who went quickly down the river to his master and collected a three-hundred-dollar reward for revealing Bibb's whereabouts. The owner and some neighbors arrived in Cincinnati, hired a small mob, and captured Bibb, who later lamented, "All my flattering prospects of enjoying my own fire side, with my little family, were then blasted and gone; and I must bid farewell to friends and freedom together." Taking no chances, the owner immediately took Bibb across the river and put him in jail overnight in Kentucky until a steamship arrived to take him to Louisville. Bibb's owner wanted to get rid of the troublemaker, to sell him down the river to New Orleans. But once the ship docked in Louisville, Bibb bolted again and once again made the perilous trip to see his wife. "We met under the most fearful apprehensions," he later wrote, because all the slaveholders in the region wanted to make an example of him. Of course, they kept a watch on Malinda day and night: "they well knew that my little family was the only object of attraction that ever had or ever would induce me to come back and risk my liberty over the threshold of slavery." It would be impossible for the couple to escape together.

Once again Bibb set out on his own, with an agreement to meet in a certain place in Ohio after all the excitement had died down. But Malinda had no faith that would ever happen: "This may be the last time we shall ever see each other's faces in this life, which will destroy all my future prospects of life and happiness forever," she told him tearfully. But he was absolutely determined to make sure she was wrong. For the third time, he successfully made his way to freedom, and after eight or nine months without hearing from his family, for the third time he dared return to slave territory to rescue his wife and child.

From there, the story gets very grim indeed. Bibb was captured again. The owner, worried that he might have told Malinda how to get to Canada and fearful that she would tell other slaves, decided to sell the whole family downriver, farther away from any free state. After a horrible sojourn in a Louisville workhouse, the family finally was taken to New Orleans and offered for sale. Eventually, a Baptist deacon bought them and brought them to his home up the Red River. One day Bibb went to a prayer meeting off the property against the master's wishes. On his way home, Malinda met him and told him of the owner's plan to give him five hundred lashes. Bibb made his move. He stole a donkey, gathered his wife and child, and set out through the insect-infested Louisiana marshland hoping somehow to escape. When they were caught ten days later, Bibb was brought back and brutally beaten, almost to death. He was kept separate from his wife and forced to sleep with his feet in stocks, but he managed to break away again. When he was captured once more, the deacon decided to sell the troublesome worker and be rid of him for good.

Some gamblers, or "southern sportsmen" in Bibb's words, who were traveling through Louisiana, saw the slave, decided he looked clever, and bought him to resell. They took him to Texas, and as he unraveled his story, they took pity on him and returned to the Red River plantation to offer to buy his wife and child. When they arrived, Malinda saw Bibb and rushed out to greet him: "Oh! My dear husband! I never expected to see you again!"

She would have been better off if she had not. The infuriated deacon stepped between them and started whipping her, much to the horror of the gamblers, who offered a thousand dollars for her and her child. But the deacon was determined to make the couple suffer, and he sent the men away to the wails of Malinda and Mary Frances, who was watching. After all that, after all the times that Bibb had had the opportunity to be free but had returned to risk capture for the love of his wife and child, he ended up a slave without a family. He and the gamblers left the deacon's property in December 1840. "I have never seen Malinda since that period," Bibb wrote in 1849. "I never expect to see her again."

The gamblers felt so sorry for Bibb that they gave him directions to Canada, sold him to an Indian, and gave him part of the money they made from the sale. After his Indian master died, Bibb found an opportunity to take off and make his way through Indian Territory all the way to Jefferson City, Missouri, where through clever subterfuge he boarded a ship to Ohio. He went back to Perrysburg for a while and then on to Detroit. There, in 1845, abolitionists who hired him to lecture against slavery collected money to look for his wife and child and try to buy them. No luck. It was a verdict Bibb couldn't accept: "In view of the failure to hear anything of my wife, many of my best friends advised me to get married again, if I could find a suitable person. They regarded my former wife as dead to me, and all had been done that could be. But I was not yet satisfied myself, to give up."

So yet again, he took the risk and returned to Kentucky one last time. He soon learned that Malinda "was living in a state of adultery with her master, and had been for the last three years." After the scene with the gamblers on the Red

River plantation, she had finally given up on Bibb and the deacon had sold her to a white man as a concubine. "From that time I gave her up into the hands of an all-wise Providence. As she was then living with another man, I could no longer regard her as my wife. After all the sacrifices, sufferings, and risks which I had run, striving to rescue her from the grasp of slavery, every prospect and hope was cut off."

Two years later, at an antislavery event in New York, Henry Bibb met "Miss Mary E. Miles." It's interesting; he never prefaced Malinda's name with a "Miss" and we never learn her last name in his narrative, but this was a different situation and he was well aware of it. They courted for a year, then, in June 1848, "we had the happiness to be joined in holy wedlock. Not in the slaveholding style which is a mere farce, without the sanction of law or gospel; but in accordance with the laws of God and our country. . . . I presume there are no class of people in the United States who so highly appreciate the legality of marriage as those persons who have been held and treated as property." Still, Bibb was defensive about Malinda because he knew that their marriage, though not legal, was true. "The relation once subsisting between us, to which I clung, hoping against hope, for years, after we were torn asunder, not having been sanctioned by any loyal power cannot be cancelled by a legal process. . . . It was not until after living alone in the world for more than eight years without a companion known in law or morals, that I changed my condition."

Harriet Jacobs: "My Story Ends with Freedom; Not in the Usual Way, with Marriage"

Harriet Jacobs was never any man's wife, but her story is still illustrative of slave marriage, because it is the tale of a woman who wanted desperately to marry the man she loved and was thwarted by the system. She came right up against the plain fact that slaves had no legal rights, that for her marriage was out of the question simply because she was a slave. That's the message she sought to convey in her *Incidents in the Life of a Slave Girl;* she was convinced the women of the North would rise up and force the men to do something about slavery if they knew what slave women suffered. But Jacobs had a problem in telling her story. Sex was not a subject anyone talked about in the mid-nineteenth century. It certainly wasn't a subject for proper women to read about. But it's central to her story. She changed her name and those of her characters for publication, and it took until the 1980s for scholars to authenticate the autobiography.

Harriet Jacobs never was subjected to the harsh physical treatment Henry Bibb describes; in fact, she was raised in relatively comfortable circumstances. She grew up in a North Carolina town where her father was such a fine carpenter that he was allowed to live and work on his own, paying his mistress two hundred dollars every month from the money he made in his business. His wife, Harriet's mother, died when her little girl was six, and the slave child went to live with a kind woman who was her mother's mistress. Not only was Harriet loved in that household, she was educated, and when her mistress died, the twelve-year-old slave hoped the woman had set her free. Instead, the young slave was bequeathed to the mistress's five-year-old niece. Harriet's father tried to make enough money to buy her, but he soon died as well.

The new household of a doctor and his wife, the parents of the five-year-old, turned out to be far less friendly for Harriet, but still she had certain advantages. Her grandmother, who had been freed many years before, was a well-known personage in the community. "Aunt Marthy" baked a type of cracker all the fancy ladies bought for their parties, and often when they stopped by her house to buy her pastries, they sought out her advice as well. No one wanted to offend her; she had once chased a white man with a loaded pistol when he insulted one of her daughters. Living in a city, instead of out on a plantation, meant that Harriet's master had to worry about his reputation as a professional man; he couldn't commit blatantly improper acts under the noses of his neighbors. Still, when Harriet started blossoming into her teenage years, the doctor started to stalk her and "to whisper foul words in my ear," trying to lure her into his bed. Remember, this was the Victorian era; this was shocking stuff to be writing about. The young slave managed by one ruse after another to avoid her master, but she was terrified living under his roof and she was afraid to tell her grandmother; the doctor swore he would kill her if she did. Speaking to the women of the North, Harriet lectured: "There is no shadow of law to protect [the slave girl] from insult, from violence, or even from death; all these are inflicted by fiends who bear the shape of men. The mistress, who ought to protect the helpless victim, has no other feelings towards her but those of jealousy and rage." Seeing the girl growing into womanhood, Harriet's grandmother worried about her situation and tried to buy her, but the doctor insisted that she belonged to his little girl and that he had no right to sell her. It was a grand excuse, which he used again after Harriet fell in love.

A young black carpenter in the neighborhood, a free man, started calling on Harriet and eventually proposed marriage to her. "I loved him with all the ardor of a young girl's first love," she wrote many years later, and he was ready to buy her, but again her master refused. "If you must have a husband, you may take up with one of my slaves," he told her. "Don't you suppose, sir, that a slave can have some preference about marrying? Do you suppose that all men are alike to her?" The doctor ripped into her: "Never let me hear the fellow's name mentioned again. If I ever know of your speaking to him, I will cowhide you both; and if I catch him lurking about my premises, I will shoot him as soon as I would a dog." She, of course, was devastated. "My lover was an intelligent and religious man. Even if he could have obtained permission to marry me while I was a slave, the marriage would give him no power to protect me from my master. It would have made him miserable to witness the insults I should have been subjected to." Also, if they had children, they would be slaves, because the children "followed the condition of the mother." She convinced her love to leave, to head for a free state, which he did, and she later declared, "the dream of my girlhood was over."

The doctor decided that it was fear of his wife that was causing Harriet to reject him, so he told her he was building a house where he could be with her. She panicked. There was a young, unmarried white gentleman in the town who started to take an interest in her, to show some sympathy for her situation. She understood she could never marry him; it was against the law for whites to marry blacks. "I knew the impassable gulf between us but to be an object of interest to a man who is not married, and who is not her master, is agreeable to the pride and feelings of a slave," she explained to her female readers. "It seems less degrading to give one's self, than to submit to compulsion. There is something akin to freedom in having a lover who has no control over you, except that which he gains by kindness and attachment." Harriet was well aware that other emotions were also governing her decision to take up with the young man. It would be a way to humiliate the doctor, and to avoid him: "I shuddered to think of being the mother of children that should be owned by my old tyrant."

As much as she justified her relationship with the young gentleman, Harriet knew she was defying all of the standards of the day; she was a scarlet woman. When she wrote about it, Harriet feared her readers might discount her story because of her sinfulness. When she was in the relationship, she was terrified about her grandmother's reaction to her out-of-wedlock arrangement. But she relished the doctor's. When he told her the house he was building for her was ready, she responded that she would never move there, and that soon she would be a mother. His furor simply kindled her self-righteousness: "but for *him* I might have been a virtuous, free and happy wife." Her delight at her master's reaction was short-lived, however, because she knew now her relatives would find out, and would be disgraced: "humble as were their circumstances, they had pride in my good character." Harriet's grandmother, particularly, was sorely saddened. But she took her in and cared for her, since the doctor's wife wanted her out of their house. When Harriet gave birth to a premature baby boy, she reflected, "It was a sad thought that I had no name to give my child." The father tried to buy Harriet and give the boy his name, but the master wouldn't hear of it.

At least her situation got Harriet out of the doctor's house. But he kept after her, determined to have her. He would threaten to sell her baby boy. Then, when, at the age of nineteen, she had a second child, a girl, he was truly infuriated. After some dramatic scenes, the doctor came back with an offer: move in with him and she and the children could be free. She refused. The consequence: she and the children would be sent to his ruffian son's plantation, where they would be treated like all the other slaves. She didn't trust the offer of freedom and she knew the plantation would be intolerable, so she determined to escape. Harriet went to the plantation, but soon did run away, to the home of a kind white woman who hid her in the attic. Hoping to smoke her out of hiding, her master threw her brother, son, and daughter in jail and kept them there for two months. Once he became convinced she really had left, the doctor traveled to New York looking for her, which cost him a good deal of money. That had one beneficial effect—he sold Harriet's children to their father to make up for his losses. Harriet knew she was endangering the woman whose house she was in, so she stole away to her grandmother's and hid in a tiny space over a storeroom across a courtyard from the house. She stayed there almost seven years.

From her hiding place, the young mother could see her children playing in her grandmother's courtyard, but she could never let them know she was there. When their father was elected to Congress, he and his wife decided to take the little girl with them to Washington, to help care for their baby. Then they promised to take her to relatives in Brooklyn who would send her to school. Through her grandmother, Harriet agreed to the arrangements and then dared detection to say good-bye to her daughter. She crept across the court-yard into her grandmother's house and waited in her room, where she hadn't been for five years. When the little girl was brought to her, Harriet said, " 'Ellen, my dear child, I am your mother.' She drew back a little, and looked at me then, with sweet confidence, she laid her cheek against mine, and I folded her to the heart that had been so long desolated." When, a few months later, the Brooklyn relatives wrote to Harriet's grandmother about Ellen's safe arrival, the letter troubled the family in North Carolina. It appeared that, con-trary to his promises, the child's father had not set her free.

One day, after she had hidden for seven years, Harriet had come down from her hole and was talking to her grand-mother in the storeroom. Carelessly, the grandmother had left the storeroom door open, and when a neighbor came to buy crackers, and went looking for Aunt Marthy, she looked in the storeroom. Harriet couldn't be sure whether she had been seen, but she was afraid to risk it. The doctor had gone to New York three times looking for her, and had never given up the chase. Though it was incredibly risky, the family de-cided it would probably be safer for her to try to board a friendly ship that was in the harbor than to take her chances with the doctor. Before she left, Harriet was determined to see her son. "It was an agitating interview for both of us. After we had talked and wept together for a little while, he said, 'Mother, I'm glad you're going away. I wish I could go with you. I knew you were here; and I have been *so* afraid they would come and catch you!' " She was amazed. It turned out he had heard a cough one day, and concluded it was his mother. From there on out, he tried to keep people away from that side of the storeroom.

Harriet successfully boarded the ship and sailed to Philadelphia and freedom. Finally. From Philadelphia, she took a train to New York and went in search of her daughter. Ellen's situation was not as advertised; she wasn't going to school and was being treated as a servant rather than a family member. Of course, the little girl couldn't do anything about her circumstances, so Harriet chose to stay in New York, where she could keep an eye on her daughter. That was just fine with the woman Ellen was living with; once Harriet got a job, she started supplying the clothes and shoes her daughter needed. Fortunately for the runaway, she got work as a nursemaid for a sympathetic Englishwoman with a new baby, who had no objection to her visiting Ellen regularly. One of those visits almost spelled the end of Harriet's freedom. A Southern relative was visiting the family, spied the fugitive, and wrote to the doctor of her whereabouts. Fortunately, the children in the family found out about it and warned Harriet. The Englishwoman then arranged for her and Ellen to go to Boston, where slave owners dared not tread. There followed an almost idyllic period for Harriet Jacobs. Her son had been sent to Boston to live with Harriet's brother, who had run away from his master on a trip north years before. Now she had her daughter there as well. She was able to get work as a seamstress and send her children to school. But then her benefactress, the Englishwoman, died, and her husband, Mr. Bruce, begged Harriet to accompany him and the baby to England. She felt she owed him that much. So she arranged for her children's education and housing and left them again.

England was an eye-opener for the fugitive slave. She kept comparing the situation of impoverished Englishmen with that of American slaves, and the English came out far ahead. "The father, when he closed his cottage door, felt safe with his family around him. No master or overseer could come and take from him his wife, or his daughter. . . . The relations of husband and wife, parent and child, were too sacred for the richest noble in the land to violate with impunity." The English better than the Americans? Unthinkable to the Northern ladies who were the targets of Harriet Jacobs's work! Grandparents were still handing down tales of the Revolution to their grandchildren. When she returned from England, Harriet went back to Boston, but before long the Bruce family needed her again. There was a new wife and a new baby.

Going back to New York was now fraught with danger because the Fugitive Slave Act had been passed, empowering federal marshals to capture runaways and return them to their masters, and penalizing anyone who assisted the slaves. When word reached Harriet that the old doctor knew her whereabouts and his emissaries were headed her way, the new Mrs. Bruce found the courage to use her own baby as a form of protection. She arranged for her nursemaid to take the baby with her to friends, figuring that anyone who found Harriet would have to return the baby; then the family might be able to help the fugitive. After about a month in the country, the coast was clear for Harriet and the baby to return to New York, but the situation remained precarious even after the news arrived that the old doctor had died. His daughter, Harriet's real owner, now married, seemed just as insistent on reclaiming her slave. She and her husband made their own trip to New York; Harriet and the baby made another escape. But Mrs. Bruce had had enough; she arranged to buy Harriet from the North Carolina family once and for all.

That should have been good news for Harriet Jacobs. It

was not. She couldn't stand the idea that she was a piece of property to be bought and sold: "A human being *sold* in the free city of New York! The bill of sale is on record and future generations will learn from it that women were articles of traffic in New York, late in the nineteenth century of the Christian religion." Still, it was a relief. And when Harriet Jacobs arrived at the Bruce doorstep, she quickly learned that she was now free. Legally. That to her was the end of the story. It wasn't the usual ending of a story aimed at women, a romance where the heroine lived happily ever after, but it was a happy ending even so. "Reader, my story ends with freedom; not in the usual way, with marriage. My children and I are now free!"

Ellen and William Craft: A Daring Escape for a Life Together

The Crafts' tale, *Running a Thousand Miles for Freedom,* sold as a suspense story when it was published in England in 1860. And it does read like a good mystery. But there's no mystery in the two central themes of the tale: the couple's abhorrence of slavery and their attachment to each other.

Both Crafts grew up in Macon, Georgia. Ellen's first master was her father; her mother was his slave. Because she looked so much like the children of the family, the mistress was eager to get Ellen out of the house, so, at age eleven, the little girl became a wedding present for the mistress's daughter. William Craft's first master decided he needed new slave stock, so he sold off William's aged parents, separating them after many years of marriage. Then, when the master started speculating in cotton, he mortgaged William and his sister to a bank, which eventually auctioned them off to the highest bidders. William was bought by a cabinetmaker. He and Ellen had grown up knowing each other, as slaves would in a town the size of Macon. Eventually they fell in love, but the young slave woman refused to get married.

William later explained Ellen's resistance to matrimony: "My wife was torn from her mother's embrace in childhood, and taken to a distant part of the country. She had seen so many other children separated from their parents in this cruel manner, that the mere thought of her ever becoming the mother of a child, to linger out a miserable existence under the wretched system of American slavery, appeared to fill her very soul with horror; and as she had taken what I felt to be an important view of her condition, I did not, at first, press the marriage, but agreed to assist her in trying to devise some plan by which we might escape from our unhappy condition, and then be married." But "after puzzling our brains for years," they could see no way to maneuver through one thousand miles of slave territory to a free state, so they finally decided to ask their masters' permissions to be married. Once wed, they decided to "settle down in slavery, and endeavor to make ourselves as comfortable as possible under that system." That's what they did until December 1848, when Craft concocted a clever scheme to make their break for freedom. Once they decided on it, only eight days later they succeeded.

The fact that Ellen was almost white, and that William could work extra for money in his job in the cabinet shop, made the daring plan possible. The basic plot was simple: she would disguise herself as a man in need of medical care in the North; he would be the slave accompanying his invalid "master." Ellen thought the scheme was silly; she couldn't imagine that she could carry it off. But the more she thought about it, the more she wanted out. So she told William that she would try to do her part if he would buy her costume. Not wanting to arouse suspicion, he went to different parts of town at different times to buy everything his wife needed, except trousers, which she made. As a ladies' maid in a city house, Ellen had a room of her own where she was able to keep all of her new things hidden.

Slaves were often given a few days' vacation at Christmastime. After all, masters didn't have to fear that they could go anywhere. No public transportation would carry them without their masters, and Georgia was too far south to worry about walking to freedom. William and Ellen each went to their owners for permission to take some time off so no one would go looking for them right away. Their masters gave them passes allowing them to travel, though neither was able to read the documents. That made Ellen realize that she couldn't write either, and wouldn't be able to register in hotels. They solved that problem by putting her right arm in a sling. Once she had donned the full costume, William thought her smooth face might also be a problem. So they put a poultice under her chin and tied a handkerchief around it. Ellen worried that traveling with men would make her nervous. For that problem a pair of tinted glasses to cover her eyes did the trick. Then William cut off his wife's hair and "found that she made a most respectable looking gentleman."

Before dawn they said a quick prayer and he peered out of her room, urging her on: "Come my dear, let us make a desperate leap for liberty!" But she "burst into violent sobs, and threw her head upon my breast. This appeared to touch my very heart, it caused me to enter into her feelings more fully than ever." They knew that if they were caught, they would not only be severely punished, they would probably never see each other again. But Ellen mustered her courage and each of them crept out of the house and went off in different directions to the train station. It was December 21, 1848. William went directly to the "colored" car; Ellen bought tickets and went to the "white" one. The cabinetmaker came looking for them, "having presentiments that we were about to 'make tracks for parts unknown.'" But the train left the station before he spotted his slave. It was the first of many close calls.

A friend of the family Ellen worked for sat down next to

her, and she was afraid he'd recognize her voice. So, in addition to being bandaged at the face and hand, she became deaf as well. Fortunately, the man got off the train before long, while the Crafts went on to Savannah, where they boarded a steamer for Charleston. Think of it, these were people who couldn't read or write, who had never been out of small-town Georgia, and now they were braving travel by land and sea through the slave states with detection likely at any time. On ship, Ellen went to bed early to avoid conversation, while William made a fresh poultice and explained his "master's" illness. They made it safely to Charleston, and for all their trepidation, they still couldn't resist going right to the lions' den—registering at the hotel frequented by that champion of the slave system, Senator John C. Calhoun. It was such a bold act that they loved telling about it. The fugitives had planned to take a ship directly from Charleston to Philadelphia, but discovered it didn't run in the winter, so they had to make the trip in many stages, sailing first to Wilmington, North Carolina. When they reached the dock, the ticket taker refused to sign for "the master" whose arm was in a sling, and it looked like the couple might be stranded in Charleston. Then a young man who had been with them on the boat from Savannah showed up, somewhat the worse for wear with brandy, and vouched for "the gentleman." Crisis averted.

From Wilmington, the travelers had to catch a train to Richmond, Virginia. A family on the train became concerned about the state of William's "master," and gave the slave a ten-cent piece, telling him to be attentive. With some irony, Craft reports, "I promised that I would do so, and have ever since endeavored to keep my pledge." Richmond meant a change of trains, this time to a ship's landing a little beyond Fredericksburg. On that train "Mr. Johnson," the name Ellen had taken, got into a conversation with a woman traveler. The woman kept talking about her slave, Ned, who had surprised her by running away. "Did he have a wife?" "Johnson" asked. Oh yes, it turned out, a sickly wife whom the woman had sold to someone in New Orleans, where the warm weather would do her good. "I suppose she was very glad to go South for the restoration of her health?" inquired "Johnson." Oh no, the slave had gone on about leaving Ned and the baby, which surprised her owner because "July" was such a faithful servant. As the woman sang the praises of the slave, "Johnson" finally asked, "As your 'July' was such a very good girl, and had served you so faithfully before she lost her health, don't you think it would have been better to have emancipated her?" "No, indeed I do not!" came the reply. The woman then launched into a tirade about the evils of freeing slaves. It was a story aimed right at women who would pity separated lovers, women who might take up the cause of abolition.

Next came a steamer to Washington, D.C., and then a train to Baltimore, the last slave port. It was Christmas Eve, and Philadelphia, the first stop in free territory, was within reach. But at the Baltimore train station, a major glitch developed. An officer, "a full-blooded Yankee of the lower order," demanded that William and his "master" get off the train, saying, "It is against my rules to let any man take a slave past here, unless he can satisfy them in the office that he has a right to take him along." In terror, they went into the office and learned that they would not be able to go farther, even though they had tickets to Philadelphia. The Crafts had no idea what to do; they were petrified that anything they said would give them away. But the other passengers clucked at the "Yankee officer" for unnecessarily hassling an invalid on Christmas Eve. And when the conductor of the train from Washington arrived and said that the pair had traveled together from there, the officer relented and allowed them to board. Christmas and freedom were in sight.

On the "colored" car, William received a good deal of advice about how to escape from his "master" once he reached Philadelphia. Though he insisted that he would not abandon so kind a master, Craft stored the information the other passengers gave him, including the address of a boardinghouse run by an abolitionist. Miraculously, early Christmas morning, they reached their goal: they arrived in Philadelphia. Exhausted, Ellen grabbed his hand: "Thank God, William, we are safe!" Then she burst into tears. She cried so long and hard that she really was weak when they arrived at the boardinghouse, so the "invalid" went right to his room. After she recovered, Ellen shed her men's clothing, joined William in the sitting room, and asked to see the landlord. The bewildered man demanded of Craft, "Where is your master?" When William pointed to Ellen, the landlord sternly insisted, "I am not joking, I really wish to see your master." They told him their fantastic story, finally convincing him they were telling the truth. The landlord told them they would be safer outside of the city and arranged for them to stay with a family of Quakers up the Delaware River. Though Ellen was wary of white people, the family members won her over when they offered to teach the fugitives the fundamentals of reading and writing. When the Crafts left three weeks later, they could write their names.

Free at last! That's what the couple believed after the move to Boston. After all those years of slavery, a few days of frightening playacting and they were now able to live together and support themselves. And for a little while they led a normal married life—he set up shop as a cabinetmaker, she as a seamstress. But when President Fillmore signed the Fugitive Slave Act in 1850, William's and Ellen's masters took out arrest warrants and sent federal marshals to collect their slaves. The good citizens of Boston took exception to the law, and harassed the marshals, who ended up sneaking out of town. By then the Crafts' story was well known, and their friends concluded that they had become such symbols for fugitive slaves that they'd be safer if they left the country altogether. Not a minute too soon, they decided to go to England.

When the Georgia masters learned how the U.S. marshals

had been treated in Boston, they wrote President Fillmore demanding that he enforce the law, to show his good faith toward the South. The president instructed a military force to go to Boston to assist in the arrest of the fugitives. Since the officers watched the port vigilantly, the Crafts were forced to go by land to Halifax, in hopes of getting a ship to England from there. They first traveled to Portland, Maine, then on to St. John's, New Brunswick, where they waited two days for a steamer to take them to Windsor, Nova Scotia. At the hotel there, one of the workers was a fugitive slave who told them his story. Soon after he was married, his bride was sold away from him and he never heard of her again. He finally escaped to St. John's, where he stayed single for many years, but eventually he met and married a woman there. One day, walking down the street, he saw someone who looked familiar; he passed her, then they both turned around and he realized it was his long-lost wife. "Dear, are you married?" were her first words. When he answered yes, she "hung her head, and wept." He then took her to meet his new wife, who was also a fugitive slave. And they decided he would stay with her, but give the first wife a weekly allowance, "as long as she requested his assistance."

The Crafts went on to Windsor, but they learned that moving north, even to Canada, did not remove them from racial problems and prejudices. William wasn't allowed to ride inside the coach to Halifax because he was black; the driver forced him to ride on the top in the rain. The coach broke down several miles out of Halifax, and after the passengers trudged through the mud into town, the couple discovered that their ship had already sailed for Liverpool. A few miserable weeks later, after a good deal of difficulty getting a room in Halifax and a place on the ship because of race, the Crafts finally left for England. The voyage was none too pleasant, and Ellen stayed sick for several weeks after they arrived in Liverpool. Even so, they were happy. Their thousand miles to freedom was more like two thousand miles with the Atlantic Ocean thrown in. But they had made it. They were finally well and truly free, and they were together.

The vast majority of slaves never could say that. It took a war, not a daring escape, to make them free. But once emancipation came, what did they do? They got married, legally. With the help of the Freedman's Bureau, or on their own, former slaves made their unions legal. The vows they had taken before God and neighbor, they now made legitimate before the state. Because, finally, they could.

NOTE: The narratives in this chapter are taken from *The Civitas Anthology of African American Slave Narratives,* edited by William L. Andrews and Henry Louis Gates, Jr. (Washington, D.C.: Civitas/Counterpoint, 1999).

Chapter Three

∞

OUR LIVES

LEAVING HOME

NEWLYWEDS IN NEW YORK

You'd think that we were facing a big decision: where to live as we started our married life together. After all, we both had good jobs, but in different cities. Steve was a reporter on the city staff of the *Times* in New York, and Cokie was producing and anchoring her own show, *Meeting of the Minds,* at the NBC affiliate in Washington. But we never talked about it. This was 1966, and like most couples in that era we simply assumed that the man's job was more important. Cokie would quit, move to New York, and start over. But first, there was the honeymoon.

CR: We went to Puerto Rico, where we were staying at a friend's apartment, and Steve had forgotten to bring a bathing suit. So the first day we went to a shop in a nearby hotel to buy him one.

SR: I went to pay for it and the clerk looked at me and asked, "Just married?" And I said, "What, it shows?" He laughed and pointed: "Your ring." I hadn't noticed but it was so bright and shiny. Once the bathing-suit crisis was resolved, everything was going along well until my back went out—it hurt like hell.

CR: He couldn't move. How pleased I was!

SR: Eventually it went away, but at certain key points in our marriage—a new child, a new job—that same muscle would start hurting again.

CR: So I dubbed it his "newfound responsibility muscle."

SR: It was a warning signal, like the canary in the mine, chirping, "Stress alert, stress alert!"

CR: Then we went to New Orleans, because my great-grandmother had not been able to come to our wedding, and we wanted to see her. Also, Steve had never been to New Orleans, so we visited relatives and ate good meals and stayed in the honeymoon suite at the Pontchartrain Hotel.

SR: You don't normally go see relatives on honeymoons, but that's still our priority. If we have a free Sunday night, usually we see family rather than anybody else.

CR: Then it was time to settle into New York. We had spent the summer apartment hunting, and at one point Steve was trying to nab a rent-controlled apartment on West Seventy-fifth Street between Broadway and West End. It had four rooms at $185 a month, and if we didn't take it instantly it would be gone. But there was an airplane strike on, so I couldn't get to New York from Washington fast enough to see it before Steve signed the lease. The people who lived there before us had egregious taste—purple-and-mustard walls, mirrors around the dining area, a fake marble floor which they tried to get us to buy at the incredible sum of one thousand dollars, which was much more money than we had. Also it was ugly and we didn't want it. So in an act of true meanness, they took up the floor and took down the mirrors. When I first saw the apartment, it had a concrete floor when you walked right in the door and horrible walls in ugly colors. One look and I burst into tears.

SR: Great! The first big decision in our marriage and she starts crying. I had already violated Arthur Goldberg's advice—don't cause a woman to weep.

CR: Then, when we came back from our honeymoon, there was a sign up in the elevator that said "No Heat or Hot Water Until Further Notice." And that became a symbol of what my life in New York was about to be like. It was not un-adulterated bliss as I went around trying to find a job and figure out my role in this new place and in this new relationship. I had no identification in my new name. So I carried my marriage certificate around everywhere, just to prove to people that I was in fact this other person I had suddenly become.

In the end it was good for us—for me—to leave Washington. But it was very hard to pick up and become another person and not have any separate identity from Steven at all. I would go job hunting and get rejected and become depressed about it. The days grew very long. It reached the point where I would say to myself, "You must do X today," so that I'd leave the house in an effort to cheer myself up. I'd scold myself, saying things like, "You must go to the bank by three o'clock in the afternoon." One day after Christmas I set a goal of returning a wedding present to Georg Jensen, a fancy New York store. But in my depressed state, I couldn't quite manage to get dressed. I decided that was all right, I could do this without getting dressed. I put on a blue coat and a hat that matched it and went to the store in my nightgown! I figured it was terribly important to fulfill my pathetic goal for the day, and if I had waited and tried to get dressed, I was likely to fail. When I arrived at Jensen's return counter, standing right there was the person who gave me the wedding present. There are eight million people in the city of New York and the friend who gave me the wedding present shows up at the same time I do at the return counter. What are the odds of that happening? I was so flustered that when the salesclerk asked, "Should I put this on your account?" I mumbled, "Yes, yes, yes," and quickly gave her my name. I didn't have an account, I was just trying to get out of there, but I couldn't move fast enough, I was caught in the act. Fortunately, the friend thought it was funny and as a gesture of forgiveness invited me to come along with him to Nelson Rockefeller's swearing-in as governor. Of course he had no notion I was in my nightgown! Like an idiot, I accepted. We got there and the room was jammed with people and TV lights, 1966 TV lights, so it was hot as it could possibly be. Everybody kept offering to take my coat. "No, no, no, I'm fine," I insisted, "I'm just fine. I'm from the South and oh, it's cold!" Then my friend asked me to lunch and at that point I had brains enough to go home. No lunch. I think I might have even mentioned to him that I was in my nightgown. It does show you that I was a basket case. I guess I didn't realize how much of a basket case. And even when I told Steven that story, he just thought I was odd.

SR: Well, I was used to your eccentricities! It didn't strike me as at all odd that you went out in your nightgown!

CR: I don't think I've ever done it since, except to get the newspaper.

SR: That wasn't the only funny story about returning wedding presents. Many of the gifts from New Orleans came from one big jewelry store—Adler's. When Cokie's mother went to Louisiana she would pack pieces of silver in her suitcase and return them for us. To make sure that the pieces remained unscratched, she would sometimes stuff them with her underwear, but one time, when she was rather hurried, she returned several presents with her underwear still packed in them. A few days later, with this great flourish, a courier arrived at her apartment and presented her with this very carefully laundered, ironed underwear courtesy of the jewelry store!

CR: But I'm curious about how you felt during this period when I was so unhappy and looking for a job and trying to figure out what my life was going to be.

SR: I think I was largely oblivious. I was focused on my own job at *The New York Times* and I was working hard and I was enjoying myself. But it does go back to that earlier assumption, that men's jobs were much more important and whatever women did was secondary. The fact that we never discussed whose job was more important was emblematic of that. But I do think that even women were not all that clear about what was happening.

CR: That's right. A lot of us, certainly including me, didn't understand how meaningful and significant work was to us. And the experiences that many of us were having—being turned down for jobs because we were women—seemed to be happening to each of us individually. We'd make bitter jokes about a prospective boss asking how many words we typed, something they never asked our male counterparts, but as far as we were concerned, that's just the way things were. It was only after we all started talking to each other that we realized we were being illegally discriminated against and that's when the modern feminist movement came into flower.

But the period where each of us was alone in our misery was a very difficult period. Nowhere was it written that women would feel this way. I expected to live happily ever after. It was a big shock and a sense of failure on my part to feel frustrated and depressed. In retrospect, I'm glad I learned the lesson then that I'm a person who needs to work in order to be happy. It saved me a lot of grief later in life.

SR: The fact that I was earning the only paycheck was not an issue in my mind, but it did bother Cokie. I used to tease her that she had, after all, brought a substantial dowry into this match—a slightly used Ford Falcon and four years left on a five-year subscription to *Esquire*. That was about it! Plus a few hundred wedding presents of course. Anyway, she eventually got a job.

CR: At the *Insider's Newsletter,* a small weekly tip sheet on politics and the markets, sold mostly to the business community. It turned out that I found something I was good at—reporting. I could learn almost anything from almost anybody. It was a great job and I loved doing it, but the newsletter folded after I had been there about a year. Then I went to work at Channel 5, an independent TV station. The ten o'clock news had started something called the action report, a nightly feature where the station solves viewers' problems—run-ins with Social Security or the Housing Authority, that kind of thing. So I produced the segments and did a good bit of the reporting for them. It was a rotten job. We'd get five hundred letters a day from people in these terrible situations and we could solve hardly any of them. I felt it was phony. And I saw some of the worst things in New York. I'd go into some building that was urine-soaked, with no electricity, and I couldn't do anything about it but rant and rave to Steven, who was covering housing for the newspaper. I discovered shortly after I took that job that I was pregnant, which I was delighted about, but that meant I couldn't leave because nobody would hire a pregnant woman.

SR: One of the big questions we were facing from the beginning was children. We were still pretty young. To have children was an added burden . . .

CR: I was dying for children. All my life I had wanted children. I loved playing with babies. I loved dolls. I had a great time with my nieces and nephews. We took a trip to Europe after we had been married for a year—Rome, Paris, London, in that order—so we were in Rome for our first wedding anniversary. Those were the days when we had two incomes and no responsibilities, and we were young enough to enjoy low-budget trips. We went someplace for supper in Rome and then to St. Peter's Square with a bottle of Asti Spumante to celebrate our anniversary. And I ruined the whole evening by crying and saying I wanted a baby. As I remember it, Steven's reaction was primarily puzzlement.

SR: But that trip provided one of the best moments in understanding each other. As any young couple comes to understand each other. We were in Florence and we were at the Uffizi Gallery. We both enjoy art but we're not overly knowledgeable about it.

CR: There's an understatement. Ignorant would be a good word.

SR: But we were determined to slog through one of the world's most famous galleries. We felt obligated to stay until closing time. It seemed the only possible option. So we were on this forced march from room to room and at five o'clock the museum closed. We thought it closed at six, so we were prepared for another hour of feigned interest. It closed at five and each of us turned to the other and whooped, "YEAH!" It was like getting a half day off from school.

CR: Liberation.

SR: It was one of those perfect moments of early marriage where you say, "You, too?" We had a great trip except for Cokie's bugging me about babies. But that soon got solved because of another big issue in our young marriage—the Vietnam War. I was prime draft material. I had gotten out of the military year by year by doing the minimum that my draft board required, taking courses in graduate school. While I worked for Scotty Reston in the Washington bureau of the *Times* I attended George Washington—the school where I now teach—and I'm glad that the department never looked up my record before hiring me. I don't think it would've sat well. Then I enrolled at New York University but I didn't work very hard, and occasionally I would even turn one of my *Times* stories into a class assignment. Eventually the university caught on that I wasn't serious and kicked me out. I'm in no way proud of it, but I tried to stay out of the war every way I could. That was certainly one of our considerations about trying to have a baby; it would mean a fatherhood deferment from the draft. In fact, we used to joke that we would name the baby Lewis Hershey Roberts, Lewis Hershey being the head of the draft system.

CR: Ironically, both of us had covered the new Selective Service law, and neither of us managed to notice a section in it that said fatherhood deferments would no longer be granted to anyone who had graduate-school deferments beyond a certain date. Once Steven was unceremoniously ejected from graduate school, I happily got pregnant. Then we learned he wouldn't be eligible for the deferment and he received a notice reclassifying him 1A, meaning the military could call him at any time. He was ordered to report for a physical exam on September 11, 1968, the day after our second wedding anniversary. So a few weeks before that, we went to visit a doctor in Bayonne, a friend of Steve's parents. The guy was a dermatologist, but still he was an M.D., and we begged, "Find something wrong with him!"

SR: He did. He found that I had elevated blood pressure because I was scared to death. I had no history of it, no documentation or anything. The doctor wrote on a prescription pad—this was the sum total of my medical history—"Steve Roberts has elevated blood pressure." And that was all I took into the exam. I had to bring an overnight bag with me because if there was some question about your physical condition the Selective Service could keep you overnight for tests. Of course, remember this was also 1968, a rather turbulent year. Cokie and I had just gone to the Democratic Convention in Chicago. I went out to the draft board and went through the process and realized that they had canceled all graduate-school deferments by then. For everybody. Most of us who were called in that day were already twenty-five. It was guys out of law school and they didn't want any of us. We were just going to be too much trouble for them. At the physical, my blood pressure still registered pretty high, so they deferred me for three months, which meant I'd be almost twenty-six and out of danger when that deferment expired.

CR: They had plenty of eighteen-year-olds, and it shows how unfair the system was. Not long after that the Selective Service changed to the lottery. In a town like Bayonne, where not many people went to college, the poor and less educated were snatched up instantly by the draft. People who had some money and the ability to get some education weren't. The poor died—the rich didn't. Even though I mightily disapproved of the way the draft worked, I was hypocritical enough to be incredibly relieved that Steven had at least temporarily escaped. I was terrified of losing him. Not long after we were married, he had been assigned to cover the Newark riots. At about midnight he called me from the hospital where he was getting a casualty count and told me he'd be home in about forty-five minutes. Hours later, when he finally made it past all of the police checkpoints, he found me huddled on the floor inside the door of our apartment. I was so scared that he was dead. Like so many other young wives of the time, I saw Vietnam as a threat to my whole future, to all my hopes of happiness. Even if Steven had gone and come home safe, he would have had a life-altering experience that I would not have shared. I knew that there were certain disadvantages in meeting and marrying young, but I thought one of the real advantages would be a long shared history, which has turned out to be true. I hated the thought of him doing something so significant without me.

SR: But the Vietnam War was shadowing our lives in other ways. I was covering the student protests around the country and sympathizing with them. Cokie's father was the third-ranking leader in the House and a strong supporter of Lyndon Johnson. Religion had never really been an issue with my in-laws, but in that period politics sure was. There was one day when Cokie and her sister had lunch with their parents at a restaurant in New York, "21."

CR: We got into a screaming, yelling fight about Vietnam, culminating in my sister and me walking out. Not a great display of maturity. The people in the restaurant clapped when we made our dramatic exit. I've been embarrassed about it ever since. It smoothed over quickly because nobody in the family was interested in having a fight last for any length of time, but it was a tense time for many families; lots of them were having those kinds of arguments.

SR: One family I wound up writing about was the Rudds. Mark was the leader of the Columbia student uprising in the spring of 1968, and his father was a military man, so it seemed like great material for a feature piece. The *Times* assigned me to do it, partly because Mark Rudd was a Jewish guy from northern New Jersey, just like me. I went out to his parents' house and rang the bell, but his mother wouldn't let me in. I turned on every ounce of charm and pulled out the names of all of these Jewish families I knew in their town, Maplewood. She was dying to talk to me, but Mark told her over and over not to dare talk to anybody in the press. Finally, she gave in and let me in, because she wanted to tell me what a good son Mark was. To prove it, she told me that on Mother's Day, she'd made a casserole, driven to Columbia, and parked behind the building that Mark was occupying. He then snuck out the back way and ate the casserole in the car with his parents. You can imagine how humiliating that story was for this great radical when he read it in the newspaper. Then Mrs. Rudd showed me her garden, proudly telling me, "My son the revolutionary helped me plant this garden." We spent a couple of hours talking, and finally, at the end of this interview, she looked at me and sighed: "Tell me, you seem like such a nice boy, have you ever done anything to upset your mother as much as Mark has upset me?" And I said, "Actually, Mrs. Rudd, I did. I married a *shiksa*" (a Yiddish word meaning a non-Jewish woman). At that point she gasped in horror: "My Markie would never do that!"

CR: Of course her son had turned the university and the city upside down. But a *shiksa*? Never!

SR: Also in this period I learned the drawbacks of marrying into a political family. The benefits were enormous—learning from inside the way political families have to deal with each other, and with their children. They have the same problems everybody else does. Only someone who has sat around those kitchen tables, after the lights go out and the cameras leave, fully understands that. But I did a stupid thing. My father-in-law was the chairman of the platform committee for the Democratic Convention and I heard from one of his aides there was going to be a negotiating session over the Vietnam plank, which was causing enormous divisiveness in the party. I wrote this modest little story about who was going to be at the meeting—there's this person and that person and Hale Boggs "representing the Southern point of view." The next morning Cokie's mother called us in tears and said, "Why does Steve think Daddy is a racist?"

CR: This was a year when my father had voted for legislation outlawing racial discrimination in housing and came close to losing his own election over it.

SR: Of course, that wasn't the context at all. I was writing about Vietnam, not domestic policy. And there are few people in this world I admire more than my father-in-law. I always say to my own children, "If you want to understand what made your grandfather great, look at his stands on civil rights." It was so shocking to me that Lindy would have that reaction, but it was a hard lesson in understanding that words have great power, particularly in dealing with a very public family. I have often said since then that it's very useful for any young journalist to be the subject of a story, preferably one that's a little unfair. Then you really understand what it feels like to be on the other side. And marrying into this family gave me that experience, at some pain, but a very important lesson.

CR: My parents were very forgiving, but the times stayed tense. We went to the Chicago convention, with Daddy running the platform committee and Steve covering the protestors outside. I was hugely pregnant and the protestors had thrown these stink bombs into the lobby of the Hilton and the smell was especially hard on a pregnant person. But my "condition" turned out to be a great advantage in the end because I was very thin and from the back you couldn't tell that I was pregnant. The cops, even in the convention hall, were so nervous that they would never let us stand still to talk. Everyone in the family had different credentials, so we'd meet in the hallways, plotting nefarious schemes like where to have dinner. A cop would invariably come along and prod one of us in the back with a nightstick: "Move on, move on, move on." I finally learned to swing around in my full pregnant glory and declare, "Do it again and I'm going to have this baby right here, right now." It worked! A very useful weapon.

SR: Exhausted after the excitement of the convention, we went to New Jersey to see my parents, who had moved from Bayonne to the pleasant town of Lakewood. After dinner on a particularly balmy night, Cokie and I decided to take a walk around their neighborhood. We had been walking for about twenty minutes when I spotted headlights behind us. The car seemed to be trailing us. "That's my mother," I told Cokie. "Oh, no, it couldn't be!" she insisted. "Wanna bet?" I was right. We might think we were grown-ups and able to take care of ourselves. But my mother wasn't taking any chances with her first grandchild; heaven knew what evil might lurk in the night! Mom's had to put up with us teasing her about that for thirty years.

When summer ended we started baby classes. We had decided on natural childbirth, which was still pretty unusual in 1968, and it was difficult to find a hospital that would allow me in the delivery room. The only hospital we could find was Beth Israel, which was downtown on the East Side of Manhattan. We lived on the Upper West Side, so it was not exactly a good choice, but it was the only one if we wanted to do this. We were convinced that if Cokie went into labor in the middle of the day and we tried to get a cab and go across town, we might not make it. But the teacher of the childbirth classes insisted it would be a long process. We had an appointment to go see the hospital on Sunday, October 20, just so we could get comfortable with the admissions procedure and see where everything was.

CR: My last day of work at Channel 5 was that Friday and the baby was due a week or two later. On Saturday, I asked Steven to screw on the little red-and-yellow knobs for the dresser I had painted bright blue, for the gender-neutral nursery of primary colors. Then I took a nap and woke up feeling lousy, but not in labor, according to all of the lessons. I cooked dinner but didn't eat it, and then, because I was bleeding, we eventually called the doctor. He was, thank God, a very conscientious soul and he said, "You better go to the hospital." So we grabbed all the stuff they said to grab. I wasn't ready. The baby wasn't due. The bag I was supposed to breathe into came from the fish store. Bad choice. At about midnight we finally hailed a cab, and by this time I was very uncomfortable and scared either that this would last another twenty hours or that I'd get to the hospital and they'd send me home. That's what the classes had led me to believe. I kept saying to the cabdriver, "Don't worry, don't worry." Because he was worrying! And he turned out to be right. When we got to the hospital, we didn't have a clue what door to go in, or what to do. Thank goodness the doctor found us and took us to a labor room. Then he did a swift exam and said, "Whoa! There's a baby coming here!" What a relief! No twenty hours, no going home, just labor and delivery to deal with!

SR: I had contracted with *Good Housekeeping* magazine to write an article about natural childbirth from the father's viewpoint. The twelve-hundred-dollar fee paid for the whole delivery. So not only was I in the delivery room, I was there with my notebook. And in between gasps she looked up and demanded, "Is that notebook sterile?"

CR: In between gasps. The baby came soon. About two-thirty in the morning. My parents were staying in a hotel in New Orleans, and when I couldn't reach them I had left a message saying, "Cokie and Steve have left for the hospital to have the baby." Then I called back a couple of hours later—I still have the messages—and said, "Tell them that Cokie has had the baby, a healthy boy, and they're both fine." And the operator answered in that wonderful New Orleans accent, "Who is this?" I said, Cokie. She said, "Dawlin', you shouldn't be on the phone. What you doing on the phone?" My mother was my father's campaign manager, and because he was in the middle of one of the worst campaigns of his life, she couldn't hang out and wait for the baby. So she flew up that night, made a quick check to see that the baby and I were okay, bought out the infant department of Best and Company the next day, and then turned around and flew home, leaving an exhausted Steven reeling from all of this. Of course for me, it was nothing but a picnic.

SR: After her flying visit, Lindy left behind a shopping bag full of all of her notes and records for the entire campaign. She called me in a panic. I was lying on our bed, dozing, not having been to sleep in forty-eight hours. I heard my mother-in-law say, "Darlin', I've left behind my shopping bag with all of my notes for the campaign." And I said, "Lindy, I've got it right here. I'll just pack it up and send it right to you." The reply: "Oh, no, I don't have time for you to do that. You have to read it to me." Well, there were dozens and dozens of little pieces of paper. Laundry slips. Envelopes. An interesting way to organize a campaign, but it worked for Lindy. Remember, I hadn't had any sleep, and there I was reading these slips of paper. "Call Phyllis three o'clock Monday for fund-raiser." And she says, "Why, darlin', you know Phyllis, she's married to Moise, and you know their kids. . . ." Lindy somehow thought it was rude not to give me the full personal history of everyone she mentioned. Finally, I snapped, "I don't need to know everything! Just let me read it." But she was incapable. She just had to tell me everything. At that moment I could've done with a little less darlin' and a lot more speed.

The next day I had to bring Cokie and the baby home from the hospital. So I went down to Beth Israel and packed them up in the car. I had put crepe paper and balloons all around the apartment to welcome them home. I got them settled and then went to work at the city room at *The New York Times*. Before I even sat down at my desk, the editor called me over. "I have something to tell you. We want to send you somewhere." And I said, "Where? Washington?" Because all I wanted in the world was to go back to Washington. My great dream was to be a reporter in Washington. "No," he answered, "Los Angeles." Now I had been west of the Mississippi for one day in my entire life at that point, covering Ed Muskie's vice-presidential campaign a few weeks before. That's how carefully *The New York Times* picked an expert to cover California. But for the last year or so the youth culture had been exploding on the West Coast, and since all the *New York Times* reporters in California were in their fifties, they had completely missed the story. My editors looked around the newsroom, picked the youngest reporter they could find, and said, "You, go tell us what the hell is happening out there." It was a great shock to me, and my first reaction was no. Where was Los Angeles? Fortunately, Cokie has always been a much more adventuresome person than me.

CR: Even though he wrote me that first note at the student convention saying never get comfortable, I was always the one saying, "Come on!"

SR: She immediately thought it was a good idea. That night I walked home up Broadway to our apartment and stopped at a bookstore and bought two books which symbolized our new life. One was *Dr. Spock's Child Care*. The other was *The Pump House Gang* by Tom Wolfe, an account of the youth culture of Southern California.

CR: All of New York was on strike that week, which made the idea of leaving sound good to me. And the truth was, the minute a baby arrives in New York, it becomes a completely unlivable city. It was one thing to be young and newly married and have jobs and enough money to go to the theater and out to dinner. The baby changed everything. Just going to the grocery store meant bringing the baby and trying to figure out a way to carry both him and the food home. When I tried to take the baby to the pediatrician for his first visit, I stood at Broadway and Seventy-fifth for half an hour trying to hail a cab and couldn't get one. Finally, in tears, I went back to the apartment, called the pediatrician, and canceled the appointment. I felt like a total failure as a mother who couldn't take care of my baby because I couldn't get to the doctor's office. I was plenty happy to leave New York.

SR: Before we left, we had to decide how we were going to celebrate the birth of this baby. In Jewish tradition there's a ritual circumcision, called a Bris, when a baby boy is eight days old. We didn't want to do that; among other things, there was no way Cokie's parents could come to New York then. But we did want to have some event marking Lee's arrival.

CR: The baby was circumcised in the hospital, which, in 1968, was an extra twenty-five dollars. Steve's Grandpa Abe called me shortly after I got home from the hospital and barked into the phone, "I want to tell you something. Whatever you do, don't circumcise that baby." Astonished, I asked, "Why?" And he said, "Because I've read all about it. Your sex life is never as good." This was my grandfather-in-law! I said, "Too late, Pop." Then I told him we were having a party to celebrate the birth of his first great-grandchild. And, despite what he saw as my precipitous action on the circumcision front, he accepted the invitation.

SR: He called me up the morning of the party and said he couldn't come. "Why?" I said. "Because I won't have a place to park." So I said to him, "Pop, if you leave now, I will go outside and lie down in a parking spot in front of the apartment and make sure it's there for you." He did come, and we have a picture of him holding his great-grandson. It was great to have family and friends around; most of my family was in New Jersey. So was Cokie's sister, Barbara, who had stayed with us after the baby was born to help take care of him. But then we announced we were moving. It was hard on my parents when I said to them, "The good news is you have a healthy baby grandson. The bad news is we're about to take him three thousand miles away."

CR: Which, now that I think about it, was really vicious of us. At the time it didn't even occur to me, but it was mean.

SR: I think that on reflection, the timing was good. There's always a balance in a young marriage. We were still working out a lot of things for ourselves, as any couple does. Exactly how to be parents. Exactly what role religion would play. Exactly how we would balance work and family. Just learning more about each other. Professionally, of course, it was a great opportunity for me to become the bureau chief in Los Angeles. But personally it gave us some space at a key time in our marriage to figure things out without either set of parents looking over our shoulders. I don't think it's a total accident that when both of our children got married they moved far away from us—our daughter to California and our son to London. At least in part they were reflecting what we had always said, that it's a healthy thing at this stage of marriage to have some time on your own.

CR: A stupid thing for us to have said!

SR: California was like another country to us. We knew nothing about it. A college friend of Cokie's who was from L.A. came over for dinner, and I remember her drawing on a napkin a sketch plan of the city, suggesting places we might live. The *Times* flew us out there to house-hunt and we couldn't find anything we liked.

CR: The houses were perfectly normal houses, houses we could have found in Cleveland or Bethesda. I was mightily unimpressed. We were in California. We were supposed to have a California house. One of them did have an avocado tree in the backyard, but that was about it. Finally, we saw an ad in the paper: "Not for everyone. Great view, Malibu, overlooking the ocean," or something like that. So, we decided, shoot, we'd go take a look at it.

SR: We were staying in downtown L.A. at the Ambassador Hotel, the place Bobby Kennedy had been shot six months before, because it was literally the only hotel name I knew in the whole city. We got on the freeway for the first time, an adventure in itself, and drove west to Santa Monica and into a tunnel. When we came out of it there was the Pacific Ocean! I had never seen it before. It was truly dramatic. We followed the directions and drove about seven miles up the Pacific Coast Highway, then turned up into the hills. We kept going up, and up, and up, thinking there must be some mistake. I remember as we were driving up, I turned to Cokie and said, "Are we out of our blooming minds?" Finally, we found the house. It was the last one on the top of the hill, nothing but open country behind it.

CR: All we could see from the driveway was this little rambler, this L-shaped California house. We walked in the door and looked directly in front of us and there, through a glassed-in living room, was a magnificent unimpeded view of the Pacific Ocean. And we said, "That's fine, we'll take it." We had not looked at a bedroom or asked the price. The landlady kept saying, "No, no, no you won't, you don't know how inconvenient it is." And we said, "In fact, we will. We'll take this house." We didn't even ask each other. We knew this was the house. This was California.

SR: We lived in that house for five years. After we signed the lease, we went back to New York, and a few weeks later, with friends lining up to take over our rent-controlled apartment, we packed up to drive across the country in Cokie's rattletrap Ford Falcon. The baby was about three months old and he traveled in a bassinet in the backseat. Our enduring memory of our trip west to our new life was seeing this fuzzy blond head poking up at us.

CR: We had many adventures on the trip. First, just to prove our anxious parents right, the car broke down as soon as we got to Washington. We visited lots of family members along the way, and I got a speeding ticket in Seguin, Texas, a town with an enormous statue of a pecan on the courthouse lawn. In Arizona we started up a mountain for a picnic lunch and suddenly encountered snow. We had to turn around and come back down to a coffee shop next to a gas station, where we asked the guys there to check the car while we ate.

SR: We came out and they had the car up on a rack and they had taken gouges out of our tires and said you need three new tires. They had circled the gouges in chalk. I figured that they vandalized it, but what was I going to do? We were about to drive across the desert. I said, "What if I don't get new tires?" The guy in the gas station said, "Fine, go drive across the desert with these holes in your tires and your new baby." So this bandit held us up, and I was helpless to do anything about it because I had to protect my little family.

CR: Also, all the way across the country we were hearing on the radio about mud slides in Malibu. We were convinced that we would get there and our dream house would be at the bottom of the hill. We finally got to California. We drove through the tunnel, out to the Pacific Ocean. We drove up and up and up the mountain, and when we got to the top, the house was still standing right where it belonged. We went in and found waiting for us a notice from the draft board that Steve was no longer eligible to be called. My other big concern—hardly of the same magnitude—was whether Pampers would flush. I put one in the toilet and it flushed right down. I was literally jumping up and down, I was so happy. Everything was right, our house was there, we were going to start a new life, everything was perfect, and then the baby just burst out laughing in this wonderful giggle. His first real belly laugh. It was a great moment.

SR: Welcome to California!

So there we were, on our mountaintop in Malibu, with lots of space and sun, a new baby, and a new life. Some mornings, when the early fog clung to the coastline, we were literally above the clouds. What we didn't have was a community— no family, no friends, not even the people we passed on the street and greeted daily in New York. In fact, we had to get in the car and drive several miles just to buy a bottle of milk or loaf of bread, let alone find a conversation. Most young marriages face the same sorts of tensions we were encountering. Like newly planted tomatoes they need plenty of room to grow and thrive, but they also need stakes to keep them from sprawling on the ground. And no stakes are more important to the sturdiness of a marriage than friendships.

CR: All of my life friendships have meant a great deal to me. Suddenly I found myself on top of a mountain with a little baby, no friends within hundreds of miles, and Steven on the road much of the time. Fortunately, lots of friends and family came to visit and it was a time when people stayed for a while when they went all the way to California. Also, Sophie Altman, my boss from Washington days, sold *It's Academic,* the show I had worked on right after college, to the NBC affiliate in Los Angeles and hired me to produce it, so I met some people at the station. Then another alum of Altman Productions showed up in California and started working with me. I had known Sylvia Rowe since Wellesley and she and her two little girls and Lee and I spent a good deal of time together. They were the only guests at Lee's first birthday party because they were the only friends I had. Steven, as usual for that era, was out of town.

SR: Cokie told me that Lee's first birthday party was the last one I could miss, but even if he doesn't remember, I look at the pictures now and feel a bit guilty about not being there. And I suppose that's progress, because I don't remember feeling guilty at the time.

CR: Our friends Terry and Margaret Lenzner lived right around the corner from us in New York and actually stood on the corner and waved good-bye when we left for California. About the time Lee was turning one, they did something so smart I've learned from it ever since. When we moved, most of our friends gave us names of people to call, saying, look up our friends, the so-and-sos. I never would do that because I was too shy, I didn't want to impose. What was I supposed to say, "Invite me to dinner?" The Lenzners did it the other way around. They called friends in California and said, "Steve and Cokie Roberts have moved there; you call them." That's exactly what happened. Monroe and Aimee Price called us and invited us to their son Gabriel's second birthday party. Lee was the littlest kid there; he was fourteen months old. I remember him sitting on the end of the picnic-table bench—not too steady there.

Millie Harmon was at that birthday party, she had kids who were three and a half, one and a half, and newborn, and we quickly became very good friends. Her middle child had a regular play day with another little girl, and when Lee joined them, I started making friends. It was a delightful community of women whose kids all played together. That summer, when I was pregnant with Becca, we went east to see our families. And while we were away, Millie's husband, Ellis, was killed. He and Tom Brokaw, who was at that point a local anchorman on KNBC, were on a rafting trip together and Tom called us with the news. It was hard to take in, to even imagine my friend Millie all alone, with three little girls and a big black Lab. After we got back to California, Millie and I started having regular Monday-night dinners together because Steve was usually on the road early in the week. One of our favorites was a pizza place, Regular John's, a kid-friendly place where we could get a glass of wine! That started a ritual, which our friends continued long after Steve and I left California. Once, when I happened to be back on a visit on a Monday, I went to dinner and discovered what had started with Millie and me taking the kids out had become a big deal with people taking turns cooking. About thirty people were there, so it had become a lot of work. But the dinners kept going because they filled such a need. Hardly anybody in California has a blood family around, and we all wanted that kind of connection.

SR: A whole group of us started spending many holidays together as well. Millie was the only California native in the gang. One Thanksgiving Tom and Meredith Brokaw, who had three little girls, came to our house for dinner, and Tom brought small boxes of raisins for all the kids. The evening wore on, the wine flowed, the kids got bored. First they started tossing the raisins around, then they jumped on them and ground them into the carpet. We were too relaxed to care, and at one point Tom turned to me and said, "Well, I guess the raisins were a bad idea." That's become a family saying ever since, when some well-meaning plan goes awry. "I guess the raisins were a bad idea."

CR: We also realized that we had to create religious rituals for ourselves. Back home Steve knew he was Jewish because it was simply part of the culture. Now, if Judaism was going to be part of our marriage, we had to deal consciously and conscientiously with the religion itself. That was particularly true for me. I couldn't make any cultural claims to Judaism, so the religious rituals became terribly important to me.

SR: I think this is especially true of mixed marriages. Each spouse has to identify with and participate in the other religion more deliberately. You always knew you were Catholic in the way I knew I was Jewish. You had the nuns, the weekly Mass, all those reference points.

CR: Absolutely. Memories of a Catholic girlhood, from a positive perspective, as opposed to Mary McCarthy.

SR: That's why our Seders became so important to us. Cokie actually started them. What we're talking about here is the special feast at Passover.

CR: The first Seder I ever went to was at the Goldbergs'. After he had been such a kind and crucial presence at our wedding, Arthur Goldberg took an interest in us. And Dorothy Goldberg and my mother had been particularly good friends, so Mrs. Goldberg made sure that we were always taken care of. They invited us to their Passover celebration at the Waldorf-Astoria Hotel, the official residence of the U.S. ambassador to the UN. It was a great evening in many ways, but for me, it taught me the importance of this festival, the fundamental message of the deliverance of the Jews from Egypt. I completely understood how central this event was to the religion. The next year, when I was pregnant with Lee, I very much wanted a family Seder but I was still too unsure of myself and too hesitant about performing my own Jewish rituals. At Hanukkah I could light the candles and say the blessings, but that was about it. (We did that quite happily one night, not long after we were married, then we went to sleep only to wake up to the smell of the burning card table, which we were using as our dining-room table. We still use that table, lo these many years later, with a little tape covering the Hanukkah disaster.) So I asked Steve's parents to provide a Seder. They gamely found a Haggadah, the prayer book which outlines the Passover service, and prepared the special meal. Steven and I drove down from New York to New

Jersey and just the four of us had our Seder. I remember in the middle of dinner, Steve's twin, Marc, happened to call and was amazed that there was a ritual meal taking place. Steve's mother, Dorothy, who had already become such a friend to me, whispered into the phone, "Cokie wanted it." I badly wanted it; I wanted to know how to inject Judaism into my household and I needed help. By the next year we were in California and we started celebrating Passover at our house every year. I went to the local synagogue and bought a Haggadah, and then I studied other Haggadahs that were available and combined them into a meaningful prayer service, which I typed up with some difficulty and copied for our Seders. I also cooked a meal I was comfortable with—a Middle Eastern meal. It seemed to me that the Bible was pretty clear about lamb being served on the night the angel passed over the Jews. No brisket of beef or boiled chicken ever made it into the book of Exodus. Also, these were people living in Egypt in springtime. I figured they had zucchini and okra and maybe eggplant. I knew for a fact they had never met a matzoh ball. So I made my annual Middle Eastern Seder, and everyone made fun of me as a *shiksa* who didn't know what she was doing. Thankfully, after a few years, the *New York Times* food section published a menu for a Sephardic Seder, a Passover meal for Jews of Mediterranean or North African extraction, and I was completely vindicated. Also, the food was better. So our Seder quickly became somewhat famous.

SR: I had not grown up with a lot of Jewish ritual at home—we never had Seders, for instance, and I only had a bar mitzvah because I asked for one. (Since I had a twin brother I only had to learn half the service!) I have never been as devout as Cokie, in a purely religious sense, but one of the things I learned from her over the years was an appreciation of spirituality, of prayer, of ritual. In a real sense, marrying a non-

Jew made me more Jewish. And I was eager to include Jewish traditions in our life together. Christian rituals were all around us, but we had to work at the Judaism part, and many of our friends came to feel the same way. When we left California, years later, one of our going-away parties was a Seder a whole month early. We all wanted to share the holiday together. Over the years friends have come in from all over to be with us at Passover, and our Seder became particularly important for my parents. They were very secular Jews, but at one point, after we returned to Washington, my father said to me, "Don't even bother to invite us to Seder—we're coming every year." They even planned their spring around the holiday, timing their trip north after a winter in Florida to coincide with the Seder. When I think of the rabbis who oppose mixed marriage in all forms, who say it can only dilute the Jewish people, I wonder what they would make of our family. Two of my siblings married Jews, but my parents always came to Seder at the home of their Catholic daughter-in-law.

CR: At the same time we were creating rituals to bring us together, we were surrounded by changes in the society that took their toll on all kinds of relationships. The women's movement was stirring all around us, and it was affecting most marriages, including ours, in at least small ways. Steve was invited by a college friend to help run a series of seminars at the Aspen Institute, in the mountains of Colorado. Rich people paid large sums of money to read the classics and get cultured. In this era—and I am told it has not changed very much—the men all sat at the table and talked about great works and the women sat up in the balcony and listened to them.

SR: And did needlepoint.

CR: It was appalling. Not the needlepoint part—I've always done needlepoint—the silence part. The women had all been

assigned the reading so they could discuss it with their husbands, but they weren't allowed to talk. So at the coffee breaks
the women would rush up to the men saying, "No, no, no,
you got that all wrong."

SR: Cokie organized a revolt and insisted that the wives join
the men at the table for at least one session. I was delighted.
Going back to our college days, I had always thought that
sharing ideas and opinions was an important part of our relationship. And it still is. Anyway, I got high marks among
the women for being on their team. But I quickly tumbled
out of the feminist pantheon when we gave one woman a
ride to Denver and I started yelling at Cokie about the route
we were taking. She kept telling me I was on the wrong road
and should ask directions; I finally pulled the car over to the
side of the road and told her, at top volume, that she could
drive if she knew so much. I found out years later from the
insightful work of linguist Deborah Tannen that not asking
directions is one of the defining characteristics of modern
maleness.

CR: We finally found the airport and flew to Washington to
see my folks and then went on to New Jersey to visit the
Robertses. Steve flew back to Denver, where we had left the
car, and drove back to California alone because I was pretty
pregnant with Becca by that time. I flew back to L.A. with
Lee, who had been a terror for five hours on the plane. Of
course, as we taxied into the airport, he fell asleep. I got off
the plane with this angelic sleeping baby on my shoulder and
Steven said, "Oh, isn't that sweet. He slept the whole way."
I handed the baby to his father, who saw that the maternity
dress I was wearing—a navy number with a double row of
brass buttons down the front—no longer had a single button
on it! Though he tried to be helpful, Steven was still fairly
clueless about this baby business. I remember at one point not
long after Lee was born, some friends were considering

whether to have a baby and I heard Steve say, "Oh, you should do it. It hasn't changed our lives a bit!" "What?" I exploded. "It seems to me everything I'm doing now I didn't do before, and everything I used to do I'm not doing now! I would call that changing my life!"

SR: I might not have been all that helpful, but I loved being a father, playing with the kids and teaching them things, just the way my father had done with me. My dad had even written a children's book about trains, based on outings we made to the local station, so I had a good role model. I was eager for another child, and as we prepared for Becca's arrival we very much wanted to do natural childbirth. I felt it made me part of the baby's life right from the beginning. After my article came out in *Good Housekeeping,* called "We Had a Baby," people would come up to me and talk about how brave I was, but Cokie would have none of it. "Oh," she was fond of saying, "did it hurt much? How about those stretch marks?"

CR: But we could find only one hospital even remotely near us that allowed fathers in the delivery room, in Culver City. It was more of a nursing home than a hospital, but we didn't want to risk driving all the way downtown. Lee had come so fast I was afraid to go that far. Steven was on the road all the time and it was an election year again. So I was afraid I was going to be on the top of a mountain by myself, but I couldn't convince the doctor to pay any attention to me and consider inducing the baby. Fortunately, Steven was there when I went into labor in the middle of the night and this time I could tell it was moving very fast. I said to Steven, "I can't make it to the hospital. It's not going to happen." We had a neighbor who was a doctor. I said, "Just tell Terry to come up here. I can't do it." Steven had a mental image of me having this baby in the house, with Lee running around. That wasn't working for him! So he kept pleading with me, "Come on, Cokie, you can do it." Then he called a neighbor, this sixteen-year-old beauty who was one of our regular baby-sitters. She had long blond hair down to her waist and would waft around with very little on. At two o'clock in the morning Steven politely, as if it were midafternoon, said into the phone, "Mr. Moss, it's Steve Roberts. I'm sorry to bother you, is Amy home?" And I screamed, "For goodness' sake, Steven! Tell him why you're calling." Oh! "Cokie's in labor and we were wondering if Amy could come up and sit with Lee." Amy was sleeping out under the full moon, but Mr. Moss, the father of four, had her at our house in about thirty seconds. Finally, Steven pushed me in the car to head for the hospital and I was convinced I'd have the baby in the Volvo wagon. It was terrifying.

SR: We were just lucky. We'd been worried that we would never get across town in Manhattan traffic and this was even worse. This was the California freeways. If this baby had come in the middle of the day, we would have been cooked!

CR: We went tearing down the mountain and across the freeways to the hospital. We had called the doctor and said the baby was coming. He went back to sleep. Not a good habit for an obstetrician. We got into the hospital and I told the nurses, "This baby is coming right now." "Sure, sure," they humored me. "No, I'm serious," I insisted. "The baby's coming." A quick exam: "Oh, the baby IS coming." In we went to the delivery room immediately, but the doctor still wasn't there. In retrospect, but believe me not at the time, it was this hilarious Keystone Kops scene, with everybody but me and the baby trying to keep her from coming. Finally, Becca just delivered herself and Steve caught her. Without his old basketball reflexes she would've landed on her head. As her feet emerged, the doctor came rushing in the door.

SR: Later he kept saying to us, "Beautiful feet, this child has beautiful feet." Because that's all he was there for.

CR: She did get a staph infection in her eyes for being in the birth canal for so long. It was so sad, this little bitty baby with this awful eye infection.

SR: Cokie's brother, Tommy, was running for Congress in Maryland and it was September 15, the day of his primary. Montgomery County has a large Jewish population, and he shamelessly campaigned all over the district that day saying he had a new Jewish niece named Rebecca. She helped him win the Democratic primary, but he lost the general two months later.

CR: My mother had said, "Don't have that baby until the fifteenth, because I want to be there for this one." I assured her that the baby wasn't due until sometime after that. But she showed up on primary day, and Mamma came straight to California. By the time I got home from the hospital, after only a day, my mother had adopted the neighborhood dog, a huge but friendly creature named Freddy. Half the dogs on the hill looked like him, because he managed to get to any dog in heat no matter how high the fence. Not only did I have a new baby and a new dog, but Lee decided that if he ever went to sleep again, I'd have another baby. So sleeping was out. Then a huge brushfire threatened the house. I kept resisting evacuation. It made it too real in a way. Finally, though, we packed up.

SR: There was a firebreak on the ridge behind us, and the question was whether the flames would leap over it. I could see the whole thing from the kitchen window.

CR: That first night we left with just the family pictures and some work we were doing and a change of clothes for everyone! That made my mother crazy because she has been burned out twice in her life, so she's very skittish about fire. We moved into a hotel downtown, next to Steve's office, and there we were—a not-quite-two-year-old, a brand-new baby with a staph infection, my mother and Steve and me. I was producing *It's Academic,* and I had to go into work just days after Becca was born. I had planned a taping for shortly before she was born, and then she came early and I couldn't cancel the taping. The station was airing news specials on the fire, and when I got there I saw this huge map with areas of destruction marked. Our friend Tom Brokaw, who was anchoring all the specials, said to me, "Cokie, I think your house is gone. Here's the map." We just assumed the house had burned down. There was nothing to be done about it.

SR: But in fact, it wasn't burned. The maps were wrong. We were able to move back into our California house, now with two kids and a bigger child-care problem, particularly since Becca soon proved to be a handful. As soon as she learned to walk, she had a habit of wandering off, leaving us all in a panic. Once, when she was just two, she managed to make it several miles down the beach before a lifeguard finally located her. It was one of those terrifying situations where we were walking with her and thought she was with us, and Becca followed the wrong people. We frantically searched the beach and tried not to think about the possibility that she had headed into the Pacific Ocean, but finally a lifeguard spotted her through his binoculars—her two little pigtails gave her away!

CR: All this time in California, I had never had any kind of decent child-care situation. At first, I hired people from an agency, but that cost a fortune. Teenagers on our hill could sit when school was out, but that still didn't solve my daytime problems. I tried to work when Steve was at home, but he was unreliable. Finally, Millie introduced us to neighbors of hers, a family of four girls, three sisters in their late teens and a baby sister who was five. They would sit for us and bring the little sister to play with Lee. It was the first child care I could count on. *It's Academic* went off the air, but KNBC then hired me to produce another show, called *Serendipity,* which featured filmed field trips for kids. Most of the filming was on weekends, when Steven was more likely to be available to help.

SR: One Saturday I took the kids to a local park. Becca was so tiny she was still in an infant seat. There was a group of guys about my age playing basketball on the court next to the playground, so I wandered over and said, "Gee, guys, can I get a game?" They said, "Sure," so I parked the baby next to the court while Lee was off in the playground. We had a good time, and the guys told me they played there every Saturday. It turned out many of them also had kids running around the playground.

CR: Who were also awfully little!

SR: So this became our regular Saturday. If Cokie wasn't working it would give her an afternoon off. I would take the kids every week to the park. She thinks we didn't pay enough attention to them, but we had a very clear rule—you could interrupt the game to take care of a kid if blood was showing.

As Lee got a bit older and could manage money, I would give him a couple of dollars at the beginning of the afternoon to buy ice pops for him and Becca at the little refreshment stand in the park. At the end of the day Cokie could tell exactly what each of them had eaten, because it was right there on their shirts.

CR: But that kind of caretaking, such as it was, on his part was unusual. The whole understanding we had was that his work mattered more than anything. It certainly mattered more than my work, and I didn't disagree with that. But it was beginning to get to me more and more. Steve worked at home when he wasn't on the road, and I was supposed to somehow keep these babies quiet and out of his hair. I was exhausted from it all. I fell asleep everywhere we went, even in the middle of a basketball playoff game at the Fabulous Forum, because I was so tired. I used to joke that everybody in California was fantasizing about sleeping with everybody else, and I was fantasizing about sleep, period. When I flew to Miami to join Steven for the Democratic Convention in 1972, I didn't want to get off the plane. It was the first time I'd had to myself in months.

SR: I was traveling a lot and missing the kids, so I tried to figure out stories where the family could travel with me. One was about an old gold-mining town, another about a protest march led by Cesar Chavez, head of the grape workers' union. At first, that didn't work so well because Cokie and the kids would hang around waiting for me to finish, and she started to feel she would be better off at home, where she could control the schedule. But then we got into a rhythm where they would go off on their own to a park or a pool and I would meet up with them at the end of the day. Fine, if we were staying someplace where they had something to do, but then I had the brainstorm of renting a big camper and touring the West. I decided to do a summertime series of pieces about Americans on the road. It didn't work out so well.

CR: First of all, it's important to understand, I think the outdoors is vastly overrated. I am not an outdoor person. When we got in this camper the thing smelled to high heaven, just start there. Then we forgot to lock the refrigerator, so as we pulled out of the driveway, the food all spilled out. I did more housework in that stupid camper than I did at home for a year. Steve would go off in the morning and interview people and I'd be stuck in a camper with two babies.

SR: Without much ability to get them clean.

CR: There were no bathtubs anywhere and the kids were pretty little for showers. Becca wasn't even a year old and she was still in diapers; she would also eat dirt. By the time I got her dressed, and turned around to get my purse, she was dirty again. Then there was the day she almost climbed out of the Ferris wheel seat when we were at a county fair in Red Bluff. Steve was off interviewing people and I took the kids on the rides. Becca wouldn't sit still in my lap, and as I desperately tried to hold on to her, she rocked the seat around and came close to falling from the top of the wheel. The guy running it thought I was just scared when I hysterically shouted at him to stop the thing, so he laughed and kept it going. When we finally got off, I told Steve he had to carry that baby in a backpack for the rest of the day so Lee and I could have some fun. Steven took Becca, but while he was doing an interview with someone from the National Rifle Association, she methodically unwound all of the crepe paper from the booth.

SR: I only found out years later that Cokie had made reservations to fly home everyplace we went.

CR: It was a hard time for young mothers. The effect of the women's movement was odd. Instead of allowing us to make whatever choices we wanted, it made us feel that the motherhood choice wasn't seen as valid. When we went out in L.A., it would have been considered gauche for me to even mention the children. I remember going to one party I didn't particularly want to go to, and I just stood off to the side, not really participating. Some women started talking to Steve, focused intently on the bureau chief of *The New York Times,* and I was completely invisible. Then the husband of one of them asked me, "And what do you do?" A question I hate. But I actually had an answer: "I produce a television show." All of a sudden it was as if the spotlights came on. These women physically turned around and suddenly I was someone who counted. What I said mattered because I had a title other than mother or homemaker. It's so obnoxious. I can't stand that. It was the first time that Steve had encountered what I had been telling him about this phenomenon—had physically seen it happen. This whole sense of a woman's worth is so discounted. It's still true all these years later.

SR: At one point during this period Cokie said to me, "You're getting better when I ask you to do things. If I ask you to take the kids or run an errand, you're happy to do it. But you don't think of these things yourself." I've learned that's a common pattern. Guys think they're helping out, but taking responsibility, worrying about decisions, is another whole leap.

CR: You still don't think about these things. You'll arrange for a house sitter when we're going on vacation, but you don't know what to tell the sitter because you don't know where the thermostats are. So there's a lot that the woman just does. No matter how enlightened we all become, we still just do it, it's so much easier in the long run. We know that we'll do it right. And we'd just as soon not ask.

SR: But it's not just that. In many marriages women say they want help, but they don't want their turf invaded, whether it's the kitchen or the nursery or whatever. So when they do accept the help, they fuss about, well, it's not done exactly the way I do it. A friend recently told me the story of a married couple where the woman got ill and the man was taking over a lot of the household tasks while she recovered.

As the woman told it, "The real present my husband gave me was not only doing all of these things around the house, but doing them the way he knew I would do them." This was an interesting insight. So often men don't think about that, which is insensitive. Or women get angry at them for not doing things exactly the right way, which isn't always fair either.

CR: Right. Part of it is noticing, though. Lately, Steve has been trying to set the table the way I like it set—putting out the right napkins with the right plates and glasses. For years he never noticed, or thought I was foolish for caring. It was also important for me to learn not to nag. That's dumb, too.

SR: But this is recently acquired wisdom. In California, we were still trying to adjust to married life, and the world around us was going nuts. The counterculture was exploding, challenging every established institution there was, especially marriage. We had not been in Los Angeles long before I made my first visit to San Francisco. A college friend was working there as a reporter, and he took me on a tour of North Beach and other hippie hot spots. I brought home a poster of the Jefferson Airplane, an early psychedelic rock group, and I felt like an anthropologist who had just discovered some strange new sect. I remember saying to Cokie, "Something interesting is happening there." But it also became quite troubling.

CR: We were both from very traditional families. We were East Coast people and this was a whole new world. But I did put the poster up over the babies' changing table.

SR: So many marriages around us were breaking up. The wife of one of my basketball buddies ran off with another woman. There was a lot of wreckage, and not just among marriages. It was among children, teenagers turning to drugs.

CR: One friend of ours said proudly that she had shed 175 pounds—25 pounds of her own and a 150-pound husband. To celebrate her new freedom she ordered a new waterbed and the guy who delivered it stayed two weeks. True story! Steve was convinced that the guy didn't have an apartment; he went around delivering waterbeds and hoping something would turn up. And these would be the conversations in the park. I'd be there pushing the kids on the swings and the person next to me would be talking about her affairs. It was very shocking, and it was frightening; could it happen to us? I instituted what I called a "have an affair with your wife" program, where every so often just the two of us would go off together for a night or two and not call each other "Mommy" or "Daddy" the whole time. All this free-floating fantasizing was going on all around us, and it made me more than a little nervous. Here I was this mom at home with two babies and there Steven was out covering the Hollywood set. I didn't mind so much the night he called me at three o'clock in the morning from the Mustang Ranch, where he was reporting on the first legal brothel. But I did draw the line at his traveling with his extremely attractive assistant to a rock concert where God only knows what would be going on in the audience. No matter how strong I thought our marriage was, I didn't see any point in asking for trouble.

SR: It was a confusing time. I was so upset, and fascinated, that I did a long series for the *Times* about divorce.

CR: One friend called in tears and said, "Can you get over here right away?" So I gathered up the kids and dashed over there. She was absolutely devastated. Her husband had just walked out. Why, I asked, what did he say? As she handed me her baby, she sobbed, "He said he wants to be a hard-living, hard-loving writer on the road." I burst out laughing. I felt sorry for my poor suffering friend, but what an exit line!

SR: During this period I wrote an article for the *New York Times* Sunday magazine about my tenth high-school reunion, and it was called "Old-Fashioned at 27." So many of my classmates felt the way I did—really lost in this new world. The assumptions we had grown up with—marry young, have kids, stay married—were all in question. I wrote about one woman's painful divorce and remarriage, only to cause her even more pain. Her new in-laws didn't know she'd been married before! Another divorced woman told me that it was her aim to "go crazy" in bed, but every time she slept with a man she wasn't married to, she saw the ghost of her grandfather, a Protestant preacher, and was convinced she was "going to hell." My job was to write about this world and understand it, and I wasn't immune from the turbulence and the temptation. One night some East Coast journalists came into town and had a party. I went dressed in the fashion of the day, and one of them cracked, "When the *New York Times* bureau chief shows up wearing red corduroy bell-bottoms, things sure have changed!" For my newspaper series on divorce, I talked to a marriage counselor who made a very telling point: the whole question about marriage was different. People were getting up every day and asking, "Do we have a reason to stay together today?" Even in the best marriages, he pointed out, there will be days when you don't have a great answer to that question, so you need an underlying commitment to each other to carry you through the rough spots. What had eroded was that commitment. "Do your own thing" had replaced "for better or worse." During this period we attended a wedding of two friends—first marriage for her, second for him. Let's start with the fact that the guy had first dated his bride's mother before discovering the daughter! And the vows they exchanged were not exactly "till death do us part." It was more like "This is cool today, but who knows about tomorrow?" If you look at the statistics it's very striking—this whole notion of disposable marriages grew steadily during the seventies, with the divorce rate reaching a peak in about 1980.

CR: Particularly in California, because so many people there came from someplace else. Many of them had gone there to get away from home—from mother and father and sisters and brothers. It makes a difference in a marriage to leave the community. Because community does two things: first, it supports the marriage, and second, it disapproves of divorce. So there is a push-pull. The lack of that support structure made California a much more rootless place.

SR: I think that's true. Now, to be fair, looking back on those years we would say that there were certain advantages to being away from home. We could work out our relationship without having to answer to any of our parents on a regular basis, and many of our friends felt the same way. But if couples had more freedom to flourish, they also had more freedom to fail, more freedom to make mistakes, more freedom to ignore the communal pressures and family expectations which help get you through the rough times that therapist was talking about. One of the key elements keeping a marriage together is the community. The people who see you as a couple. The people who expect you to stay married, who reinforce the importance of marriage. Whether it's the high-school buddies you played basketball with or the other young mothers in your kids' play group. So there were enormous pluses and enormous minuses in our situation.

CR: In the middle of all this turmoil a life-shattering event forced us to come to an understanding of what was truly important in life. My father was on a campaign trip with a colleague in Alaska, and his airplane was lost. The news hit the wires in late afternoon California time when I was at home feeding the babies. A friend called solicitously asking, "What can we do to help?" And I said, "With what?" She said, "About your father." I tensely demanded, "What about my father?" Her husband, a reporter, then got on the phone and explained to me that Daddy's plane was missing in Alaska.

I started frantically trying to reach Steve. The people in his office kept trying to protect me, saying he's not here. I screamed, "You've got to find him." And they said, "Cokie, he knows, he's trying to get home to tell you."

SR: My editor had called me immediately, and I made the judgment, foolishly it turned out, to go home to tell Cokie in person. But it was a long drive, and many of our friends were reporters, too, and they all had access to the wires. When I walked into the house, I realized immediately that she knew. She was standing there in tears, still feeding the babies.

CR: The next day I went to Washington and Steve stayed home with the kids. It was the first time that I understood that our little foursome wasn't the sum total of my responsibilities. I had other people to care for and care about, and I needed to be with them to care for me. No matter what was going on in our household, it didn't matter. When I got to Washington—my parents' house, of course, was filled with people—my mother said, "Thank God you're here. We're leaving for Alaska." I said, "You're out of your mind. Your entire support system is here, and here's where we'll get the best information." She shot back, "If you were missing in Alaska, Daddy would go looking for you." Which pretty much ended the argument. So we all got on *Air Force Two* and headed for Alaska. Lee turned four while I was in Alaska. What did you do on his birthday?

SR: Not sure, but I do remember buying him a black football jersey as a birthday present that he wore for years.

CR: It turned out that my mother was absolutely right about going to Alaska. If we had not had regular briefings from the military and seen the terrain and learned as much as we did, I can't imagine we would ever have been reconciled to the fact that the plane was never found. And the military stepped up its search because we were there asking questions. They brought in spy planes, whose pictures subsequently rewrote the map of Alaska. But then I left and went straight to Los Angeles, for Lee's fourth birthday party, which was the next day, at Disneyland. My friend Millie had gotten the cake and the party favors. Winnie the Pooh was running for president—talk about surreal!

SR: It was the fall of '72, right in the middle of the presidential campaign. Winnie probably had a better chance than George McGovern, the Democrat running against Richard Nixon. As the election approached, *The Washington Post* was beating our brains out with stories about Watergate. Woodward and Bernstein had written that many of the dirty tricksters who worked for the Nixon campaign were based in Southern California, so I had to cover that story while all the rest of this was going on.

CR: Right before Daddy went to Alaska, my parents had been in California raising money for the Democratic congressional ticket. They were in L.A., and while Mamma was working on some other campaign event, Daddy took the kids swimming in his hotel pool. He spent a nice long day with them and me. That was the last time I ever saw him.

SR: We learned something in this period about the importance of mourning rituals to a family and to a marriage. Because the search for Hale's plane continued for months, Lindy was not ready to have any sort of service for a good while.

CR: It was so strange in so many ways. For some reason, I had always had a fear about someone disappearing and never being found. I remember when a plane sank into Lake Pontchartrain and when another one crashed over the Grand

Canyon and no bodies were ever recovered. I would always think, reading those stories, that would be awful, to not know with certainty that someone you loved was dead. Little did I know that I would someday be in that position myself, and I was right: it is awful. No matter how much I intellectually accept the fact that the plane must have gone to the bottom of the cold, deep Prince William Sound, emotionally I've always half expected my father to turn up someday. For years, after I moved into the family house, I didn't change the kitchen wallpaper because I was afraid he might find his way home and then think strangers were there. Eventually, of course, the paper got so dirty I had no choice. But I've always had a tremendous amount of sympathy for the families of the missing-in-action. Some of them truly believe that their lost soldiers are still roaming the Vietnamese countryside, but most just want to claim the bodies, to know for sure what happened, and to be afforded the commonplace dignity of burying their dead.

SR: The next year I was assigned to cover the return of the POWs, and I could share with many of their families that special pain of losing a loved one, yet being deprived of certainty, of the chance to mourn and heal. Covering that story also provided an insight into marriage: many of the young couples broke up after the men returned, because their foundation was too shaky to take the weight and pressure of such a long separation. The older couples, who had time to build a life together before the husbands became prisoners, stood a much better chance for survival.

CR: In Daddy's case, the fact that he was missing caused all kinds of complications. First of all, he had to get reelected to Congress. He didn't have an opponent, but still, for various technical reasons, he had to be actually elected. So he was, even though he had been missing for weeks by then. Being away from family at that time was very hard. I was worried sick about my mother, and I was so grateful to my brother and sister-in-law, who were in Washington. I kept asking, what would we do if there weren't three of us siblings, each with spouses who can help?

SR: Lindy was resisting having a memorial service because it would be something final and she said many times that it would be breaking faith, that Hale might still be found. But finally, when Congress reconvened in January, his seat was declared vacant, and the next day there was a huge service in New Orleans, with massive contingents from Congress and the Nixon Administration. The Boggses' old friends Lyndon and Lady Bird Johnson also came, and President Johnson died only a couple of weeks later. The night before that service about thirty of us—including my parents and many of Lindy and Hale's old friends—had dinner in a private room at Antoine's around a big round table. People were uncertain about how to act. One of them asked us, very nervously, is it all right to talk about Hale? And we said, of course, that's why we're here. It started slowly, but gradually the evening turned into this rollicking wake of funny stories about his life. Afterward, my mother said to me, "That's what I want you to do for me." And in fact, we have done something similar— a night of memories and stories—for my dad and a number of others since then. It was a moment in marriage when you realize that sharing grief is part of the journey. It is part of what you do for each other.

CR: Another thing you do is back off, don't try to fix it. When I finally realized that I would never see my father again, I was so profoundly sad, I think it was hard for Steven. I was the youngest child and my father had always taken great delight in me. Losing him meant that never again would I be loved in quite that way. And knowing that he would never know my children broke my heart. There was nothing Steven could do about any of that, and it was tough for him to handle.

SR: That's true. But I also missed my father-in-law in my own way. I always dreamed that when we eventually returned to Washington, I could learn from him about the ways of Congress and politics, and I never got that chance. When we did come back, and I started covering Congress, I would search out many of Hale's old friends, sit at their feet, and hear their stories, receiving from them what I might have gotten from my father-in-law. And I wanted to pass on to my children tales of their grandfather, to keep alive their sense of a man they would never remember.

CR: During the search for my father, I couldn't stay in California worrying. So I moved east with the children for a few weeks, where at least I could be somewhat helpful to my mother and we could do our worrying together. It was, fortunately, at a time of hiatus in the TV show, otherwise I guess I would have quit. The fact that the TV tapings had fallow seasons worked both for me and against me. It gave me time off, but it made me antsy. During the antsy times Steve and I started writing together.

SR: The whole world wanted to know what was happening in California, and I had a lot of offers to do magazine pieces, but I couldn't get to them all. So we hit on this plan—Cokie would do most of the research, I'd write the piece, she would edit it, and we'd use a double byline. She had always been my best editor, so this was simply an extension of what we'd already been doing. And a good way for her to get out of the house. We did a whole series of pieces. One was for *Seventeen* on teenage mothers keeping their babies, a brand-new trend. We also did some travel articles. It was fun writing together, and it added a different dimension to our relationship. I've always had a lot of confidence in Cokie's ability, at times more than she had in her own.

CR: It was also extremely useful for me. Steve had a name already. For me to have my byline with his on stories in good magazines was very important. In truth, I wasn't writing much. He was writing, I was editing. In later years that changed. But it was important to my professional development; I learned a lot and the public recognition made a huge difference when we went abroad. It made me feel that I could do something professionally, not be lost.

SR: She talks about going abroad. After almost five years in California, as much as we loved it, it was time to do something else. So I went to New York to talk to my bosses about our future.

CR: It was October of '73, and as soon as he left, another huge brushfire swept through Malibu. Rather than stay up all night monitoring how close the flames were coming, I decided to leave. I packed up the kids, and the dog, and went to Millie's house. It was just before Halloween, and the kids insisted on wearing their full costumes. When we got to a police checkpoint on the Pacific Coast Highway, off to the left of us was a huge wall of fire; it looked like a holy card of hell. The policeman checked the car, where he beheld a little witch and a little ghost! And Freddy the dog! At least it gave him one good laugh on a terrible night. The fire passed quickly, and Steven came home from New York with wonderful news—the *Times* had offered to move us to Greece!

SR: It was the perfect time for a foreign adventure. The kids were at a highly portable age—three and five. Cokie's show had won a bunch of awards, but to her credit, she understood—even better than I did—that the experience of living abroad would far outweigh the costs of putting her career on hold one more time. My one regret was my parents. Now I was taking their two grandchildren even farther away from New Jersey. But my twin brother and his wife did more than their share, having produced two daughters and a baby boy, to help fill the grandchild gap.

CR: At that point I thought of California as home. I could easily imagine living there the rest of our lives. But when the offer came to move to Greece, I was ready! I think women make a mistake when they say no to a great opportunity because it doesn't fit exactly into a career outline at the moment. First of all, even in terms of a career, the experience of living abroad can be very useful. But secondly, it's terrific in terms of broadening life. I was terribly excited about the prospect, and right after we learned the news I went to New Orleans, where my mother, who had been elected to fill my father's seat in Congress six months earlier, was being honored by B'nai B'rith. I unthinkingly burst into a room full of people and blurted out, "We're moving to Greece!" Here she was, a widow of only a year, and I was moving thousands more miles away. Mamma handled it, as always, completely graciously, but it must have hurt.

SR: We might have been the parents of two children, and recognized professionals, but we didn't always act like grown-ups. The worst example of continuing childishness came that Christmas when we went east to see the family and to celebrate Cokie's thirtieth birthday. This was at the height of the oil embargo and the East Coast was really suffering from shortages, much more so than in the West. For weeks before we arrived, my mother fretted, warning us that driving would be difficult, that there were long gas lines everywhere. I got very annoyed with her, which I normally did not do. I kept saying, "Look, Mom, I am the *New York Times* correspondent in California, I travel all over the country by myself, I can handle it!" Well, we went to Washington and borrowed a car from Cokie's brother to drive to New Jersey and then we went into New York for a day. When we started back out to my parents' house, we discovered there was very little gas in the car, so we got in a long line. After inching forward for blocks we finally reached the pump just as the station ran out of gas. We edged into another line, but that station ran out before we made it to the pump. Then, as we went searching for gas, the car ran out, right in the middle of an intersection. We managed to get it to the side of the street and go to the *Times,* where the truck dispatchers conjured up a few gallons—enough to get through the tunnel to the Jersey side. So, after snapping at my mother for weeks that I could handle this situation, I had to call my parents and say, we've run out of gas, please, come get us. It was one of the hardest calls I've ever had to make. Years later I had reason to remember it when a similar thing happened to Lee. He had had more than a few driving mishaps as a teenager and was eager to show us that those years were over. On his way home from college he had a flat tire and changed it. Then he had another flat tire and he didn't have a second spare. It was after midnight and he had no option but to call us. I got in the car and drove two hours to pick him up. As we headed home he turned to me: "I hope you understand how hard it was for me to make that phone call." And I answered, "I do, Lee, because I've been there." When I told him the story about running out of gas, he was thrilled!

CR: After our East Coast misadventures, we went back to California to start packing up. But before we left for Greece, I had to fulfill my TV contract to produce twenty-six episodes of *Serendipity.* The *Times* was ready for us to go and we had to stay until I was finished. That was the first time my work took precedence. Steve was great about it, saying, "If you have to stay, you have to stay. We won't go in January, we'll go in March." The movers were at home packing up around me while I sat at my typewriter frantically trying to finish all the final paperwork, so I wasn't paying much attention to the packing. Months later, when I was in Athens unpacking, I kept smelling this awful odor that got worse and worse as I dug deeper into a big box. Finally I got down to the problem: the movers had packed a full potty seat! A friend of mine had been visiting with her one-year-old right before the packing started. There was also a dead mouse, but I think he died along the way. Probably the stench from the potty seat got him. My inattention to the packing also deprived us of a moment of sentiment that it turned out we had each been anticipating. In *Fiddler on the Roof*, Tevye's last act before leaving home had been to remove the mezuzah, the symbol of a Jewish household, from the door. My sister's husband's Irish-Catholic mother had given us a mezuzah as a wedding present (she also sent her family's christening gown at the appropriate points), and separately, we each imagined Steven taking it down as we got in the cab to leave for the airport. But when he went to get it, he discovered the mezuzah was already packed up and on its way to mark our next doorpost, our doorpost in Greece.

SR: As we got ready to move, we worked hard to get the kids, who were then three and five, interested and excited about their new home. Cokie put up posters all around the house of the Acropolis and the Agora, and other Greek temples and monuments. Becca kept looking at the posters and the books we showed her. Finally, she said with tears welling in her eyes, "Daddy, are we going to have to live in one of those tumbled-down houses?" She thought all the buildings in Greece were ruins. But they weren't. In our future was a lovely house, surrounded by orange and lemon trees, in the first suburb north of Athens. The name of the street was Agias Sophias, which translates as both Saint Sophie and Holy Wisdom. And we would need plenty of the good saint's wisdom, and protection, for our little family during our years abroad.

The romantic notion of a foreign correspondent, to quote our old California friend, is of a "hard-living, hard-loving writer on the road." No spouse or kids at home to limit options or nurture guilt. But we had learned from our days in California—a foreign country to most Americans, after all—that it was actually better to live abroad as a family. Not only did you take your best friend and lover with you, but children, more focused on circuses and cookies than parliaments and politics, provided a fresh view of the cultures you were covering. The hard-living, hard-loving types came home to empty apartments and out-of-date address books. Steve came home to the life and laughter—and yes, the stresses and strains—of St. Sophie Street. One of the stresses was Cokie's work. She was eager to move, and give up her job, but she also knew that she needed something stimulating to do in Athens. Producing TV shows was out—they were all in Greek. Part-time reporting for American radio seemed like a good bet. But Steve's sensitivity to the situation was not all that great, as a stopover in London on our way to Greece made clear.

CR: Before we left for Greece, I went to talk to the networks and said, "Look, I'm learning Greek, I'll have access to Steve's Telex, I'll be involved through him in all the news, can't you use me?" CBS handed me a tape recorder and said, fine, file for radio. But I knew I couldn't count on that; I needed to hedge my bets and talk to everyone I could. My next stop was Westinghouse, which at that time had a big radio network; there, I also got some encouragement. At NBC, which is where I'd been working, I was told to call on the London bureau chief when we stopped there on the way to Greece. I dutifully made an appointment at NBC in London, but Steve wanted to buy a Burberry's trench coat. He couldn't sit for the children while I went to NBC because, he insisted, he couldn't be a foreign correspondent without the right trench coat. So I missed my appointment at NBC.

SR: I don't remember the story quite that way. I was all for Cokie working, and encouraged her to become a radio reporter, because I thought that medium would use her skills well. But was I also self-centered and insensitive at times? Without a doubt. And the trench coat *was* cool. Lots of rings and pockets and epaulets. It made me a feel a bit like Snoopy, getting off a plane in a new country, carrying my typewriter and muttering to myself, "Here's the world-famous foreign correspondent. . . ." But in many ways it was the kids who adjusted to their new life first. One of my earliest images of Greece is putting Lee in school and watching him disappear down the corridor with his new teacher.

CR: It was so easy with Lee because there was an American school and he was able to start kindergarten right away. But he did have one complaint: "Didn't *The New York Times* know that I just learned to read when they sent us here?" With a different alphabet he couldn't read the billboards and street signs. Becca was much harder to find a place for. Eventually, a slot opened at the one American-style preschool and she happily went off on her own, at three and a half, to "The Early Childhood Education Center." Just hearing her pronounce the name was worth the price of tuition.

SR: After we'd been in Greece only a few weeks, it was time for the Orthodox Easter, their most important holiday. A military government was running the country and the foreign press corps was invited to an Easter celebration at an army base outside of Athens. The soldiers were performing all the traditional rituals, roasting a lamb and dancing, and we were sitting there and watching, still feeling a bit tentative and out of place. We looked around and Lee and Becca had dashed out onto the dance floor and were dancing with the soldiers! I turned to Cokie and said, "Well, I guess we've finally arrived in Greece!" Or at least two of us had. That was actually the only pleasant encounter we had with the military regime. It was a tense time, with many Greek nationalists either in jail or out of the country. I had to be very careful in talking to people about the government because I could get them in trouble with the junta. The Nixon Administration backed the regime, so it was particularly dicey for an American journalist. Fortunately, the government did not last long after we got there.

CR: When we first arrived, I was frankly less concerned about the grand goings-on of government than I was about the everyday business of finding a house for us to live in and schools for the kids. We were lucky on the house front, we found one quickly, but our stuff took a good while to get to Greece, so we lived in this rather cramped apartment hotel. That was a challenge. I did do one smart thing—airfreight about four boxes of toys so the kids had things to play with. In Greece, parks and playgrounds are closed during siesta and I had to keep the children quiet because people were sleeping. I kept suggesting that they might sleep, too, but they didn't see siesta as a charming Mediterranean custom, they saw those afternoon hours in bed as nap time for babies.

SR: But even the toys were a hassle. When I went to customs to collect them, the young guy who was checking the boxes was fascinated. Greece didn't have anything like these fancy American toys, and he kept playing with them. Finally, I gave him a plastic helicopter and said, "Here, take it." It was the closest I had ever come to bribing someone.

The kids adapted very well. They never learned a lot of

Greek because they both were in English-speaking schools, but they did learn one critical Greek phrase, *exi biscota, parakalo,* which means "six cookies, please." There was a bakery at the corner, and they could walk there with their drachmas in hand and buy cookies. For children who had been driven everywhere they ever went, they loved being able to do things on their own like that.

CR: That first spring, right after we arrived, we went down to Corinth and the kids were climbing around the ruins. Archaeological sites make wonderful playgrounds for kids, because they can run until they tire out. It's not like a museum, where they have to behave and be quiet. The back of the site at Corinth had clearly been a row of shops, and the children set up imaginary stores there while we toured the site with the guidebook. When we came back to the kids, we found Becca hawking her wares. "What is your shop, Rebecca?" "It's a statue shop." "And what are you selling?" "I'm selling statues from Corinth, Delphi, and Santa Monica!" That was the known world of Rebecca Roberts!

SR: One of the first friends we made in Athens was the real estate agent who helped us find the house. We didn't know that it was across the street from where George Papadopoulos, the colonel who had run the military junta, had lived for seven years. The whole street had been closed off during his reign, but he had just been deposed in a coup, by another group of colonels, which is why the house had come on the market.

CR: There was still a little guardhouse across the street, which was great because it was so safe.

SR: The stories were that Papadopoulos had used our house for his family, or maybe for his mistress. We were never quite sure. The kids found in one of the drawers a set of hair curlers, and they kept waving them around saying, "We have Mrs. Papadopoulos's curlers!"

One of our first evenings in Athens our real estate agent invited us out to dinner at a Greek taverna. We came to love tavernas. Talk about family values. They were these wonderful, informal spots, often with gardens, even in the middle of the city. It was a perfect place to eat with young children—they could run around and not bother anybody. We usually asked for five chairs for the four of us because Becca would often conk out in the middle of the meal, stretch out across two chairs, and go to sleep. During our first taverna experience, our agent served us a goat from his home island. One of the things we learned quickly was that all Greeks were very proud of their origins. Their village or their island had the best—the best olives, the best wine, the best tomatoes, whatever. The agent was very proud of the goat, and I innocently asked him how he had managed to get it from his home island to Athens. "On a leash," he replied. I had a mental picture of this smiling little goat, walking onto the ferry, headed for slaughter in Athens! It dimmed the pleasure of the meal a bit.

CR: We had had a Seder with our California friends a month early, but now it really was Passover, so we celebrated with a little ceremony in our apartment hotel, just the four of us. There was a synagogue in Athens, old and very traditional. I asked Steven to go down to the synagogue and see if there were stores in the neighborhood selling matzoh. I told him to get some pita bread if he couldn't find matzoh, because at least it's unleavened bread and in a pinch we could substitute it for matzoh. Steven came home with a piece of cheesecake! I said, "What is this? We're having a Seder with a piece of cheesecake?" And Steve answered, "Well, it's Jewish."

SR: Hey, you have to be ready to adapt to new cultures.

CR: After about three months things were settling down. The kids were in school, we had moved into our house, and we already had guests, a couple from New York who had been friends from Washington days. I was thinking about sending a cable to CBS saying I was ready to do some work, could they use me?

SR: We were sitting in the house on a Monday morning, talking with our friends, and the Telex—sort of a private telegraph machine—rang upstairs. The message: "Assume you know. Coup in Cyprus. Makarios presumed dead." I didn't know. So I quickly called the Reuters office and learned that a group of right-wingers associated with the military government in Athens had overthrown Makarios, who was both the archbishop and the president of Cyprus. Immediately the airport in Nicosia closed down, so no reporters could get onto the island. Over the next few days dozens of reporters from all over the world gathered in Athens, eager to fly to Cyprus as soon as possible. Finally, we got a call on Thursday that the airport was opening and a flight was leaving immediately.

So I raced to the airport and found myself in the departure lounge surrounded by all these war correspondents wearing fancy bush jackets and safari suits. They all seemed to know each other, and they kept saying things like, "Hey, remember that day in the Golan Heights?" I was sitting there in a drip-dry sports shirt, watching these guys and saying to myself, "I can't cover this war. I can't even dress right for this war." But I had actually been to Cyprus once, a few weeks before. During that period when the airport was closed, I'd written a long background piece on the politics of Cyprus, which ran that morning on the front page of the *International Herald Tribune*. I got on the plane still feeling very shaky about my role when I noticed that all these self-important war correspondent types were tearing my story out of the *Tribune* and stuffing it into one of the many pockets of their bush jackets. Then I realized: "I may not have the right clothes, but at least I know where this island is, and most of you don't!"

The first two days were very calm. I went over to the Turkish sector for dinner with two other *New York Times* correspondents who had flown in from Israel and Lebanon. But at five o'clock Saturday morning I was rudely rousted out of bed by machine-gun fire. I dashed to the window of the hotel, which was right on the border between the Greek and Turkish sectors, and Turkish paratroopers were dropping out of the sky. The Greeks had machine guns on the roof and were firing down into the Turkish sector. Shortly after I was woken up by gunfire in Cyprus, Cokie was woken up by a phone call in Athens.

CR: It was CBS telling me the Turks had invaded Cyprus. I cried, "Oh, my God. Steve's there." The person on the phone said huffily, "Well, we have correspondents there as well." He thought I was being competitive on Steve's behalf, not that I was worried about my husband. Then he asked me to file a radio spot.

SR: The main CBS stringer in Athens was in Cyprus with me. They didn't have anybody but Cokie.

CR: I had not heard from CBS since my visit in New York, but now they wanted Greek reaction to the invasion and they had my phone number, so the folks there thought it was worth trying me. I had never filed a radio spot in my life. It was very early in the morning, so there wasn't anything going on, what was I going to do? I didn't know anybody. I woke up the live-in baby-sitter, a young Canadian woman who was in Greece for the summer, and told her I was leaving to do a radio report. I drove by the Greek Pentagon—which was right near our house—no action there. Then I went to the

Reuters office, where the bureau chief, Neocosmos Tzallas, a good friend of ours, was already working. Fortunately, Neo had an old friend, an opposition politician named Averoff—he later became defense minister—and Averoff was able to find out what was happening and fill us in, so I was able to file a spot. From there on out I was filing every hour, but at times the whole country's communication system broke down and I couldn't get a phone line out of Athens. The father of one of Lee's friends was duty officer at the American embassy one night and tipped me off that they had agreed on a cease-fire in Cyprus. I had a world beat but I couldn't get the story out. Our borders were closed. Banks were closed. It was chaos. And I didn't know where Steven was. For a little while I didn't know whether he was alive or dead, until the *Times* got word to me that he was safe. Meanwhile I was filing constantly. The events in Cyprus triggered a reaction in Greece, and the civilian politicians started moving against the military junta. I'd been working twenty hours straight for days, which was fine because I was so scared about Steve, and it was all very exhilarating. But the baby-sitter was getting pretty tired. On her birthday, I promised I'd be home for dinner and we'd cook some steaks and have a nice party. I got in the cab to go back home from the Reuters office and all of a sudden it was like Mardi Gras and New Year's Eve all at once. In all the cars, people honked their horns, and on the street everyone was shouting and jumping up and down. Just then the radio in the cab announced that the junta had fallen! I hopped out right at the Presidential Palace, where the civilian leaders were meeting, and turned on my tape recorder to capture all the sound. Flower stalls line one whole side of the building. I ran into one stall and commandeered the guy's telephone. Without so much as a by-your-leave, I took the phone apart and stuck these little alligator clips into the receiver, which is the way you filed from a tape recorder in those years, and produced a spot. The flower-stall owner was screaming at me, convinced I was with the CIA, taking his phone apart. I calmed him down and bought some flowers. It was an incredibly exciting moment.

SR: That night CBS called Cokie's mother and asked, "Do you have a picture of your daughter?" Lindy was alarmed. "Why? Is something wrong?" And CBS said, no, but her radio report is the only news we have out of Greece; we want to play it as the lead of the TV news and we want to run her picture along with it. So just days after Cokie started working for CBS, she led the Walter Cronkite show. Not a bad beginning.

CR: All of this time, which seemed forever but was in fact about a week, Steven and I hadn't been able to talk to each other, and usually, no matter where we are, we talk at least once a day. It was the longest period of our lives that we were out of touch—even now, twenty-five years later, it's still the record. It was just terrifying. I didn't know what his situation was. My own situation was pretty scary. It was hard for me to get money to buy food. The banks were closed and credit cards didn't exist. Fortunately, the kids thought it was pretty neat, with all these tanks in the street.

SR: I wasn't able to talk to Cokie because I went to the British base in the south of the island, hoping for better communications. But there were about twenty or thirty reporters and only one phone line we could use, so whenever it was my turn, I'd call my office in London to try to dictate a story.

CR: At one point the *Times* called your father to tell him you were okay, and he said, "I didn't raise my son to be a war correspondent!"

SR: I agreed with him. And anyway, the new civilian government in Greece was an even bigger story, so after about a week I was able to hop a British air force flight to London, and get back to Athens the next day. I had left behind a wife who was obviously a very accomplished woman but didn't know squat about being a radio reporter. I returned home to find out that she had been filing constantly for a week and was now a veteran foreign correspondent. It was one of the more bizarre moments in our marriage. Friends in California tell tales of driving along, listening to the CBS all-news station, hearing Cokie's voice from the radio and practically driving off of the freeway. I wasn't the only one surprised.

CR: That week established me with CBS, and later that year the foreign editor came to Greece and said that they were interested in hiring me as their woman in Europe. There was just no way on earth I could do that. Steve was away all the time, I'd be away all the time. Talk about unfair to your children! But it was fine to say no to that. It was flattering, but it would have been wrong. We were able to spend a lot of time traveling together, often with the kids. And *The New York Times* was beginning to understand that the spouses of their correspondents were important to the whole operation. So they agreed to pay my way occasionally when I traveled with Steven, and that helped a lot.

SR: When Cokie traveled with me, she'd often call CBS and offer to work. At one point we went to Italy during an election campaign, and when she called New York they said, "Thank God you're there. Our radio correspondent has just been taken to the hospital." Cokie wound up covering the whole Italian election for CBS radio. It posed a bit of a problem for me because my editor used to drive into New York listening to CBS and I would propose all these stories and more than once he'd say, "I already heard that story on CBS from Cokie." What he probably didn't realize was that he was also paying for her to scoop me.

Even though Cokie wasn't working anywhere near full-time, having her own press card, her own identity, was very important in those years. She had legitimacy in the international press corps and with government ministers, and had access to press conferences and briefings. She had an independent role beyond foreign correspondent's wife. Secondly, I think it meant that she could absorb and process the experience in a very different way. Everything became grist for a possible story.

CR: I started doing freelance pieces for little magazines, and then we wrote some travel pieces together for *The New York Times* and a big Sunday magazine piece. Like Steven, I was able to write on a variety of topics and I enjoyed putting together different stories for different publications, plus the radio and occasional TV work when news broke.

SR: We had both become interested in how modern archaeologists were proving that many of the ancient myths had a basis in fact. The magazine article focused on an excavation on the island of Santorini, in the middle of the Aegean. A village had been sealed in by a volcanic explosion, just like Pompeii, except this was from the Bronze Age, 1200 B.C., more than a thousand years before Pompeii. The site had been discovered accidentally by a shepherd and it was in the early stages of excavation. So we went to the island with the kids and the baby-sitter and left them together one morning at the little villa we had rented. Cokie and I spent this absolutely fascinating morning going through the dig with the caretaker explaining it all to us, and I became convinced the explosion on Santorini had led to the myth of Atlantis.

CR: The caretaker's grandfather was the shepherd who had first stumbled on the find and this was the family property.

SR: Normally, in any ancient site the walls are at most three feet high, but here was a Bronze Age city with ruins preserved to the second story. In fact, they had discovered a bench on the second floor with a hole in it. The archaeologists had originally proclaimed that this must be a shrine; that's what they always said when they couldn't explain something. Then they discovered the network of pipes leading from the hole and realized it was indoor second-floor plumbing more than three thousand years old. Some of the houses in the surrounding village didn't have such luxuries. Then we went to a late lunch, Greek style.

CR: We went to this little teeny beach which had maybe three buildings on it. We had hired a cab for the day, and we asked the driver to recommend a taverna. He said, "That one on the end, the guy who runs it is also the fisherman." The place had at most two tables, and a little lettuce garden out back. Santorini is famous for its wine because the volcanic soil produces delicious grapes; tomatoes, too. The fisherman showed us his fresh-from-the-sea catch and we picked out a couple of fish. Then he and his wife brought our rickety little table right out to the water. While we were waiting for the fish to cook we ate the fresh-picked lettuce, with some cheese and wine. Then on came this unbelievably fresh fish, grilled perfectly, and Steve looked at me and exulted: "We're on assignment for *The New York Times*! We're getting paid to do this!" That was maybe the single best moment of our entire stay in Greece. It doesn't get any better than that.

As Steve says, working was important for my identity and sanity, but it also helped to keep my hand in professionally so that when I did come home, I had clips to show, and broadcasts to bolster my résumé. But I also wanted time to be a mother and volunteer in the community. I was PTA president one year and very involved with the school. I remember setting up a spook house for the elementary school at Halloween, and it wasn't easy. This wasn't a country where I could run down to the local hardware store and buy fluorescent paint. After I finally found the paint through some theater group, I prevailed upon an appliance store to give me a huge refrigerator box. I got inside the box and painted all these spiders and eyes. I am the world's worst artist, but I was the only one willing to do it. Turns out the rest of the mothers were wise to steer clear because that fluorescent paint is poison!

Becca was in a ballet class run by a Frenchwoman who missed her calling as a marine drill instructor. We American mothers were considered the renegades, we were not nearly strict enough with our five-year-olds, but I was the only one daring enough to drive into Athens. It was ten minutes away, but traffic was so terrifying that a lot of foreigners wouldn't go near the city. I remember risking my life to buy the little ballet outfits, but I ended up with the wrong shade of blue and that was a huge deal to the teacher. So our little American girls all wore a paler shade of blue. How humiliating!

SR: We knew why we were there—we were there for my job. Cokie never said, it's my turn, or my career is being thwarted. But she did establish herself as a journalist apart from me. Once we attended a press reception in honor of Constantine Caramanlis, who had been in exile in France during the military government and now was back as the country's newly elected premier. He was a very courtly, very patrician man with a great eye for a pretty lady. When he made his entrance, he took one look at Cokie from across the room and made a beeline for her.

CR: I was avoiding him because the paparazzi surrounding him scared me to death. I had been hit in the head more than once by one of those cameras. But Caramanlis was what you'd call single-minded if there was one woman in the room.

SR: Cokie's Greek was pretty good but it wasn't perfect, and she was trying desperately to think of the Greek word for "congratulations."

CR: Which is *synharitiria*.

SR: But the only word that stuck in her mind was *synagrida*, which actually means "red snapper"! As Caramanlis was bearing down on her, she was about to say, "Red snapper, Mr. Premier."

CR: It was one of those moments where the Holy Spirit came upon me, because just as I was about to say "red snapper" the right word popped into my head and I didn't disgrace myself. But I also learned a lot about myself in those years. Steve was traveling much of the time and often I resented that. I can remember one night in California taking the garbage down the driveway and thinking, "This is a pain. I would like to live with someone who is here and takes the garbage out." Then I thought if we weren't married I'd have to take it out every night. But still, like most people, I think, I would occasionally gripe—maybe I can find somebody else who will take the garbage out. When we got to Greece I was alone a lot. And it was a difficult country to live in because it was neither first world nor third world. There weren't modern conveniences, but there wasn't easily hired help either. And because we weren't with the government or the military, I was living much more on the local economy than most of my American friends. The *Times* was very generous; it paid for half the school and gave us a housing allowance, so we weren't impoverished by any means. It was simply a question of coping. I remember, for instance, my search for charcoal to use in a little grill I had bought. I knew there had to be charcoal someplace; tavernas with grills dotted the countryside. Finally, I discovered that charcoal was sold at lumberyards, since it was burned wood. I bought the equivalent of a hundred-pound bag of huge pieces of charred wood and brought it home. Then I drove the car over it about twenty times to break it up enough to use for cooking. Accomplishments like that, as minor as they were, gave me a wonderful sense of competence. I didn't need Steven to do those things; in fact, he would have told me I was nuts to drive over the charcoal, but it worked. I realized that I missed Steven enormously, but what I missed was his company, the companionship, the conversation, the laughs. I could take out the garbage by myself, even if I didn't like it.

SR: There's now a lot of talk about society recognizing the economic contribution that housewives make, and this was a classic case. There was simply no way I could have been a foreign correspondent without Cokie's help.

CR: Essentially, I managed the office as well as the house. If I didn't do it, Steven would have had to hire someone else because he was on the road so much; bills wouldn't have been paid. For a single person, it would be very difficult not to have some support system in place. Being a family meant we were connected to the community. We had a completely different experience living in a foreign country with children than we would have without children. And Greece was a delightful place to be with children. No one thinks of them as nuisances; they are accepted everywhere. We spent many a winter Sunday in a country restaurant having a long meal while the kids ran around with the other children there. In good weather we packed picnics to enjoy in some wildflower-studded field. Early on, Steve instituted a Sunday rule. The family had to spend Sunday together and make no other plans. As the kids got older they chafed under that stricture, and I did, too, sometimes, but it turned out to be very wise to guarantee time together.

SR: I was the culprit who broke the rule one time. The phone rang one Saturday in Athens and I heard this familiar breathy voice on the other end, "Mr. Roberts, this is Jacqueline Onassis." At first I thought it was a joke, but in fact it was Mrs. Onassis. She had started working as an editor at Doubleday and she wanted to talk to me about writing a book about Greece. It was a subject she knew a great deal about, and she had been reading my articles. Obviously, I was flattered, and intrigued. But when she asked Cokie and me to join her at a friend's house for Sunday lunch, I blurted out, "But we have a Sunday rule." She told me that was the only time we could meet, so I essentially asked the kids for their permission and we went to lunch with Jackie Kennedy.

CR: She was very gracious about the children. As we were leaving she pulled me aside to say, "Tell your children that I'm grateful they let you come, and tell them that President Kennedy loved and admired their grandfather very much." It was a lovely moment. But Steven didn't want to write a book about Greece, he just wanted to write for the newspaper, which continued to mean a lot of traveling.

SR: Leaving a family behind means separation, and guilt. Once in California, when I was packing for a trip, Cokie said she was sorry I was going, and I gave some stupid reply like "Well, dear, I have my job. . . ." And she just looked at me and said, "Aren't you glad I'm going to miss you?" It was a telling moment; I've never forgotten it. And in recent years I've had occasion to remind her of the same story, as she leaves town to cover a story or attend some event. But in the end I think it's easier having a family. Cokie was paying the bills and managing the office, but her role was much more than that. Psychologically it was very important for me to know that the family was there to come home to.

CR: From my perspective, as a woman alone a lot of the time, children forced me out of my own innate shyness. I *had* to go to the park. I *had* to go to the school. I needed to form a community for the children's sake. I would hate to have to move to a new place without children. For women particularly, I think the sense of universality of mothers in a park is enormous. It doesn't matter what language anyone speaks, we all respond in the same way when a child falls. I think that it would have been awfully tough to have been there without children.

SR: We all see things through the lens of our own narrow experiences, and living abroad provides a different perspective. I always thought that the key word in the term "Jewish mother" was "Jewish," that the mothers of my tribe were particularly attentive, and at times overly attentive, to their children. But spending an afternoon in a Greek playground was a revelation. Here were these women, all acting like "Jewish mothers"—some of them even fed their kids, a spoonful at a time, as they pushed them on swings. It made me realize that the key word is "mother," not "Jewish," that all mothers in all cultures share common traits. I'm not sure I would have learned that if I'd never gone to a playground.

CR: But things could get confusing, not just for us but for the kids, too. Steve's folks had given us a children's encyclopedia and the kids were leafing through it one day and saw a picture of a Ku Klux Klansman in full regalia. Of course that was intriguing, what was that? I made an attempt to explain the Klan and their hatred of people who were different. A few months later we're sitting on the beach in Crete and Rebecca suddenly burst into tears. When I asked what was wrong she sobbed: "I'm getting really, really, really brown and I'm Catholic and I'm Jewish and we're going home to

America where the Klan is going to get me!" Oh dear, that was my child's view of America.

SR: Our view of religion evolved during those years. We were a Catholic-Jewish marriage living in an Orthodox country and traveling regularly to the Muslim world. Not only did we celebrate our own holidays but we celebrated the local holidays as well. One of our favorites was Orthodox Easter, and even in our suburb of Athens our neighbors kept a custom common in their home villages and islands. At midnight everybody would gather in church, and it would be totally dark. We went to our local church, St. Sophie, which was just a few blocks away. The priest would light one candle and say, *"Christos anesti,"* Christ is risen. Then he would light one worshiper's candle, and gradually, candle by candle, the flame would be passed from hand to hand.

CR: So the church gradually goes from pitch darkness to full light—with no electricity, only candles. Everyone's expected to live close enough to a church to be able to walk home with a still-lighted candle, and we did. Then, following the tradition, we made a sooty cross on the doorpost with the flame. It's ritual clearly taken directly from the Passover story—the paschal mark, telling God to bless and protect the house and "pass over" the family as He carries out the ten plagues against their enemies.

SR: Living in that part of the world often reminded us of how Jewish and Christian traditions are so intertwined. That made it easier to raise the kids in both religions and celebrate everything! They, of course, loved getting all those presents, and had no sense of irony when they chose their own treats. Once we were on the island of Rhodes for the first night of Hanukkah, where Becca picked out an olive-wood cross for her present. Another time we were in Egypt shortly after

Passover and Lee bought an Arab headdress with the money my folks had sent him for the holiday. Our Seders have often included non-Jews and mixed couples, and several of our celebrations in Greece were quite emotional. We had one friend, a German woman whose father had been an officer killed in France during World War II. She asked to come to the Seder, very much as a gesture of reconciliation. To this day, it's one of the most moving Seders we've ever had. Another friend with German origins, a correspondent from an American publication, also asked to come one year.

CR: And he had a black Southern Baptist wife, just to add to the ecumenical spirit.

SR: Our friend Neo, the Reuters correspondent, had been very kind to us and we invited him to the Seder one year. But he was running a wire service, he had to be on constant call. If you went out to dinner with him, he was always jumping up and going to the phone. But at the Seder, to our amazement, he never moved once. Toward the end he started getting itchy and asked if the ceremony was over. When we said, yes, it's over, he leaped for the telephone! He had made this incredible gesture of friendship, telling his office not to call him until the Seder was finished. Seders were very important to us in Greece, as were all of our religious rituals, because they connected us to home and to our roots.

CR: But they were also a lot of work! Making potato pancakes for Hanukkah in that kitchen was not easy. Remember that this was pre-Cuisinart. I grated everything by hand. But after the cheesecake fiasco I did find matzoh. We actually lived right around the corner from Greece's only real supermarket and for a price you could get many imported things. Many of our American friends had PX privileges on the military base, but they weren't supposed to shop for unauthorized people, like us, and boy, did they follow the rules! Something like matzoh they could justify for religious reasons, but peanut butter, no. Our standard request from America, the things I could never seem to find locally, were Tabasco, peanut butter, grits, chocolate chips, and Fig Newtons. The fresh figs in Greece were beautiful, but they never learned to "Newton-ize" them like Nabisco.

SR: One family that came often to our Seders, and still does, were the Friedmans. Townsend was Jewish, a diplomat in the American embassy, and his wife, Eli, was a Brazilian Catholic. They were raising their two girls in both religions, just like us, so it was perfect. In one of the Seder rituals, the youngest child opens the front door to see if Elijah, the messenger of God, has come. One year we sent out Elisa, the younger Friedman girl, and she disappeared for a while. When she finally wandered back in we asked if she'd seen Elijah, and she replied, "No, but I saw God." It was one of the high points. I told the story recently at her wedding dinner.

CR: One year, I guess it was our first real Seder in Greece, Lee asked, "Daddy, when you were a little boy and both of your parents were Jewish, did Elijah come?" He thought Elijah was boycotting me, the *shiksa*! But I took very seriously the responsibility of making both religions part of our family life. The Catholic church I usually went to was a pretty chapel in the neighborhood where the priest said one Mass in Latin. With so many foreigners attending, that was the easiest common language. It had a little yard with swings and rabbit hutches and the kids loved to go, but when I wanted them to hear and understand a Mass in English, we'd attend the Anglican church.

For Jewish High Holy Days we'd join the armed forces. The U.S. military owned a hotel near the airport, and one year at Rosh Hashanah, the Jewish New Year, when Steve was out of town, I took the kids to morning services. The military would bring in a visiting rabbi and I found him sitting out on the balcony of his room, looking out at the water. I knocked and asked, "Sorry, are there Rosh Hashanah services here?" He explained that at services the night before, the other families had decided not to come back again, but he was hanging around in case anybody showed up. So I said to him, "Here we are." The kids were four and six. It was perfect. He pulled out the Torah and let them see it and touch it. And then he pulled out the shofar, the ram's horn that is blown to signal the start of the year. He let them try to blow it and of course they couldn't, but it was a neat thing to try. Then we all went downstairs in this American hotel and the kids had real American ice cream and the rabbi and I had American beers. Happy New Year!

SR: My grandparents had come to America from what's now Russia and Poland, and like many Jews of my generation, I grew up in a very different world and felt little connection to the lives they had led. Right before we moved to Greece, I was contacted by a representative of Amnesty International who wanted to feed me information about the Greek military government. We met in a restaurant in the Los Angeles airport and she told me her own story. As a young Jewish woman in Italy before the war, she came home one day to find her parents gone, arrested by the Fascists. She fled in terror, joined the underground, was captured and tortured. As I listened something deep inside me just gave way. I started sobbing, right there in the restaurant. She was talking about my people, my heritage, and I realized that moving to Europe would give me a chance to reconnect to that heritage. So as we traveled over the next few years, we got in the habit of looking for signs of Jewish settlement.

CR: And sometimes we found signs when we weren't looking. We were riding bikes on the Greek island of Chios, just off the Turkish coast, and it started to rain. We hid under this clump of trees for shelter and it turned out to be an old desecrated Jewish cemetery. It somewhat undid us.

SR: The gravestones were in three languages.

CR: Right, they were in Hebrew, Ladino, and Italian. The island had belonged to Italy at one point.

SR: Ladino is the Sephardic version of Yiddish, both languages that Jews spoke to each other. Ladino was a corruption of Spanish, the way Yiddish was a version of German. On another occasion I was in Salonika, a port city in northern Greece, once a thriving Jewish community that had been totally wiped out by the Nazis. Behind an Orthodox church I found a large pile of headstones with Hebrew writing on them. The Nazis had torn up the Jewish cemetery and the priests had tried to collect and preserve whatever relics they could find. It was one of many moments during those years that brought me closer to my own history. But the experience that was most meaningful to both of us was a trip we all took to Israel, our common Holy Land. We took a children's Bible along to read with the kids as we visited the sites where the stories had taken place.

CR: This Bible had been approved by so many priests, rabbis, ministers, and psychologists that it sometimes verged on the ridiculous. We were at one of the holiest spots in Jerusalem, which is supposed to be where Abraham almost sacrificed Isaac. But that crucial story had been excised from this Bible, apparently because children would be upset at the thought that their fathers might actually kill them. But Lee was such a pain in the neck that day that I was feeling a certain sympathy for Abraham! I didn't care what the psychologists said, I was telling the story!

SR: We talked a lot about how Mommy and Daddy were of different religions. It was an obvious and easy place to deal with the subject, since both traditions were right there, side by side. One night we were going to dinner in Jerusalem and we were telling riddles to keep the kids amused when Lee piped up, "I have a riddle." Lee's riddle? "What does a Christian and a Jew make?" When we were stumped he supplied the answer: "Me!" I subsequently wrote an article for *The New York Times* about this trip, and when I quoted this line the editor refused to believe that Lee had actually said it. He said it's too cute, too perfect, couldn't possibly be true. I said, "You take it out and I'm taking the piece back and you're not printing it." So eventually he did put it in. But when the piece was published, it stirred up a tremendous reaction.

CR: He wrote about everything.

SR: But that was part of my job. The fact that I was living with a family and taking these kinds of trips broadened what I saw and wrote about. My grandmother had a sister who had escaped from Europe during the Holocaust and moved to Israel. We went to visit her, and her son, on that trip, and she took me over to a photograph on the wall, a photograph of her father.

CR: This was Steve's first sighting of his own great-grandfather.

SR: I choked up and I brought the kids over and showed them this very austere man in a beard. "This is a picture of your great-great-grandfather." Lee peered up at the picture: "Oh, he looks like a Greek Orthodox priest." That was his frame of reference. A bit of cultural confusion there. But that was not the part of the article that got people so upset; their anger went much deeper.

CR: The fact that he was married to me was the main problem.

SR: True. The mere fact that I had married a non-Jew set people off. We got letters saying, "You are carrying out Hitler's work." Others said, "How dare you take this mongrel family of yours to Israel." But the part that was most controversial involved my grandfather. Early in this century he had been a Zionist pioneer in Palestine, and a number of letter writers said, in essence, "Your poor sainted grandfather, how upset he would be if he were still alive to know that you had married outside the faith." To this day, when I think about those letters, they enrage me. The truth of the matter was that in his declining years, when my grandfather often didn't recognize his own children, he would ask for Cokie because she had been so kind to him. Here were all of these people imposing their own prejudices and thinking they must know what was true for us. It hurt Cokie's feelings but it infuriated me. It reminded me that there is still a lot of hostility toward mixed marriages. Still a lot of people who can't get past their own fears and blind spots. The reaction caused considerable pain to both of us.

CR: In fact, we had even thought, up to that point, that Israel would make sense as our next assignment. It's a fascinating country which holds great meaning for both of us; it's a great story and it didn't require too much travel, or serious study of a foreign language because so many people there speak English. But after Steve's piece came out I thought, boy, would this be a mistake.

SR: A couple of years later I finally got a chance to vent my anger. After we came back to America and we were both covering Congress, we were traveling with a member back in her home district in northern New Jersey. We were standing in a shopping center watching the congresswoman greet constituents and she would occasionally introduce me. One older woman recognized my name and snapped, "Oh, you're the Steve Roberts who wrote that article about Israel." I stiffened as she added, "You're older now, you must know better now the mistake you made." Years of resentment just came spilling out . . .

CR: I was so embarrassed.

SR: I started screaming at this woman, "Yes, I did write that article. And the more I think about it, the more I know I was right, not wrong. You are the most bigoted, prejudiced person I've ever met." Cokie was standing a few yards away—the woman never saw her—and she captured the whole tirade on her tape recorder.

CR: This was not a good moment.

SR: It *was* a good moment. It was a great moment. It was a moment of release and vindication. But it also reinforced something I deeply believe. You can stay true to yourself while respecting and embracing another tradition. You don't lose your identity by loving someone else, you enlarge it. And you should not let others impose their prejudices on you.

CR: That trip to Israel was one of many we took with the kids and they became quite seasoned and easy travelers. Still, we always wanted to have another baby, but it never happened. I kept saying, "This doesn't make any sense. The only time in my life when I have both the time and the help and no babies are showing up." I made some efforts to determine the problem, but my experiences along those lines were fairly unpleasant.

SR: We already had two, and we had covered both sexes, but I think we're both sorry we never had more. We even had names picked out, Sam and Molly, whose real name would have been Miriam, after my grandmother.

CR: Finding ways to amuse the two we had was a constant challenge. There was no TV—only one channel and it was in Greek. There were few amusement parks or movies geared for kids. It was by and large reading and imagining, and years later both kids realized what an advantage that turned out to be. Without television they never formed the habit. When they returned home, they found their friends would walk in the house and turn on the TV. They never did that and still don't. Years later they revealed that their return to America presented them with one socialization problem: all the kids in school talked about *Brady Bunch* episodes. They pretended to watch as well and found it was pretty easy to fake it. The story lines didn't vary much.

SR: No TV was fine with me. My dad had been a writer and editor of children's books, and to him the tube was the enemy, a threat not only to our minds but to our living standards. I loved making up stories for the kids, and on one trip to Morocco, in the old city of Fez, the streets were too narrow to accommodate trucks, so the garbage was picked up by donkeys. Every night I spun out a different story about the adventures of a garbage donkey. On trips around Greece we would drive our green Fiat station wagon, and taking off from the Beatles song "Yellow Submarine," we made up endless verses to our own version with the chorus "We all live in a green automobile!" But the Fiat never quite had the proper papers, and one night, when we were supposed to take an overnight ferry to Italy, the port officials wouldn't let us on the boat.

CR: Our whole vacation depended on us making this ferry.

SR: It got more and more testy. The guy at the port yelled at Cokie and Cokie yelled back in her best Greek. Lee got frightened and finally burst into tears. Cokie screamed, "See, you made my child cry." He shouted back, "No, *you* made your child cry." Finally, in exasperation, he waved us onto the ferry with about two minutes to spare. When we woke up the next morning in Italy, we warned the kids, "Our papers are still not good, so we are likely going to have a problem getting off this boat." Lee got this sly look on his face: "How am I going to know when to cry?"

That trip also provided one of those tiny moments in marriage when you realize you've changed in some way. After we talked our way into Italy, we set off on a long drive eastward to spend the night in Naples. We didn't have enough Italian money for the last toll on the road.

CR: We were exhausted. We had two kids in the car. It was well past bedtime!

SR: I tried to give the toll taker dollars, but when he didn't take them, instead of getting into another endless argument, I just drove away.

CR: And I said, "Yes!"

SR: The guy was yelling at the top of his lungs.

CR: For years Steven wouldn't have done that.

SR: If I had not been married to Cokie, I'd probably still be at that tollbooth.

CR: He would've been a totally law-abiding citizen. What a great influence I am. But dealing with the Greek bureaucracy would make anybody a lawbreaker. There was the day the children and I staged a sit-down strike in a Greek police car.

SR: The whole notion that anybody in Greece would pay a parking ticket is ridiculous. People didn't pay taxes, why would they bother with tickets?

CR: So if you parked illegally the cops would take the license plates off your car. I had actually gone through the process of getting my license plates back once before and it was endless. I had to go to the police station and walk around from one person to the next—the underemployment was enormous, so everybody had these little bitty teeny jobs—one person would stamp my paper and direct me to another person to stamp it, one stamper worked in the barbershop! It was awful, it took all day long, and then they told me to come back another day. It had me completely crazy. I was not ever going to let that happen to me again. The street I was parked on had spots reserved for foreign press, but other cars were illegally parked there, forcing me to find another spot. Since I was only going to be there about ten minutes, I illegally parked. When I came back outside, a cop had taken off my license plates. I tried reasoning with him. Hah! Then I started shouting. "Let's go to the Ministry of Information! Let's go right now!" He growled a few words, then ignored me. So I put the children in his car and climbed in after them. Lee flipped through a stack of plates on the floor and pointed: "Here's our license plate right here." By this time I had certainly succeeded in getting the cop's attention. He kept ordering me to get out of the car. I refused, leaving him with the choice of dragging a woman and two children out onto the street or giving me my license plate back. It was a hard choice for him because it involved losing face, stepping down. It's something most men have trouble with, Greek men in particular. Finally, he gave me my license plate. It was a wonderful moment because the children went between thinking this was the most fun thing they had ever done in their lives and being totally terrified that we were all going to go to jail because of their crazy mother. But they were on my team. They were pretty good about hanging in there with me. Adapting to a culture is easier with children because they give you an incentive to cope.

SR: The same is true for traveling with kids. Then it's important to live on their schedule and not yours. We'd go to places like Egypt and spend the morning exploring tombs and the afternoon sitting by the pool, because the kids couldn't manage another educational outing after lunch. We learned their schedule was a lot more relaxing and fun, and shared that knowledge in a newspaper article we wrote together about traveling with kids.

CR: And we got a letter saying, "I've sat next to families like the Robertses in Europe and I hated having those brats all around me." Can't please everybody.

SR: Living in Greece also gave us a chance to observe marriage in other cultures. One of the things that we ran into a lot was the marriage of a Greek to a non-Greek, often an American. Talk about a mixed marriage!

CR: They made our situation look much easier.

SR: In one case, a Greek man had gone to America for graduate school and met a fellow student. He was this dashing romantic foreigner and they agreed to get married and move back to Greece. Once home, he reverted to type and became a domineering sexist. At that time, most Greek men treated their wives that way. But this was an educated American woman. She was not having it. At one point the guy's parents tore down the old family house and built a three-story apartment building on the site—one floor for each of their three sons. That did it. The American woman absolutely refused to move into the same building with her husband's two brothers and sisters-in-law. It was a huge scandal.

CR: The family couldn't get over it. The parents moved into the third apartment, thinking they would keep it warm until she came to her senses. But her husband caught on and backed her up, and in the end they moved back to America. It was too hard.

SR: Some customs stayed the same as they had been for centuries, others were changing rapidly, and many families were faced with a cultural crunch. I interviewed one woman in northern Greece who was a master weaver. With tears in her eyes she showed me a closet full of gorgeous things—bedspreads, tablecloths, pillow cloths—she had made over the years for her daughter's dowry, or *prika* in Greek. But the young woman had gone to work in Germany, met a Greek boy there, and rejected all her mother's handiwork as "old-fashioned." The couple only wanted "modern" things. The mother was heartbroken. We heard a similar story in Crete, but there the mother was selling the weaving, so we proudly display her daughter's dowry in our house.

After the Cyprus war I talked to some families in the refugee camps who told me an interesting story. Because everybody had left their home villages and family wealth behind, young women were liberated from the tyranny of the *prika*. They could get married without one. The camps were a bit like California—people were freed from the traditions that had restricted their choices, but they had also lost the community support systems that helped keep marriages together. I told this story recently to a Greek friend, who told me about his own father, an immigrant to America in the late thirties.

According to custom, the man could not hope to marry until he had helped his three sisters acquire their *prikas* and find husbands. During World War II he served in the American army and lost touch with his family back in Greece. When the war was over, he discovered that his sisters had all married without dowries—wartime had been like the refugee camps in Cyprus, customs had changed under the pressure of events. So my friend's father was free to marry! When he got the news, his son says, it was the happiest day of his life.

CR: The gardener who tended our citrus trees had three little girls, and he was already worried. When I would go to America I would bring back sheets and things for their dowries. And they were still babies.

SR: The "cultural crunch" I was talking about affected many marriage customs. Greek girls would come in from the villages to Athens for school or work. In the normal course of things they would have romances and sexual experiences. But some of these young women were still expected to go back home and marry a man that their family had picked out for them. In the more traditional areas, the mother-in-law, the mother of the groom, had the right to inspect the bride to make sure she was a virgin. That led to a thriving business among plastic surgeons who would re-create hymens for these deflowered brides. I recently interviewed a woman on the radio who described a similar situation in New York, where young women from Latin cultures have the same operation revirginizing themselves before getting married.

CR: These conflicts could be very painful. One woman we knew, who had moved her family to Athens in order to work, told us her daughter had been engaged and engaged meant sex was permissible. Then the guy broke the engagement, at which point the girl was unmarriageable. She was eighteen and her mother said, "I don't know what to do about it. I would know what to do if we were back on the island." Which meant murdering the guy. And no local island jury would have convicted her.

SR: Living abroad put extra stress on many marriages, but fortunately, we found many of the trials and tribulations pretty funny.

CR: When Steve's boss came in from New York, we decided to entertain him at home, which was a big deal. We had invited fancy people, cabinet members and diplomats to meet with the foreign editor of *The New York Times*. The day started as a disaster when I got up in the morning and found a note from the latest baby-sitter saying she had left to go home to Australia. She was supposed to be helping me with the dinner. I cooked a big turkey and whipped up lots of interesting salads because it was hard to keep everything hot. A friend of ours dropped by during the day, the wife of the *Times* correspondent in Beirut, who had evacuated to Athens with her children during the civil war in Lebanon. We went into the kitchen so I could get organized, and I realized the turkey was missing. Where was the turkey? It was the centerpiece of the meal and it was nowhere. Gone. It had disappeared from the kitchen. I looked outside and there was a stray cat dragging my turkey. The cat had come in through the kitchen window and taken the turkey out the same way. I dashed outside, reclaimed the turkey, brought it back inside, and washed it off. The cat had only gnawed on the bottom of the turkey, so when I turned it right side up it looked just fine. I pleaded with my friend, "Steve's job is in your hands. If you ever tell what I've done with this turkey, he's finished!" I had no choice. The stores were all closed. It was the turkey or nothing. Fortunately, I had been very good to this woman and she said, "I promise you, I promise you!"

SR: After she left Beirut, there were times her husband couldn't reach her by phone, but somehow he could dial through to my Telex. Occasionally he would call me on the Telex and say, "Would you call my wife on the phone?" I would call her and read her messages he typed out on the Telex. She would reply and I would type back. So I was the link between these two people who were not having a happy time in their marriage. The husband would write, "Tell my wife I love her." And I would say, "He says he loves you." And she would say, "Tell that creep to get back to Athens in the next two days or I'm leaving." I would type out, "She says she loves you, too."

CR: We kept that marriage together for a year longer than it would have survived otherwise, though eventually the couple did split. But in that situation families always helped each other out because the pressures and the dangers were very real. The father of one of Becca's friends was an undercover CIA agent, and when the station chief was assassinated right before Christmas one year, my first instinct was to call the mother of Becca's friend and offer to help, because I knew the station chief's widow would need her. But we had never openly acknowledged that we knew her husband's real job. It was a dilemma. Finally, I called the house and, without any explanation, offered to take her little girls for a few days. She was deeply grateful and in fact no explanation was needed. It's one of those situations where actions matter and words get in the way.

SR: After more than three years in Athens we had to decide where we were going to go next. When we first went abroad, we had told *The New York Times* that we wanted to live in Asia, and they had penciled us in for Bangkok as our next post. But I had been in heavy travel jobs for close to nine years, and I was tired of it. I kept remembering a famous story told by another *Times* correspondent in those years named

Henry Kamm. Kamm's little boy had noticed that when his father left on a trip, he always carried his little blue portable typewriter. So one time he wanted his daddy to stay home so badly he hid the typewriter. The parents tore the house apart until they finally found it in the back of some closet. I didn't want my kids to start hiding my typewriter. So as the time came closer to go to Asia, I balked.

CR: I was dying to go.

SR: But I felt I was missing a lot of the kids' lives and I didn't want to live that way anymore. Besides, I had always wanted to go back to Washington. That was the place where I felt my career would grow and flourish. And since I was not a career foreign correspondent and not proficient in languages, I was not high on the foreign-desk priority list for a new assignment. So when I turned down Bangkok, things got pretty tense. We were not getting any clear answers about our future and the *Times* had already named my successor in Athens.

CR: He was there measuring the drapes.

SR: The kids were increasingly upset about it and one night, literally in the middle of the night, I got a phone call from the new Washington bureau chief, Hedrick Smith. He said, "I hear you're having trouble finding another foreign post. If you want to come back to Washington, I'd really love to have you as part of my team." After months of not feeling wanted by the powers that be in New York, I was thrilled to have someone offer me a job that I had always dreamed about. Cokie had a different view.

CR: We took a vacation trip to Yugoslavia over July Fourth of 1977, and that was when we had it out about coming back here. Lee wrote a postcard to Steve's parents saying, "I wish my parents would stop yelling at each other." I dutifully mailed it. I didn't feel it was my job to censor his communication with his grandparents. I had reached a point where I was proficient at being a foreign correspondent's wife. I had carved out a good life. I did my pieces for CBS Radio and wrote for several magazines and did my community service; I had put together a package of things that worked for me. I felt that our kids were still young enough and our parents were still young enough for us to be away for a few more years and not have it disrupt anyone's lives very much. The learning experience was incomparable. I was particularly eager to go to Asia because I had never been there, and I've still never been there except to Japan. I know myself well enough to know how I learn. If I'm living somewhere, then I'll read every single book ever written about it and get involved in the culture and learn a huge amount. But I'm never going to sit here in Bethesda and read a book about Thailand. It's not going to happen. I thought moving to Asia would be a wonderful opportunity and I was certain I could find my place. I had figured out how to do this. I was traveling with Steven a certain amount of the time, and when he was away, the kids and I had our own routine. In fact, when he finally did move back in full-time, I gained about twenty pounds. I was not used to dinners every night. To me, moving to Bangkok seemed like absolutely the right thing to do. On the contrary, moving to Washington seemed like the worst possible thing to do. To me it was like dying. I was coming back to where I grew up. I was thirty-three years old and it was like being buried alive. I didn't want to do it.

It wasn't fair to Steven because I expected him to make a new adventure possible for me through his job. I didn't consider myself master of my own fate. I remember feeling helpless and blue, and not knowing quite how to get myself out of it. I went to the archaeological museum to cheer myself up and I passed by a store with a pretty dress in the window. I thought, buying that would give my spirits a boost. But then the dress ended up costing more than I usually spent, and that just depressed me more. When I told Steve about it, he stole out and bought me the dress. As silly as it might seem, that made me feel a good deal better. At least he showed he cared, even if he couldn't do anything much to fix the problem.

I suppose I could have been expected to think it was my turn, that I would want to go back and restart my career. But I didn't feel that way at all. I was doing enough that interested me so that I didn't feel stultified in any way. We didn't need the money of a full-time career because we could live abroad on a *New York Times* salary quite nicely. So I didn't feel that pressure to work. But the minute we got back to the U.S., that pressure was very real.

SR: It was a very hard decision. I had been gone from Washington at that point for twelve years. I felt that it was time to start focusing on what my long-term career would be, covering politics and policy in Washington and around the country. Another foreign assignment, as interesting as it would be, was a sidestep. I think in all honesty that Cokie had other feelings about Washington. I think this was the one place in the world where she was known as Cokie Boggs, Lindy and Hale's daughter. While her father had been dead for five years, his memory was still strong and her mother was a member of Congress. As we said earlier, there was a real value to a young couple moving away and being on our own and not having to live up to the expectations of family, particularly a famous family like Cokie's. I also think that Cokie was concerned about coming back into the job market. She was obviously very accomplished as a foreign correspondent's wife; she was also increasingly accomplished as a journalist. She had done a lot of radio reporting.

CR: And TV. A good bit of TV.

SR: And magazine writing. In fact, as we were coming back, a major piece she had written about Turkey for the *Atlantic* magazine was just being published.

CR: That helped.

SR: In retrospect, it's astounding to think she was insecure about competing in the Washington job market, but I do think that was part of her concern.

CR: Of course it was. It was a huge part of my concern. First of all, I didn't even want to have to be in the position to go look for a job. I'd done that before. It's horrible. I didn't want to do any of it. The only part that appealed to me at all was being near our extended family. Ironically, I thought that going to Bangkok was more familiar than coming back to Washington. I didn't know what it was going to be like to be a grown-up here, raising children here, all of that. It was going back to my childhood in a way. I didn't know how any of that was going to work out and I didn't much want to learn.

SR: Cokie was obviously wrong about her job prospects but she was right about one thing. Once we returned to Washington we would never leave. More than twenty-two years later we're still here, still in the old family house where Cokie grew up, and we were married. Bethesda is not as exotic as Bangkok, but it's home.

Chapter Four

OTHER LIVES

NEW PLACES,

NEW ROLES

PIONEER MARRIAGES

The move west—early in the country's history across the Appalachians, later across the Rockies—made marriage a necessity. Men moving to set up homesteads knew they needed women in order to make it; they couldn't expect to clear the land, build the house, plant and tend a garden, care for the animals all by themselves. The living was hard, but the lure of making it someplace new appealed to American men from the beginning. Their wives often objected to being uprooted from home and family, as their letters and diaries tell us. Even so, hundreds of thousands of them eventually did make the difficult and dangerous trek across the prairies and peaks. Between 1840 and 1848, fewer than nineteen thousand people went to settle California, Oregon, and Utah. By 1860, almost three hundred thousand more had joined them. The discovery of gold accounted for much of that migration, but the real pull of the West was toward the land—a place to possess, and make produce, and pass on to children. Those dreams could not come true without marriage.

Every time America pushed westward, the men went first. They so outnumbered women that they would advertise for wives. In the early 1800s, Nettie Harris, a young woman in upstate New York, answered an ad in her local newspaper: "Every respectable young woman who goes to the West is almost sure of an advantageous marriage, while, from the superabundance of her own sex in the East, her chances for success are not greater than those for disappointment." Off she went on a flatboat for Iowa with about forty other women. A magazine of the time described what happened when they arrived at the dock: "The gentlemen on shore make proposals to the ladies through trumpets: 'Miss with the blue ribbon in your bonnet, will you take me?' 'Hallo, that girl with a cinnamon-colored shawl! If agreeable, we will join!' The ladies in the meantime are married at the hotel, the parties arranging themselves as the quire sings out, 'Sort yourselves, sort yourselves!' " Romance clearly did not enter into the picture.

Once married, these women could expect to work alongside their husbands in the business of survival, while they struggled physically and emotionally. Bearing babies every couple of years was the norm; too often so was burying them. Bearing the loneliness of the isolation of the farms was sometimes almost as trying. The women's letters are filled with longing for their mothers and sisters and female friends. They seized on any opportunity to socialize, especially weddings. And these hardscrabble pioneers loved to dance. All of that comes through in their records.

What's hard to glean from their writings is how husbands and wives felt about each other. And there's no going back and asking them, so we are left with their own scant renditions. Some of the diaries are downright funny in their sparseness of language. When Amelia Stewart Knight left Iowa for Oregon with her husband and seven children in 1853, she kept an account of her days on the trail, as many people did.

But she never tells us that she's pregnant for her eighth child, until the last entry, after five months of traveling. What she does tell us about is the weather.

> Friday, April 15th. Cold and cloudy, wind still east. Bad luck last night. Three of our horses got away. Suppose they have gone back. One of the boys has gone after them, and we are going on slowly.

> Saturday, April 16th. Camped last night three miles east of Charlton Point in the prairie. Made our beds down in the tent and the wet and mud. Bed clothes nearly spoiled. Cold and cloudy this morning, and every body out of humor. Seneca is half sick. Plutarch has broke his saddle girth. Husband is scolding and hurrying all hands (and the cook) and Almira says she wished she was home, and I say ditto, "home, sweet home."

That's about the closest we ever get to sentiment. Then it's back to the weather, through May, June, July, and August.

> Wednesday, Sept. 14th. Still in camp. Raining and quite disagreeable.

> Thursday, Sept. 15th. Still in camp and still raining. (I was sick all night.)

> Friday, Sept. 17th. In camp yet. Still raining. Noon—it has cleared off and we are all ready for a start again, for some place we don't know where . . . [She breaks off, then picks up.] A few days later my eighth child was born. After this we picked up and ferried across the Columbia River utilizing skiff, canoes and flatboat to get across, taking three days to complete. Here husband traded two yoke of oxen for a half section of land with one half acre planted to

174

potatoes and a small log cabin and lean to with no windows. This is the journey's end.

The trials of the trail—the disease, death, the danger of children falling out of wagons, getting run over or lost, the fear of Indians—are well documented in letters and diaries. Everyday life stories are harder to come by from a taciturn and proud people. One scholar in the field calls it "the history of the inarticulate." Fortunately, some of the pioneer women managed to find their voices and tell the stories of their marriages.

George and Keturah Penton Belknap: Always a New Frontier

Even in the early days of this nation, people from many different countries came together to form uniquely American unions. One of Keturah Penton's father's parents was English, the other Irish; one of her mother's parents was Swedish, the other Dutch. Raised in New Jersey at the time of the Revolution, Johon and Magdalena Burden Penton migrated to Ohio in 1818, to what was then the frontier. The trip meant a wagon ride over the Alleghenies to Pittsburgh, where they then went by boat to Cincinnati. About sixteen miles away, in Hamilton County, Penton bought land and found work helping some nearby settlers thresh wheat. His wife and oldest daughter would spin flax in the winter for summer linens, wool in the summer for winter warmth.

The fifth child, Keturah, was born in 1820, and started keeping a journal when she was fifteen years old. She recounted how the family lived in a log cabin until she was six, then moved to a farm near Cincinnati, where her father truck-gardened and brought his produce to market every day. Everyone in the family worked. At night, after a day on the farm or at the market, the boys shucked corn to sell as meal. The girls helped on the land, hired out as baby-sitters and dishwashers to more fortunate settlers in the area, and spent their evenings spinning and knitting. When Keturah was sixteen, the family moved again, this time to northern Ohio, one hundred and twenty-five miles and five long days by road from Cincinnati. The new move meant more backbreaking work, building the log cabin and clearing the land. To help make ends meet, Keturah hired out as a housekeeper for seventy-five cents a week, and a washerwoman for twenty-five cents a day. That was her life, and what she expected to remain her life until, at the age of nineteen, she listened to some motherly advice.

One day, as she was getting ready to go care for a sick neighbor, Keturah's mother lingered over her tea and Keturah "thought she looked a little sad. Like she wanted to say something that was hard to say." After some coaxing, her mother blurted out, "Kitt, if I was you I would get married and be fixing up a home for myself and not be a drudge for the whole country. There is plenty of these fellows that want you and could give you a good home, and with the tact you have you could soon have a nice place of your own." Keturah objected, insisting that she didn't want to leave her parents. Her mother counseled that if Keturah could better herself, she had no objections. "They could get along very well now they had land enough cleared to make them a good living on, and if I stayed till they died, I would be an old broken down old maid and maybe so cross nobody would want me and then would be kicked about from one place to another without any home." It's a pretty good summary of the attitudes about marriage at the time.

Given permission, Keturah started husband hunting. First prospect: a young preacher on the circuit. But the presiding elder of the church warned her against him, telling her "not to waste my talents on so unpromising a youth." She got rid of him in short order. "The next one that appeared on the scene was a rich young doctor, but he was too lazy to practice and he did not know how to do anything else. He had been raised in the South and had slaves to wait on him. So he was no good." Then came "an old bachelor with hair as red as fire. He had two sections of land and lots of money. He said it was waiting to be at my disposal, but he was too stingy to get himself a decent suit of clothes. So he was shipped pretty quick." Finally, along came a man in a stovepipe hat. George Belknap had decided to come to a church meeting at the Penton house, even though there was another meeting at his own, a thinly veiled excuse to start calling on Keturah, with visits that "became more frequent and more interesting." That's about as close to romance as we get.

On one of his calls, Belknap announced that his family was preparing to sell their place and move west, and "if we went along we must bring matters to a close pretty soon. So him and mother had a long talk out by the well that evening in the moonlight, and before morning it was settled that we would be married on the third of October, 1839. So then we had to get ready for the wedding and also for the journey." The journal tells us nothing at all about the wedding, but a good deal about the journey. Two weeks after they were married, Keturah and George set out in a two-horse wagon, traveling through Ohio, Indiana, and Illinois, camping out along the way, buying food from farmers. They expected to spend the winter in Rushville, Illinois, until they heard about some property they could buy from the Indians in Iowa, so they hazarded a mean snowstorm, with Keturah driving the horses and George driving the stock, rushing to claim the land. They bought the parcel, with a house on it, from a family who had not yet finished paying the Indians. Collecting enough cash to make the final payment meant working all the time. The men planted and made rails, the women cooked and made cloth. Keturah did the spinning, her mother-in-law the weaving. While the men tended the fields, the women tended the farmyard, collecting enough eggs and making enough butter to sell as well as eat.

Even in those hard times, the young married couple understood that it was important to get away for a bit. "George and I are going to take a vacation and go about ten miles away to a campmeeting. There are four young men and two girls going with us, but I made them promise there should be no sparking." The young people behaved admirably and that fall each of the girls was married to one of the men. After the meeting, Keturah announced, "Now we have had a rest and have got strengthened both soul and body—we will go it again." Back to work, day and night. But it was paying off. The hogs sold well, there was enough wheat to sell as flour, and their dreams of building the first frame house on the prairie seemed close to reality. In between planting and harvesting, they would work on the house. Oh, and by the way, "August the 20th, harvest is over and we have the sweetest little baby girl. We call her Hannah." The house wasn't ready for that winter, so it was another season with the in-laws. But Keturah was coming into her own; her Christmas dinner was a great success. The next spring she hosted a party for twelve "nice old ladies." After chicken and pound cake like her mother used to make, "my name is out as a good cook, so I'm alright, for good cooking makes good friends."

Companionship on the prairie made life bearable, and George appears to have been an amiable husband. After spinning yarn during the day, in the evening Keturah would twist it for weaving, "while George reads the history of the U.S., then we read some from the Bible together and have prayer and go to bed feeling that the sleep of the laboring man is sweet. My baby is so good and she don't seem much in my way." They moved into their new house, and all seemed perfect with the birth of a boy in March 1843, but then, in November, little Hannah died of "lung fever." Keturah called it the first real trial of her life, and she expected to spend the winter mostly in the house. Fortunately for her, weekly prayer meetings were held at the Belknaps', so she could regularly see her neighbors. A year later another baby boy arrived, but six months after that, Keturah passed "through another season of sorrow" when their three-year-old boy died. Then, in a few months, the arrival of a baby girl brought this sad journal entry: "We have another baby, such a nice little girl, only six pounds at first and it is a month old, not much bigger than at first. It has never been well, so we have two children again for a while, neither of them are very strong." In the same entry, though, Keturah goes on to give the news. "The past winter there has been a strange fever raging here. It is the 'Oregon fever,' it seems to be contagious and it is raging terribly. Nothing seems to stop it but to tear up and take a six month trip across the plains with ox teams to the Pacific Ocean."

The Belknaps resisted the fever for a while. They went east instead, on a trip to see Keturah's parents. She and the baby were both sick, and she was heartsick knowing once she went back to Iowa they would be Oregon bound—there was no way to hold back the men once they heard of new lands to conquer—and she would never see her parents and old friends again. "It was hard for me not to break down but they all thought in about two years we would come again." On the way back west she boarded a train for the first time, for a seventy-five-mile trip that took half a day, which greatly impressed Keturah because a wagon would have taken three days. Once they arrived in Iowa, everyone was bustling, getting ready for the trek west: "the loom was banging and the wheels buzzing and trades being made from daylight till bedtime." The Belknaps' house had been sold, but she didn't want to move in with her in-laws until it was time to go. "For the first time since our marriage I put my foot down and said 'will and won't.'" They moved into another house, and there, their baby girl died. "Now we have one puny boy left. So now I will spend what little strength I have left getting ready to cross the Rockies."

Keturah busily went about making clothes for the family to last for a year. "Have cut out four muslin shirts for George and two suits for the little boy, with what he has that will last him (if he lives) until he will want a different pattern." Poor woman, she'd buried three children and has every expectation of losing her fourth as she prepares to leave everything she knows behind, yet again. The neighbors helped pull her through, pitching in with the sewing, and her husband kept her company. Traveling in a covered wagon meant the women had to make the cover; Keturah spun the flax for a huge piece of linen, which her mother-in-law and a friend wove into cloth. With Keturah spinning away, George read to her. Finally, the months of preparation were finished and in April 1848 they were ready to set out for the edge of the continent. Keturah couldn't face going to church the last Sunday, after they had already made their farewells, "so George stays with me and will take a rest, for tomorrow will be a busy day."

The big day came and "Father Belknap's voice was heard with that well known sound: 'Wife, wife, rise and flutter.' " As Keturah took her place in the wagon, the preacher came by and "told me to keep up good courage and said, 'don't fret, whatever happens don't fret and cry. Courage will do more for you than anything else.' " That could be the motto of the pioneers, something to embroider on the wagon covers. Keturah kept a detailed journal of life on the trail, including this entry twelve days into the trip: "We all started but had only gone about five miles when a little boy was run over by the wagon and instantly killed. We then stopped and buried the child. We were near a settlement so he was not left there alone." In addition to the sad observations, Keturah noted the funny ones. After four weeks of traveling, they hit Pawnee Indian territory and thought it wise to join a larger company for defense. With so many people, some rules needed to be established and leaders selected, not easy tasks, according to Keturah: "They have quite a time with the election of officers—every man wants an office."

A posse of men rode into the camp from the west, warning about attacks, and some in the party started agitating to go back home. "In the next wagon behind ours a man and wife are quarreling. She wants to turn back and he won't, so she says she will go and leave him—that these men will furnish her a horse and she will leave him with the children and he will have a good time with that crying baby. Then he used some very bad words and said he would put it out of the way. Just then I heard a muffled cry and a heavy thud as though something was thrown against the wagon box and she said, 'Oh, you've killed it' and he swore some more and told her to keep her mouth shut or he would give her some of the same." Just then the man was summoned to take his turn keeping guard, "so he and his wife were parted for the night. The baby was not killed. I write this to show how easy we can be deceived."

As they journeyed on, Keturah's diary petered out. "For want of space, I must cut these notes down and will pass over some interesting things. Watts and the sheep pulled out and fell behind. . . . The old mother Watts said after they got through, 'Yes, George Belknap's wife is a little woman but she wore the pants on that train.' So I came into notoriety before I knew it." Her last entry from the trail is about her boy, Jesse, who was very sick with "mountain fever": "I have held the little boy in my lap on a pillow and tended him as best I could. I thought in the night we would have to leave him here and I thought if we did, I would be likely to stay with him. But at day light we seemed to get fresh courage."

The Belknaps reached Oregon and the men set off for the California gold mines. In April 1849, Keturah, once again keeping a journal, wrote, "We women folks began to realize that we were the providers for our families . . . we had to rustle for our families and also for the church." When the men returned with little to show for their adventure, they started serious farming. But George Belknap couldn't stay put. Though Keturah was a respected personage in the settlement, acting as nurse and midwife to the immigrants, and friend to the Indians, he uprooted the family again, moving in Oregon, and then, in 1879, to Washington. Ten years later, they celebrated in style their golden wedding anniversary, but still they weren't settled. They lost the farm in 1895 and moved in with their children. George died in 1897, but Keturah lived until 1913. Her grandfather had fought in the Revolutionary War, her parents had been some of the early settlers of the first frontier, then she and her husband moved with the nation ever west. She buried six children in the course of her journeys; five others survived her. Their children understood that their grandmother's primitive and hastily written journal told the story of what it took to extend the country from coast to coast.

Elkanah and Mary Richardson Walker: Talk to Me

Mary Richardson might have been born female at a time in history when a girl could not expect to have goals of her own, but she had ambition—she wanted to be a missionary. To fulfill her mission one thing was necessary: she had to be married. Born in Maine in 1811, Mary was known for her scientific interests and her wit, and she was ready to share her feelings, at least with her diary. She started keeping it when she was a twenty-two-year-old not particularly interested in marriage: "I see very few men that are perfect enough to please me." A couple of years later, however, her tune began to change: "my attention has been called of late to the subject of matrimony." But Mary was not at all happy with the man who was making her an offer: "Ought I to bid adieu to all of my cherished hopes and unite my destiny with that of a mere farmer, with little education and no refinement? . . . In a word, shall I, to escape the horrors of perpetual celibacy, settle down with the vulgar? I cannot do it." Pretty risqué stuff for an aspiring missionary in 1836! She didn't settle down, petitioning instead to the American Board of Commissioners of Foreign Missions for an assignment, but was told she must be married. A mutual friend introduced her to Elkanah Walker, who also wanted to do missionary work.

The first impression wasn't very promising: "I saw nothing particularly interesting or disagreeable in the man, though I pretty much made up my mind that he was not a missionary, but rather an ordinary kind of unaspiring man who was anxious to be looking up a settlement." But then she read the letter he brought her, and it was clear they had the same goals in mind, which presented her with a quandary. "The hand of Providence appeared so plain that I could not but feel that there was something like duty about it, and yet how to go to work to feel satisfied and love him, I hardly know." Soon, though, he grew on her: "I have no more doubts as to being able to love him." There were times after that when she did have doubts, but they stayed married, and eventually happily married for many years to come. But it was a rocky road along the way, both literally and figuratively.

The other suitor stayed after her, telling her that "people did not think I was cutting a great cheese" with Elkanah. The competitor for her affections succeeded in raising her doubts: "Can it be that I have been mistaken?" Then, when Elkanah sent protestations of desire—"I love you, therefore I want you," he wrote to her; "to fold you in my arms, hear from your faithful lips that I am still your dearest one would be sweet, sweet indeed"—she melted. "Oh, Elkanah what a desolate being should I be if you should forsake." She at least believed herself to be head over heels in love. In December 1837, word came from the missionary board that they should expect to leave in April to go "beyond the Rocky Mountains." They set a wedding date for March, but even as they prepared to be married, tensions between them cropped up. In January, she received a letter from him which "contained such severe criticism as I almost feel as if I could not bear it. . . . I will however retaliate a little by just letting him know that I have noticed a thing or two in him as well." Shades of Abigail! This was not going to be an easy match. He might have gotten some sense of that when the bride wore black to the wedding, to show the grief she felt in leaving her family, even though she had always wanted to go to the missions. A week after she was married, Mary wrote, "Nothing gives me such a solitary feeling as to be called Mrs. Walker. . . . My father, my mother, my brothers, my sisters all answer to the name Richardson. The name W. seems to imply to me a severed branch."

Soon she was truly severed. Mary and Elkanah, along with two other couples, left Missouri, the "gateway to the West," in April of 1838. Mary was already pregnant, and seemed at sixes and sevens about how to behave. "Should feel much better if Mr. W. would only treat me with more cordiality. It is so hard to please him I almost despair of ever being able. If I stir, it is forwardness, if I am still, it is inactivity." Here were these newlyweds, crammed together with two other couples in close quarters, traveling difficult terrain and trying to get to know each other all at the same time. A few days later she recounts, "Had a long bawl. Husband spoke so cross I could scarcely bear it, but he seemed to pity me a little when he found how bad I felt. Today has been very kind." That didn't last long, however; a couple of weeks later she was fretting again: "Husband sick. In a big worry lest he does not feel as well satisfied with me as he ought." She, too, was sick, so much so that she was bled as a treatment; she doesn't tell us by whom. But by June she was feeling better, and reflecting on her husband: "I can but believe he loves me. I, however, experience some anxiety on this account. But I think I am gaining ground." She wanted desperately to please him; still, she had trouble staying cheerful, never feeling really well, wanting to cry, fearful of danger: "A long journey before me, going I know not whither, without mother or sister to attend me, can I expect to survive it all?" The group did follow a strenuous course. One day in July they rode thirty-five miles without stopping, and she was four and a half months pregnant. Emotionally, though, things were getting better: "Becoming every day more fondly attached to my husband. Indeed he seems every day to become increasingly kind and I am more and more confident of my ability to please him and make him happy." Making *her* happy turned out to be another matter altogether.

Finally, on August 29, 1838, after 129 days, Mary and Elkanah reached Oregon, where fellow missionaries feted them with melons and salt salmon and pumpkin pies. It was a great celebration, joined by a few dozen Indians. Then came reality—nine adults and two children in one house over the winter, while Walker and one of the men who traveled with them searched out their ideal spot for a mission. Mary truly missed him: "I can hardly refrain from tears every time I think of him. . . . I have so good a husband. . . . I have enjoyed his society so much." When he returned in October, she was much relieved: "Was glad once more to see my husband and he appears glad to see me and I suppose he really was for he has no faculty of making believe. Could not sleep all night for joy." Over the fall Mary wrote a good deal about how much she loved her husband, and worried he might not love her as much. He could completely undo her with a word: "Slept little last night. Mostly in consequence of something husband said to me." Her chief complaints, though, had to do with the other women. Mary thought they let her work too hard establishing their household, considering her pregnancy. Soon she was grateful for their company.

Mary woke early in the morning on December 7 and realized she was in labor. The ladies came to her aid, but they knew she had a while to go before the baby. After about four hours, "felt as if I almost wished I had never been married. But there was no retreating, meet it I must." A couple of hours later a baby boy arrived, and when Elkanah returned from his travels that evening, it was with "plenty of kisses for me and my boy." Mary had a hard time nursing and she missed everyone at home; maybe this missionary life wasn't such a good idea. She was filled with self-doubt: "I have desired to become a missionary and why? Perhaps only to avoid duties at home." She now had a new home, a log cabin they moved to in January, and new worries about her husband. She still didn't seem to be able to please him, and she wanted to fervently. Romance was her goal: "I can never with all my care make myself what he would like me to be. I never intended to be the wife of a man that did not love and respect me from his heart and not from a stern sense of duty. . . . I am tempted to exclaim, woe is me that I am a wife. Better to have lived and died a miserable old maid and with none to share and thereby aggravate my misfortune. But it is too late." Later that night, Mary told her husband how bad she felt and he apologized, assuring her he loved her: "So I think I will try to feel better." Still, her entries continue to complain of his harsh words, of her upset at his unhappiness with her. Meanwhile, Mary was beginning to fulfill the mission she had so long sought, to teach the Indians; she was also pregnant with another child, and trying to cope with frontier life. A wall of the house fell down one day; another day, after doing the milking, Mary "found it necessary to call my husband." He arrived, and quickly called a doctor, and on May 24, 1840, a baby girl was born. Mary had now settled into her life well enough that she was able to take up the household chores— ironing, baking, washing, milking—within a few weeks after the baby's birth, and her missionary work soon after that. By the end of July, she tells us excitedly about her teaching: "think I succeeded pretty well as the children seemed pleased. . . . I gave them a lesson in geography on an egg shell which I had painted for a globe." Soon, she voiced the cry of all busy women: "It is all I can do to get along, do my work and take care of my children. How I can answer a single letter I do not know."

With two children, and finally performing her missionary work, Mary started casting a critical eye toward Elkanah, instead of just worrying what he thought of her: "Have felt the past week several times as if I could no longer endure certain things that I find in my husband. . . . What grieves me most is that the only being on earth with whom I can have much opportunity for intercourse manifests uniformly an unwillingness to engage me in social reading or conversation." He wouldn't talk to her! Who knows why not, we don't have his side of the story, but he was driving her crazy. At home she would have been able to visit with her mother and sisters, to share secrets with female friends, but on the frontier she had only her husband. She wished she could make up for his lack of conversation by "improving my mind" but she had too much to do, she needed his company. Mary became increasingly introspective: "My husband and children seem to engross my heart and I fear they will be taken from me." But her fretfulness did not get in the way of her work; she made such notations as, "Cast wicks and dipped nineteen dozen candles." Occasionally there are notes about news from home—which she refers to as "the United States"—like this one in May 1841: "I am not pleased with the course my brothers are pursuing in regard to certain young ladies." Over the months, Mary seemed to get into a rhythm of housework and teaching, if her diary is to be believed, and then in March 1842: "Rose about 5 o'clock . . . got my housework done up about 9. Baked six more loaves of bread. . . . Nine o'clock pm was delivered of a son."

Mary was overwhelmed, and soon truly depressed, a word she actually used in her accounts, instead of the term of the era, "melancholy." Her oldest boy was a hellion and she didn't know how to handle him, the younger boy was underfoot, the work was never ending, the weather was miserable, her husband was absent either physically or emotionally or both. What a relief it would have been to be with her mother! As she baked eighteen loaves of bread one day, Mary pined, "What a handy thing an oven would be." But they were progressing in the mission. They had a printing press and used it to provide the Indians with a primer in their own Flathead language. The Walker family was progressing as well. Another boy was born in March 1846.

The baby boy, Jeremiah, was healthy and she had an easier time nursing than with the others, and Mary seemed to settle down some; by now she was thirty-five years old. She also took up her old interest in science, getting her husband's "permission to pursue collecting a few objects in natural history." And, for a little insight into the mores of the frontier: "Teacher's daughter had a child born. Her father was enraged and threatened to shoot himself." Then, in December 1847, came the horrible news. The Whitmans, the couple they had stayed with when they first reached Oregon, had been murdered by Indians, along with others in their mission. It became famous throughout the West as the "Whitman Massacre" and scared off some future settlers. What happened to the ones who escaped? That was Mary's worry, along with her fear that her family, too, despite their friendship with the Indians, might be attacked. And she was once again ready to have a baby; a nine-pound boy was born a couple of weeks after the Walkers received news of the Whitman slaughter. The couple had been in Oregon just ten years and had produced five children. As hopeful as she now felt about the prospects for her family, Mary no longer expected success for their mission: "I fear our labors for the Indians must soon cease. . . . The hope of our seeing them much better than they now are, fondly as I would wish to cherish, is all hope against hope."

And so, after all that, they abandoned the mission. Mary had married Elkanah because she wanted to be a missionary, and missionaries needed to be married. The missionary part didn't work; the married part did. After the massacre, the Walkers settled in the Willamette Valley in Oregon, living simply and raising eight children. After almost forty years of marriage, Elkanah died; by then it was his company that Mary missed: "I think of so many things I want to tell Mr. Walker, I realize more and more how much more I love him than anyone else." Either he had started talking to her somewhere along the line, or she had decided to talk to him regardless of response. They had actually made the trip all the way back to Maine once, after the railroad made it possible, but she didn't stay there with those female friends she had so longed to see. Mary Richardson returned with her husband to the frontier, which had become their home.

Clyde and Elinor Pruitt Stewart: Married in Haste, No Cause to Repent

Not all pioneers were married. Single men, and occasionally single women, would set out on their own to try to establish homesteads in the West. One who thrilled to the enterprise was Elinor Pruitt, a hardworking woman who expected to make it on her own. But she ended up getting an assist, and some affection, from Clyde Stewart, a husband who delighted her.

Elinor Pruitt was born into a poor family in Fort Smith, Arkansas, in the late 1870s. She took over as caretaker for her brothers and sisters as a young teenager, after her parents died. She went to work for the railroad, moving steadily west and managing to educate herself enough that she wrote articles for the *Kansas City Star* after she got married at the age of twenty-two to another worker for the railroad, Mr. Rupert. Four years later her husband was killed in a railroad accident, leaving his wife with a baby girl, Jerrine. To support her daughter and herself, Elinor moved to Denver, and hired out as a laundress and housekeeper to a woman named Mrs. Coney, who became her friend. But the young woman wanted to homestead, and in 1909, after she heard about the wide-open spaces of Wyoming from a friend, Elinor quickly placed a newspaper advertisement asking for a job on a homestead. A Scottish rancher looking for help, who happened to be traveling through, saw the ad and hired her. Instead of a journal, Elinor wrote letters about her adventures to Mrs. Coney, which were published as a book, *Letters of a Woman Homesteader,* in 1914.

Traveling by train and stagecoach, it took three days for the Scottish rancher, Elinor, and Jerrine to reach Burnt Fork, Wyoming. When they arrived, the new employee deemed everything "just lovely for me. I have a very, very comfortable situation and Mr. Stewart is absolutely no trouble, for as soon as he has his meals, he retires to his room and plays on his bagpipe, only he calls it his 'bugpeep.' It is 'The Campbells are Coming' with variations, at intervals all day long and from seven to eleven at night. Sometimes I wish they would make haste and get here." Never losing her humor, Elinor shows herself a woman of endless energy and boundless optimism, easy to please, and eager to file for her homestead. After about six weeks in Wyoming, she did, choosing land adjoining Stewart's and declaring herself "a bloated landowner." The trip to the filing office meant taking Jerrine by wagon through snowstorms, meeting wolves along the way, enjoying the spectacular scenery even so, and then returning home to Mr. Stewart. "If you will believe me, the Scot was glad to see me and didn't herald the Campbells for two hours after I got home. I'll tell you, it is mighty seldom any one's so much appreciated."

Mr. Stewart soon married Elinor, but she didn't want to tell her old employer. Instead, her next letter, in September 1909, dwells on the joys of the busy summer just past. Mr. Stewart had been unable to find enough men to do all the work, so, without asking, one day when he was out looking for help, Elinor took out the mowing machine, which she had learned to operate as a girl. "I had enough cut before he got back to show him I knew how, and as he came back manless, he was delighted as well as surprised. I was glad because I really like to mow, and besides that, I am adding feathers to my cap in a surprising way. When you see me again you will think I am wearing a feather duster, but it is only that I have been said to have almost as much sense as a 'mon,' and that is an honor I never aspired to, even in my wildest dreams." This was a woman who worked day and night and seemed to love it, but she would occasionally take a day, ride up into the mountains with Jerrine, and just bask in the beauty, without any need of consort.

At Thanksgiving, a young woman in the neighborhood got married at the Stewart house, where "our dinner was a success, but that is not to be wondered at. Every woman for miles around contributed." Elinor draws a picture of homestead weddings, where first the justice of the peace came, then an enormous dinner was served immediately in order to finish before the obligatory and much-anticipated dance. "Dances are never given in the home here, but in 'the hall.' Every settlement has one and the invitations are merely written announcements posted everywhere." The accounts of Christmas also paint a happy scene; still, Elinor had not let on that she was married to the man of the house. The following April, she gave a clue. She told her former boss that she had built her homestead house adjoining Mr. Stewart's, "so that I could 'hold down' my land and job at the same time." Then she made a tantalizing admission: "I have not treated you quite frankly about something you had a right to know about. I am ashamed and I regret very much that I have not told you." In the next letter, Elinor decides to "confess and get it done with. The thing I have done is to marry Mr. Stewart. It was such an inconsistent thing to do that I was ashamed to tell you. And, too, I was afraid you would think I didn't need your friendship and might desert me."

That didn't happen, clearly, because Elinor kept up her correspondence. In the next letter she tells Mrs. Coney, "I have been a very busy woman since I began this letter to you several days ago. A dear little child has joined the angels. I dressed him and helped to make his casket. There is no minister in this whole country and I could not bear the little broken lily bud to be just carted away and buried, so I arranged the funeral and conducted the services. I know I am unworthy and in no way fitted for such a mission, but I did my poor best, and if no one else is comforted, I am." It's one of the few sad moments Elinor recounts over four years. Some letters show the playfulness in her marriage, like one she wrote in the fall of 1911, where after a long story about tricking Mr. Stewart into taking her to town, Elinor suddenly closes with this news: "I am not going to let my baby prevent me from having many enjoyable outings. We call our boy Henry Clyde for his father. He is a dear little thing, but he is a lusty yeller for baby's rights." She did keep taking her "outings," camping trips with Jerrine and the baby on which they encountered all kinds of excitement, be it horse thieves or snowstorms, in between many hours of work on the ranch, where she still insisted on making money to pay off her own homestead.

Finally, two and a half years after she arrived, Elinor decided to tell her friend all about her husband and her marriage. She said she hadn't before because "I could not even begin without telling you what a good man he is and I didn't want you to think I could do nothing but brag." She was also still embarrassed by the speed with which she married him. "But although I married in haste, I have no cause to repent. That is very fortunate because I have never had one bit of leisure to repent in. So I am lucky all around. The engagement was powerfully short because both agreed that the trend of events and ranch work seemed to require that we be married first and do our 'sparking' afterwards." Elinor explains that they had to "chink" the wedding in between the planting because "Wyoming ranchers can scarcely take time even to be married in the springtime." He sent for a marriage license by mail and called the neighboring justice of the peace to come for the ceremony; she fixed up a dress, cleaned up the house, and cooked up a meal. "Everything was topsy-turvy, and I had a very strong desire to run away. But I always did hate a 'piker,' so I stood pat." She described how she had wanted to "stay foot-loose and free" but first she wanted to try homesteading, so there she was.

Also, Elinor revealed that the dead baby she had written about was her own. "For a long time my heart was crushed. He was such a sweet beautiful boy. I wanted him so much . . . so you see our union is sealed by love and welded by great sorrow." Over the next two years, "God has given me two more precious sons. The sorrow is not so keen now." To read her high-spirited letters, it would have been impossible to know that Elinor had been grieving. She was always cataloging her blessings, among them her "clean, honest husband, my kind, gentle milk cows, my garden which I make myself." As happy as she was with her husband, Elinor wouldn't let him on her land. She was a great proselytizer for homesteading as the answer to poverty: "any woman who can stand her own company, can see the beauty of the sunset, loves growing things, and is willing to put in as much time at careful labor as she does over the washtub, will certainly succeed." She goes on to explain all about the Department of Agriculture's role, and how the homesteaders can experiment with different seeds. "I would not, for anything, allow Mr. Stewart to do anything toward improving my place, for I want the fun and experience myself. And I want to be able to speak from my experience when I tell others what they can do." Slowly, over the months, she opened up more about Clyde. In June 1913, four years after she arrived in Wyoming, Elinor wrote, "I am as proud and happy as the day I became his wife. I wish you knew him, but I suspect I had better not brag too much, lest you think me not quite sincere."

In the last letter, written in November 1913, Elinor rejoices in her success. "I set out to prove a woman could ranch if she wanted to . . . now Jerrine and I have put in our cellar full, and this is what we have: one large bin of potatoes (more than two tons), half a ton of carrots, a large bin of beets, one of turnips, one of onions, one of parsnips, and on the other side of the cellar we have more than one hundred heads of cabbage." She lists the pickles and preserves she's made over the summer, the ten cows milked twice daily, providing enough butter to pay for a year's supply of flour and gasoline, plus the chickens and the turkeys. "In all I have told about I have had no help but Jerrine." Clyde's mother came in the summer and helped with the cooking and the babies, but Elinor proudly concludes, "I have tried every kind of work this ranch affords and I can do any of it." She didn't need her Clyde to support her. She needed him to love her, and he did.

Elinor Pruitt Stewart's experience with marriage was not the norm; she enjoyed it but didn't need it. For most of the men and women of the plains and prairies, it was just the opposite—they depended on each other, they sought comfort and stability. After all, these couples were picking up their lives, shaking up their societies, reinventing their relationships. Romance was a little suspect, passion distracting. Marriage was a partnership, a bargain—he stayed sober, did the clearing and the plowing and the planting and the harvesting;

she produced children, did the gardening and the cooking, the pickling and preserving, the spinning and the sewing, the candle making and the animal tending. The basic contract's made clear even in some of the songs of the time:

> [He]   *Go tell her to make me a cambric shirt . . .*
>   *Then she can be a true lover of mine.*
> [She] *Go tell him to clear me an acre of land . . .*
>   *Then he can be a true lover of mine.*

It might not have been the stuff of hearts and roses, but it worked. These practical people stayed together and settled the country.

NOTE: The writings of Keturah Belknap and Mary Walker have been taken from *Women of the West,* by Cathy Luchetti and Carol Olwell (New York: Three Rivers Press, 1982). We corrected spelling and punctuation for easier reading. Elinor Pruitt Stewart's *Letters of a Woman Homesteader* was reprinted by the Mariner Books division of Houghton Mifflin in 1988.

IMMIGRANT MARRIAGES

We can both trace our origins to Europe—Cokie's family first came from England early in the seventeenth century, Steve's from Russia and Poland three hundred years later. And we both grew up with a strong interest in our foreign-born forebears and the stories of their journeys. Immigrants have generally tried to transport the customs of the "old country," wherever that was, to their new homes, and invariably, those customs have crumbled under the pressures to be "modern" and "American." When it came to marriage, couples quickly discovered that the old rules no longer applied. They were free to make choices and cross lines that would have been unthinkable for their parents.

In this section we focus on Steve's tribe, Eastern Europeans, and in that world, the concept of romantic love was pretty foreign. Couples were often brought together by their parents, sometimes with the help of a professional matchmaker. Reporter Lillian Wald, writing about the immigrant Jews of New York early in the century, quoted a shocked father as saying, "What? Let a girl of seventeen, with no judgment whatsoever, decide on anything so important as a husband?" Alfred Kazin, in his lovely memoir, *A Walker in the City,* says of his parents' generation: "Their marriages were neither happy nor unhappy; they were arrangements." And he describes how stunned he was to hear his cousin and her friends talk about their romances: "They were the first grown-up people I had ever met who used the word *love* without embarrassment. 'Libbe! Libbe!' my mother would explode whenever one of them protested that she could not, after all, marry a man she did not love. 'What is this love you make such a stew about? You do not like the way he holds his cigarette? Marry him first and it will all come out right in the end.' "

Similar stories run through all immigrant communities. In writing about our Greek experience, we describe Cypriot families fleeing from war who discover that in a refugee camp, the old custom of needing a dowry to get married has been destroyed, along with their home villages. Today in California, parents place ads in Indian newspapers seeking appropriate grooms for their daughters. But those traditions are struggling to survive. One of Steve's students at George Washington University describes a family of Indian immigrants with three daughters. The parents demanded that the oldest girl, a doctor, enter an arranged marriage. The second daughter, while on a longer leash, was barred from attending her senior prom with a date. By the time the third daughter hit high school, the parents allowed her to fly to Mexico on spring break with a bunch of friends. In just a few years, the new culture of California had overwhelmed the old culture of India. Every Sunday, Cokie is struck by the banns of marriage announced in the church bulletin: the couples might all be Catholics, but there are a lot of O'Hearns marrying Garcias and Nitkowskis marrying Nguyens.

For the first generation of immigrants, as Kazin points out, marriage was often an arrangement, not a romance, and in some ways that was a whole lot easier. Expectations were lower and community support was greater. But there was no escaping the change. As these immigrants and their children adapted their Old World customs to the New, one of their hardest adjustments was coping with a culture where everybody was making "such a stew" about love and marriage.

Irene Gut Opdyke: Only a Girl

In the fall of 1956, Irene Gut was having lunch in a small coffee shop on New York's East Side, near the United

Nations. The place was full, and a tall man with glasses asked politely if he could share her table. When he sat down, he looked at her more closely and said, "I know you." The man was William Opdyke, and he did know her. They had met more than six years before, in a displaced-persons camp in Germany. She was a young Polish woman then, a refugee from the war, and he was an American working for the UN. That day in the camp she had told him her story, and he had never forgotten it. Or her.

We learned Irene's full story during several long interviews that expanded on her memoir, *In My Hands*, a book aimed at high-school students. The tale starts in September 1939. Irene was a seventeen-year-old nursing student in the city of Radom on the day the Nazis invaded Poland. Raised a strict Catholic, she had never kissed a boy and wanted to be a nun. As the German forces pushed eastward toward Radom, she and other medical personnel joined the outmanned Polish army and fled to the forests of the Ukraine. One night she and several soldiers slipped into a nearby town on a bartering mission. She was posted as a lookout when a Russian patrol came by and spotted her. "I was brutally violated, beaten and left in the snow to die," she recalls. "But I did not die. God did have other plans for me."

Another Russian patrol found her and brought her to a hospital. After recovering her strength, she went back to Radom in search of her family, but she was conscripted to work in a hotel serving the German high command. The back side of the building looked down into the Jewish ghetto, and after watching from a window as a Gestapo force swept through the area, gunning down helpless victims, she decided to act. The next day she stole some food from the hotel and pushed it under the ghetto fence.

A few weeks later she saw a Nazi officer fling a Jewish baby into the air and then shoot it with his pistol as the baby's mother watched. Something cracked deep inside her. "Like a little child, I have tantrum with my maker," she recalled, her English still tinged with a Polish accent. "But in the morning, there was an answer in my soul, in my heart. God gives us free will, to be good or bad. I asked God at that moment for the opportunity to help." A resistance fighter was born. Gradually she took bigger and bigger steps: from stealing food and passing secrets to hiding Jewish fugitives and raiding Nazi convoys. As her work got riskier, she realized she could be discovered and executed at any moment, but the knowledge that she "could only be killed once" kept her going. In her memoirs, Irene writes: "I only wanted not to die in too much pain, and to foil the Germans as much as I could before I went."

Transferred by the Nazis to the Ukrainian city of Ternopol, she met a group of Jewish laborers assigned to the laundry she was running for the German officers. Through her contacts with the laborers she smuggled food and intelligence to the Jewish underground hiding in the nearby forests. But when word came that the Gestapo was planning to liquidate every Jew in the city, including the slave laborers, her friends were suddenly facing mortal danger. She promised she would help, but one of the men, older and gloomier than the others, dismissed her with a shrug: "You're only a young girl. What can you do?"

Quite a lot, it turned out, but Irene refuses to take all the credit. "I believe a miracle happened," she says simply. The German major she was working for commandeered a large villa and put Irene in charge of the housekeeping. Designed by a Jewish architect, the basement of the villa contained a network of secret rooms and passages, and just hours before the Gestapo arrived, she hid a dozen of her friends in the major's house.

They lived there for nine months. During the day, after the major left, the Jews would emerge from the cellar and help Irene run the house. At night they would return to their hiding place, and one frequent dinner guest was the local head of the Gestapo, who never knew he was eating meals prepared by Jews living literally beneath his feet. The scheme was working well until one of the Jewish women discovered she was pregnant. The group decided to abort the baby—any other course was too dangerous—but Irene pleaded with them. Wait, don't let Hitler have this life, too. The Russians are advancing and something could happen.

But then danger appeared from another direction. One day Irene was walking back to the villa and ran into a crowd blocking a square where a gallows had been built. A Polish couple and their two small children were being hanged for hiding a Jewish family. Irene was so upset that when she got back to the villa, she forgot to lock the front door behind her. Two Jewish girls, about her age, came up from the basement to console her, and suddenly, without warning, the German major walked in.

He did not know that ten others were in the cellar, but he was still furious. That night the Nazi officer exacted a bargain from Irene: I'll protect your friends if you become my mistress. The next morning, she writes, she fled the major's bedroom and filled a tub: "I sank into water so hot it made me cry, and my tears plinked into the water as I scrubbed myself. This was worse than rape." And yet she kept her bargain with the major. "I had banked on his affection for me for too long, used him for too long," she writes. "I could not be surprised now that it had come to this accounting." And besides, she adds, her shame "was a small price to pay for so many lives."

Sixteen lives in all, plus the baby conceived in the basement of the villa. With Russian forces approaching Ternopol, the Nazis fled and Irene smuggled her charges into the forest, to join the Jewish underground, and that's where the baby was born a few months later. The German major took Irene with him on the retreat westward, but she managed to evade him in the city of Kielce and join a band of Polish partisans who were harassing any target they could find, German or Russian. She took the *nom de guerre* "Mala," Polish for "little," and fell in love with the group's leader, Janek. They were planning to marry and settled on May 5, 1944, as their wedding day. Three days before, she was at the home of Janek's parents, trying on her wedding dress, when her groom burst in the door, surprising her. "It's bad luck to see the bride in her dress before the wedding," his mother scolded, but he had news. A German transport was moving through the area that night and he would lead a raid against it. Irene pleaded with him not to go. "But, sweetheart," he teased, "I'm the fearless leader." Janek was killed in the ambush and buried in the forest.

With her love lost and her heart shattered, Irene made contact with some of the Jews she'd helped to save. The Germans were gone, and the Jews felt free to emerge from hiding, but the Russian occupation weighed heavily. Irene was particularly anxious to see the baby, Roman Haller, who'd been born in the forest, and her eagerness dulled her survival instincts. Just blocks from the Hallers' house, she was arrested by Russian police and interrogated for days about her partisan comrades. Again she escaped, but there was nothing left for her in Poland. If she looked for her family, she would place them in grave danger. In a final irony, her Jewish friends found her a forged transit pass with a Jewish alias, Sonia Sofierstein. With her blond hair dyed black, she took a train to Germany, and in May of 1946, she settled into life at a DP camp near the city of Hessich-Lichtenau. She'd been in the camp more than three years on the day, in the summer of 1949, that William Opdyke arrived to interview the residents.

It was a rabbi in the camp who introduced them. As she remembers: "We had six languages between us but not one in common—except the language of laughter. We could not help chuckling at the predicament we were in. He called across the room to a colleague, and in a few moments we had another American with us, one who spoke German." Opdyke asked a few questions but mainly let her talk. As she writes in her memoir: "I left nothing out. I think I wanted to shock him, to tell this well-fed American what a simple Polish girl was capable of. Opdyke had been taking notes, but he finally just put his pen down and stared at me. For a moment, I feared that he did not believe what I had told him. He said something to the interpreter in a gruff voice. 'Mr. Opdyke says he feels honored to have met you, and that the United States would be proud to have you as a citizen.'" In our conversations with her, Irene embellished the story: "I liked him very much, a man with black hair with lots of silver in it. Tall, very distinguished, that reminded me of my father." But she says sternly, "there was no romance" at the time. He was married, and he left without giving her an address or a telephone number in America.

Later that year she arrived in New York aboard the troop-ship *John Muir,* which was carrying refugees from Europe. The Jewish Resettlement Organization found her a place to live in Brooklyn and a job in a corset factory, but they could not replace what she had lost: "I was alone without money, or family, or marketable skills." After getting her first wages from the factory, she remembers: "I was so proud of myself— I could earn money!" But she lived quietly, still nursing her emotional wounds. When we asked if she had any social life in those years, Irene replied: "No, no. I was scared of men. I didn't want to have anything to do with men." She deliberately dressed to hide her beauty, in drab dark clothes, without any makeup. Still, one day when she was heading for work, a group of young men whistled at her. "In Poland, they do that for prostitutes, and when I came to the factory, I was so upset," she says. "I asked the other girls, 'Why did they do that to me?'" But she got a quick, amused reply: "In America, when they *stop* doing that you're in trouble."

After several years in the corset factory, Irene met Ruth

Altman, a Jewish dressmaker originally from Poland. Ruth hired Irene for her business and the two women became friends and roommates. They went to movies and plays together, and the chill that had gripped Irene's heart for so long began to thaw. "I was already six years in the United States and I quieted down," she remembers. "I started having dreams. I wanted a normal life." Then one day Ruth sent her on an errand, and Bill Opdyke sat down at her table. During lunch, he explained to her that his wife had died, and as they were finishing, he asked, "May I call you?" Irene's English was still so poor she had trouble explaining to him where she lived, but he figured it out. On their first date they went to a nightclub and everybody else was laughing at the jokes. Irene didn't get most of them, but apparently it didn't matter. They danced instead—"he was a wonderful dancer and played the piano beautifully"—and she went home and prayed that he would call her again. He did, and when he proposed six weeks later, Irene remembers: "I was ready to accept. I was a woman, I wanted a child."

They were married quietly, on November 14, 1956, and Irene invited only two guests, Ruth Altman and Ruth's mother. In the wedding pictures she is wearing a silk cocktail dress, with a short white veil—nothing like the fancy gown she was trying on that day, more than twelve years before, when her beloved Janek was killed. But she is clearly happy, slender and blond, beaming up at her husband who is almost a head taller. When it came to sex, she was both very innocent and deeply scarred, and as she puts it: "Bill knew my story, so he was very gentle with me."

She was so inexperienced that when she got pregnant a few months later, she didn't know the signs. But when she started asking for some Polish food she hadn't eaten in years, a friend took her to the doctor and he confirmed her condition. Bill was fifteen years older, he already had three children by his first marriage, and Irene was nervous about how he would take the news. He was pleased for her, but not exactly a modern, engaged father. After their daughter, Janina, was born—named for Irene's favorite sister back in Poland—Bill "never changed a diaper, he didn't know what to do, he was more like a grandfather."

Their time together was happy but brief. Bill was stricken with Alzheimer's, and as Irene recalls: "He became a man I did not know. He would go into these rages and I thought he did not love me. It's the most painful sickness, people change in front of your eyes." Money was running low, the family was in danger of losing their house. And then, says Irene, "a miracle happened—again." A rabbi who knew her story interceded. The Jewish old-age home in the area took in Bill Opdyke, a Christian, without charging a fee, and he died there five years later.

Today Bill and Irene's daughter, Janina Opdyke Smith, is the mother of two sons, and the grandmother of two girls, and Irene says proudly, "I'm a great-grandmother now." Her marriage did not last long, but it lasted long enough. The man who gave her a new home in America also gave her something else. He gave back her life.

Abe and Miriam Rogow: A Photo in the Window
Sam and Norma Weiss: A Book of Poems

These are two family sagas that Steve has told for years. For this book he interviewed several elderly relatives, filling gaps and correcting mistakes, and he retells the stories here.

My grandfather, Abe Rogow, was always a restless person, full of schemes and dreams. As a boy, he helped his father in the textile business, running errands and collecting shipments of cloth at the train station. His hometown of Bialystok, now in eastern Poland, was then under Russian domination, and his older sister became an early convert to Bolshevism. Family legend has it that his sister would occasionally ask young Abe to pick up a package for her, and since he was well known at the station, no questions were asked. But they should have been. His sister's packages contained copies of *Iskra,* the Leninist newspaper, that were being smuggled into Russia. If the bundles had broken, and revealed their contents, Abe would have been shot on the spot, but fortunately for me that never happened.

It was Zionism, not communism, that fired Abe's imagination, and he was still a teenager when he stole money from his father and made his way to Palestine. I have a photo of him working on the first road ever built in Tel Aviv, and his plan was to settle there and help build a new Jewish state. One problem: if a young man was drafted into the czar's army, and failed to appear for induction, the penalties on his family could be severe. So after a few years away, Abe returned home, a *chalutz,* a pioneer, with the dust and the dash of foreign lands still clinging to his clothes. He would go into the army, save his parents a problem, and see what happened.

Meanwhile, a young woman named Miriam Wasilsky had come to Bialystok from the village of Eishishok, probably to find a job and a husband. She had her picture taken by a local photographer, and he displayed it in his shop window as a sample of his work. While Abe was waiting for his draft notice, he had a lot of time on his hands, and as he roamed around Bialystok, he noticed the photo of the girl. Every day he'd pass the shop window, and gradually he fell in love. As the legend goes, he finally met Miriam one night at a gathering of young people and stammered, "You're the girl in the photograph."

Soon they agreed to be married, and I have a set of photographs taken at about this time. The date on one is stamped 1912, and it shows my grandparents gazing straight into the camera, their heads tilted toward each other, barely touching, as they faced a very uncertain future. She's wearing a dark dress, with a lace panel at her throat, and a slightly saucy expression. He's wearing a white shirt with a banded collar, in the Russian style, and looks a bit nervous. There's another shot, of Miriam alone, that shows why Abe fell in love with her. Her huge dark eyes leap through time and space, looking directly into mine. And as I look back at her, I find myself thinking, "Oh, Grandma, if you knew then what I know now . . ."

Under Russian rules, once you were drafted you were the responsibility of the army, not your parents, so Abe hit on a scheme. After he joined up, he'd escape as soon as possible, get back to Palestine, and send for Miriam. His mother aided the plan by making him a special cap. On one side it looked like an army cap, but when you flipped it over, it became a civilian hat. As he left for training camp, he put on a layer of his own clothes under his uniform, and as best I can tell, he spent no more than a couple of hours in the service. The first time the train stopped, he leaped out, stripped off his uniform, flipped over his cap, and took off.

Abe wound up in Odessa, a Black Sea port where ships left for Palestine, but since he had no papers and was a deserter from the army, he couldn't sail legally. As he used to tell the story, he met a family with twelve children. And when the youngest one died, he stepped in as the oldest child and everybody else moved down one rung. Of course, the genders on the papers no longer matched, but the customs officials were too lazy to check. They lined the kids up on a bench, counted twenty-four knees, and allowed the family to board.

When he finally got back to Palestine, Abe realized it was not a good place to bring a young bride. The Arabs were rebelling, World War I was approaching, and he decided to switch course. He wrote to Miriam and said, meet me in New York, not Tel Aviv. She already had a brother in America, who would take her in until Abe arrived, but Grandpa did not make a good first impression when he landed in his new country. Getting off the boat, he tried to look debonair by twirling a cane. My mother says Miriam's brother was so incensed at the greenhorn that he took the cane, broke it in half, and snapped at Abe: "In the United States, we don't use canes."

Grandma's brother tried to break off the relationship as well, but he didn't succeed. These two young people had risked too much and come too far to be kept apart. After they were married, my dad was born a year or two later, in 1916, and the family settled in Bayonne, New Jersey, not far from where my mother's family, the Schanbams, were also living. In fact, Abe Rogow and Harry Schanbam met long before their children married—and never liked each other. Harry's family owned a dairy farm, and one story has it that Harry fired Abe from a job delivering milk. Years later, after Abe became quite successful, Harry would brag that he gave Abe his start in this country. But he'd usually leave out the part about firing him. My parents were still living in Harry's house by the time I was born in 1943, and Abe and Miriam lived just a few blocks away. I have from those years another photo I cherish: my brother Marc and I are three or four, dressed in our Sunday best, white shirts and navy blue short pants, and sitting on a couch with our grandparents. Miriam is much grayer and heavier than in her earlier pictures, but you can still see flashes of the girl Abe first noticed. The girl with the slight smile and smoldering eyes. The girl in the photographer's window.

The other family fable starts back in Eishishok, Miriam's home village. As a young man, her father, Max, was a bookbinder, hardly a lucrative trade, and as my mother remembers the story, Max "spent more time reading books than binding them." He fell in love with Bodonna, a girl from a wealthy family, which looked down on the poor bookbinder. I always heard that Bodonna was sent away to break up the romance but her granddaughter, Norma Weiss, says that Bodonna and

Max were actually engaged, and that she went to America assuming he would follow her. "He never got here," says Norma. Whatever the details, we know this: before Bodonna left, Max bound a book with his own hands, inscribed it in Yiddish, and gave it to her as a going-away present. My father always said it was a book of love poems. Norma insists it was a Bible. I'll accept her version, grudgingly, but I prefer my father's.

In any case, Bodonna took the book to America, and the two young lovers never saw each other again. They both married others and had many children. I have a photo of Max and the woman he did marry—my great-grandmother—a rather stern and unappealing person, to tell you the truth. Surrounded by his family, Max wears a skullcap and a full beard, and there's my grandmother Miriam in the back row, as always looking fearlessly forward. After Miriam came to America and married Abe, she was joined by her other brothers. One of them was a monument carver by trade and his life was shadowed by tragedy. In 1925, while his wife was pregnant with their seventh child, he died in a flu epidemic. The first two children, twins, had died at birth, a son had died in an accident, and the latest blow was too much for his wife. She suffered an emotional and physical collapse and could no longer care for her children. The four surviving kids were sent to the Brooklyn Hebrew Orphan Asylum, where they remained until they went to work or were taken in by relatives.

The oldest boy, Sam, was a real go-getter. At age fourteen, he got a job as a mail clerk at the Classy Coat Company in Manhattan's garment district and was soon taking care of his younger siblings. "He became our father," recalls his sister Pearl Bronstein. Sam was rising quickly through the ranks of the garment trade when he went to a social club in the Bronx one evening and met Norma Kass. Norma's father was also in the garment business, but her family was not pleased with her new beau, who had been raised in an orphanage and seemed to have no family background. Norma's grandmother was particularly upset, and today, more than sixty years later, Norma can remember the old woman complaining, "Who is he? Who's his family? What's what?"

Sam was not about to be thwarted, so he asked his aunt Miriam, my grandmother, to come with him and meet Norma's family, to show them that he did have relatives of his own, that he was somebody. So Abe and Miriam made the trek to Norma's house in the Bronx, and things started stiffly, with the grandmother sitting over in the corner and not saying much. But Miriam was a gregarious person and the group fell into conversation about the old country and where they were all from. Finally the grandmother broke in and started asking questions: You say you're from Eishishok? Your name was Wasilsky? (Weiss was the Americanized version.) Your father was Max the bookbinder? Please. Just a minute.

She went upstairs and after a while brought down a book, a book inscribed to her in Yiddish by a young man many years before. The grandmother was Bodonna, the girl who left for America and never saw Max again. She had never forgotten her lost love. She still had the book he had given her, a book he had bound with his own hands. And now their grandchildren had found each other. There was much rejoicing. All was forgiven. Bodonna gave her blessing and Sam was embraced. Soon they were married, at a synagogue on the Grand Concourse, a large boulevard running through the middle of the Bronx. After the wedding, the guests trooped to a restaurant around the corner for a meal, and Norma remembers how happy her grandmother was that day. "She was so excited, she went around telling everybody" the story. And the match was a good one. Sam and Norma were married for sixty-three years before he died in 1998.

There is a footnote to the story: Sam wound up owning

his own business and hired his father-in-law to run one of his factories. He was so respected in the garment trade that after his death, a scholarship was named in his honor at the Fashion Institute of Technology. Norma, who insists that Max gave Bodonna a Bible, not poetry, does not know what happened to the book, but that's all right. To me, his gift will always be a book of poems, and I know where it is. In my heart.

Lilly and Ludwig Friedman: A White Wedding Dress

If you buy a wedding ring from Lilly Friedman, she won't charge a commission. And sometimes you'll get more than you bargained for. "I tell them stories," says Lilly, sitting in her tiny jewelry shop on Manhattan's Lower East Side. "When a young couple comes to me, I'm always very excited if I see that things go well."

Lilly has quite a story to tell, but you wouldn't know that just looking at her, a shy, soft-spoken woman of seventy-five who is about to become a great-grandmother. It is a story of one woman's strength and spirit, of her refusal to give up her dreams, simple dreams, really, of a home and a husband and a white wedding dress. But they were not simple in Czechoslovakia, not in 1944, not when the Nazis were doing everything possible to exterminate her family and her future.

Lilly was born and raised in the small Czech village of Caricha, where her ancestors had lived for generations. There were only twenty-five Jewish families in the whole place, "but we lived very good," she remembers, baking their own matzoh and building their own synagogue, where Lilly's father presided as the rabbi. Things changed in 1939, when Germany's Hungarian allies occupied the area and "made our lives miserable." Jews were forced to wear yellow stars and barred from shopping in stores, traveling on trains, or running their own schools. Lilly's older sister, Celia, had gone to America in the mid-thirties to live with an aunt, and the family was desperate to join her. "We always wanted to go out but we didn't have a chance," says Lilly. Celia sent tickets for her father and two brothers, but when they got to Lisbon, they didn't have the right papers for America and the boat—one of the last escape routes from Europe—left without them and they had to return home.

In 1944, the Gestapo moved into Czechoslovakia and Lilly and her whole family were put on a train for Auschwitz. "But we didn't know what to expect," she recalls. "We never heard of Auschwitz, we never heard of the crematoriums." At the camp, her father and two brothers were separated out and never seen again. Lilly, her two younger sisters, and a cousin were dispatched on a work detail, where they basically moved rocks from one place to another, and were then sent back to Auschwitz. By this time they knew what to expect and "we were sure we wouldn't survive," she says. But they did for one reason—the Nazis needed healthy workers—and the four girls were assigned to a weaving factory that ran twenty-four hours a day.

By January 1945, the Russians were advancing from the east and the Germans retreated, taking their workers with them, marching through fierce winter storms and shooting anyone who faltered. One of Lilly's sisters, Fayge, couldn't walk, so the three other girls carried her most of the way. Czech villagers living along the route would sometimes hide vegetables in the snow for the Jews to eat, but by the time they got to the camp at Bergen-Belsen, most of the survivors were half-dead. "From here we don't go," said Lilly's cousin. "Either we die or get liberated."

So many people were dying so quickly that the corpses were just stacked in a corner of the room where the prisoners slept. Lilly remembers being told to remove a pile of clothes from one room and finding the bodies of dead babies wrapped in the bundle. "I became hysterical crying," she says, "those babies are always with me." Somehow, all four of the girls made it through: "We held on to each other and we helped each other however we could. If one of us got a piece of bread, we cut it into four and everybody got a piece."

On April 15, Bergen-Belsen was liberated, but as Lilly remembers that day: "We were so sick when the British came, we couldn't walk. We had typhus, our hair came out, everybody had sores and frozen toes." After getting emergency medical care, and enough food to regain their strength, the girls were moved to a displaced-persons camp near the German town of Celle. "It was a very sad life but we all wanted to live," says Lilly, who was then twenty years old. "We lost everything, we lost everybody, but we still wanted to go on with life."

Soon Lilly started noticing a tall man who worked in the camp kitchen: "We were so thin we were always standing in the line, and he was also very thin, because he was also liberated on the fifteenth of April." The man's name was Ludwig Friedman, although Lilly now calls him by his Hebrew name, Aaron, and as they started talking, they realized their home villages were only thirty kilometers apart in Czechoslovakia. "At night he used to bring a little more food for me and my sisters," Lilly recalls. "I felt so sorry for him. I didn't see how thin I was but he was tall, six feet five, and he was *so* thin. He had a pair of sneakers, some kind of white shoes, and I said, at least don't wear those white shoes, you look terrible in them."

At first, Lilly was not taken with Ludwig: "I said to my sisters, 'He looks terrible,' and my sisters said, 'What do you care? Food he brings us. So?' I couldn't see how I could fall in love with him." But time passed and Lilly changed: "We went out, we talked, we both had very little education, so we talked about what we would do, what kind of jobs we would have. Most of the time we were with the girls, with the family, and little by little, I started to see he doesn't look so bad as I thought." Little by little, other survivors were also regaining their health and vitality. Some who were musicians before the war begged and borrowed instruments and occasionally played for dances, often after synagogue services. Lilly was a quiet girl, but Ludwig was a good dancer, so when the young people got together, he was the "life of the party" and Lilly liked that about him, he brought out her fun-loving side. "Sometimes he made me jealous, he would dance with other people, and I didn't like that," she admits. But when other boys tried to dance with her, "he would not let anybody near me, he was terrible about that."

Soon they were getting serious. "We were religious people, you can't just hang out," she says with a laugh. "We went for a walk in a park, and on the way home he says, 'Look, Lilly, why are we schlepping around? Why don't we get married? I would like it if you should be my wife.'" Such boldness would have been unthinkable back in Caricha. Lilly's father probably would have arranged a match for her. If not, his approval of her choice would have been essential. But the village life Ludwig and Lilly once knew was gone forever, and he felt free to tell her: "I wouldn't dream of this before the war, but now we could get married, we could be very happy, we're entitled to it." The young couple was discovering what all immigrants realize: one way or another, the old rules don't apply. They had no parents to ask permission from, no community to please but their fellow survivors. They could make their own decisions, and when Ludwig proposed, Lilly was eager to accept: "I felt very much to have a home of my own. I didn't want to be in camp. I wanted to make a home for me and my sisters."

But this was still 1945, only one other wedding had taken place in the camp, and Lilly asked Ludwig: "How will we get our wedding together? Do we just go to the rabbi and get married?" He answered: "No. I get you a beautiful dress, a white gown, and I give you everything you really wanted. We're going to be married the way you want." A hard promise to keep, but Ludwig was a clever and resourceful fellow. He'd made friends with an English sergeant, a supply officer for the camp and something of a fixer, the sort of guy who could get you anything—for a price. And when the sergeant told Ludwig he had a German parachute for sale, Lilly recalls her husband's reaction: "Right away it hit me—this could be made into a gown!" Money was worthless, the local economy operated on a barter system, and Ludwig established a price with the sergeant: two pounds of coffee plus some cartons of cigarettes. (Lilly and Ludwig didn't smoke cigarettes or drink coffee, so when those commodities were included in relief packages sent from abroad, they would always save them for use as currency. They were better than cash.)

When Ludwig showed his purchase to Lilly, she exclaimed: "Oh, my God, where did you get this?" And he replied: "I bought it, maybe you could do something with this." Indeed, she could. She brought it to a friend named Miriam, an accomplished seamstress, who said: "We could do something with this, definitely." She worked for two weeks, Lilly remembers: "Everybody was very excited, so everybody went to look for the dress. I said she will never finish it if people will be interfering all the time." In fact, when Miriam finished the dress, she had enough material left over to make Ludwig a shirt. "I don't think I could describe the feelings I had about that dress, that gown," Lilly says today, fifty-four years later. "It was something a young girl dreams to have."

The wedding was set for late January of 1946 and the preparations began, helped immeasurably by a British woman named Lady Rose Henriques who had come to Germany to help care for the survivors. "We cooked, we baked delicious pies," says Lilly. "We couldn't get nothing, but that Lady Henriques, she could get it for us. It was beautiful how she helped out. Everybody helped out. We set beautiful tables, and we had guys who used to play, so we had music."

Ludwig borrowed a truck from the English sergeant "and

went to ring bells to bring people to the wedding." Somehow, at a local hothouse, he found Lilly a bouquet of white lilacs, her favorite flower, to carry at the ceremony. The wedding was held in a makeshift synagogue, located in an old house. And then the couple and the guests marched through a snowstorm to a kosher restaurant that had been set up to feed the religious Jews. "Soldiers were marching, people were marching, whoever went along joined the wedding party, it was very exciting," says Lilly. "It was a joy to have the wedding. This was a survival, really something we wanted so much to have." Over four hundred guests were still celebrating when the curfew came at eleven and the restaurant closed down, so the party moved back to the camp. "We had music, we danced, we danced all night."

The wedding set off a "chain reaction," says Lilly. About two thousand girls from Czechoslovakia were housed in the camp at Celle, and as she remembers with a laugh: "There were a lot of boys liberated, too, so the chances were good. Boys and girls started to date, to go out and get married and live again and not think about what happened to us. Because if you thought about it, you couldn't go on with life." Lilly's younger sister Fayge met a Polish Jew named Max and wanted to get engaged, but Lilly was concerned. Her sister was only nineteen, but Fayge retorted: "I feel like a hundred years old, not nineteen, and I love Max and I want to get married, too." Besides, the old rules didn't apply to Fayge either. She told Lilly she'd get married anyway, whatever her sister said, so Lilly gave the couple her blessing.

But there was also the issue of the dress. Many brides wanted to wear it, but Lilly said, no, Fayge gets it first, then others can have it. Lilly took up the hem a bit, the dress fit Fayge "very nice," and then it started making the rounds: "It just went from one to the other; they didn't even bring it back to me." She stopped counting after about eighteen brides, and Lilly figures more than twenty women wore her dress. Each one took it in or let it out, made it longer or shorter, and for Lilly, the gown took on symbolic meaning: "When they asked me for the dress, I told them, I would like that this dress should represent a beginning for us, for the survivors. We got married and we want to live and build Jewish homes and show that Hitler didn't succeed in what he wanted to succeed."

Meanwhile, Lilly had lost touch with her sister Celia, the one in America. She enlisted the help of a Canadian soldier who was going home on leave, and he put an ad in the *Forward,* the Yiddish newspaper in New York, telling Celia that her three sisters were all alive and looking for her. A friend of Celia's saw the ad and the family was reunited by mail, but Lilly was desperate to see the sister she had not seen in twelve years. Her daughter Miriam was born in 1947, and when President Truman agreed to take in a hundred thousand additional refugees the next year, Lilly pressed Ludwig to go to America. He preferred Israel, but agreed to her wishes, and Celia sent the baby a little sweater and a hat with pom-poms to wear on the journey. "If I don't recognize you," said Celia, "I'll recognize the baby."

The family settled in the Brownsville section of Brooklyn and Ludwig found a job in construction, but after he hurt his back and couldn't work, he opened a kosher butcher shop on Flatbush Avenue called "L&L," for Lilly and Ludwig. Two boys were born, and as Ludwig's dream of moving to Israel faded, the family moved to a nicer neighborhood in Sheepshead Bay. After the children went to school, Lilly started working in the jewelry business, where she had a relative, and it turned out she had a talent for selling. Eventually Ludwig closed the butcher shop and joined her selling jewelry, and he died in 1992 after almost forty-seven years of marriage. The tiny shop she still runs today is also called "L&L," in honor of their years together. Celia is also dead, but the three sisters who survived the war together, Lilly, Fayge, and Eva, are all still alive and living within a few blocks of each other in Brooklyn. Lilly has seven grandchildren, and the oldest, Miriam's daughter, is pregnant. "My God, my fourth generation," says Lilly. "I couldn't believe it. When I was in the camp and struggling to survive, to live, I'd just ask God for a piece of bread. And now I have a home and children and grandchildren and I'm expecting a great-grandchild. It's the biggest gift God gives me."

And what of the wedding dress? When she came to America, Lilly put it away in a closet, protected by a plastic box. "Every time I cleaned the closet, I'd say, what's going to be with that gown? This is not even good for a garage sale." But she was wrong. One of her nieces told a curator at the Holocaust Museum in Washington about the dress, and it's now part of an exhibit detailing the history of the displaced-persons camps in postwar Europe. Lilly is very pleased because putting her wedding dress on display completes a journey she started in 1944, when she first got on the train for Auschwitz: "We wanted to live, and to tell the story, this was our most important thing. To tell the story that happened, so that it shouldn't happen again."

Chapter Five

OUR LIVES

COMING HOME

FAMILY HOUSE

"Coming home" is one of the most resonant phrases in the English language. It means returning to comfort, to security, to familiar people and places and things. Cokie had moved into the house on Bradley Boulevard when she was eight years old. We had some of our earliest dates there and were married in the garden. Now, eleven years, three cities, and two kids later, we were very different people. We knew we belonged at the grown-ups' table at Christmas. But coming home has another meaning. Comfort can lead to constriction, familiarity can mean a loss of freedom and privacy. Family can feed your spirit and fuel your anxieties, open windows and impose obligations. These were the tensions we faced as we moved back to America, back to Washington, back to the old house and the old neighborhood. Back home.

CR: My mother could not have been more accommodating. She threw us a big welcome-home party with Greek food and decorations on what turned out to be our eleventh wedding anniversary. She turned over her room to Steve and me and moved into my old bedroom with Becca. She gave us her closets and dresser, and put all her stuff under the bed she and Becca shared. It was more than a little strange for me, with Becca in my old room, Lee in my sister Barbara's old room, and Steve and me in my parents' room. The house had not changed since my father had died; some of his things were still in their bedroom, even though it was almost five years since his plane had disappeared. My mother's mother had been living there, with a full-time housekeeper to help look after her, so Mamma had not even thought about leaving the big house in the suburbs for something more convenient downtown. But the previous April my grandmother had died, and Mamma was reaching a point of decision about the house. She knew that I loved the house, had always wanted to live in it, had in fact picked it out when I was eight years old, but she didn't want us to feel pressured to move in. She encouraged us to look at other houses, and we did.

SR: We had so many things to do and buy. We needed two cars! We bought one real jalopy, which lasted about three weeks. I needed new clothes because I hadn't gone into an office regularly for nine years. Fortunately, the neighborhood public school was a good one, so the kids' situation was easy to settle, and we had waited until almost the first day of school to arrive in Washington so they could plunge right in.

CR: House hunting was a real shock. When we had left the area, many people who worked in the *New York Times* bureau lived in my family's neighborhood, and usually on only one salary. By the time we got back, there was no way on earth anyone could do that. The growth of the government during the sixties and seventies had drawn all these well-paid lawyers and lobbyists and consultants to town and they had driven real estate prices through the roof and interest rates were at an all-time high. It became clear that to live in what was just a regular house, we had to have more money and that meant I had to find a decent job, not something to occupy and amuse me. The obvious place to start was CBS, since I had worked for them in Greece, but the bureau chief crisply told me that foreign stringer was one thing, Washington staffer quite another. I made the rounds of the networks soon after we arrived in town, but it was Steven who found me a job.

SR: I had worked in the *Times* bureau thirteen years before, but there were many new faces, including the one at the desk next to mine. I introduced myself and she said her name was Judy Miller and that she had just started working at the newspaper. I asked where she came from, and when she said National Public Radio, my reaction was "What's that?" Public radio was then about five years old, but for four of those years we'd been in Europe and I had no idea what she was talking about. When Judy described public radio, I said, "I've got a wife crying herself to sleep every night. I'm desperate about finding her a job and that sounds like the perfect place. What do I do?" Judy said, "I know they're hiring because they are replacing me. Call Nina Totenberg." Nina knew friends of ours and had heard we were coming to town and agreed to help, at least partly because she wanted to make sure NPR hired more women. It was the first time I'd seen the old-girl network in action, but not the last. So the next morning I brought Cokie's résumé downtown with me so she didn't have to make a special trip, and Nina came downstairs and met me outside the NPR offices. Since then, she's become one of our dearest friends. A few years later, in another gesture of female solidarity, Cokie was an usher—an usher, not a bridesmaid—in Nina's wedding.

CR: Nina got me in the door. But NPR still didn't hire me. For a while I was on a weekly retainer. None of it was certain.

In fact, even though I was filing stories almost daily, I wasn't hired for a long time. I remember Steve's sister got married in October, and when we flew up to Boston, I cried the whole way. I couldn't see how any of this was ever going to get resolved. Nobody was hiring me, we couldn't afford to live anywhere, I felt like I was a child in my mother's house. It was all a mess, though I loved the work itself. When I was finally brought on staff in February 1978, it was at the lowest-level reporter's salary. That made it tough in terms of buying a house, but we were eager anyway to get that settled. By that time we had been living with my mother for six months. Her things were still under Becca's bed, ours were still in storage, and the situation was unnerving for everyone.

SR: At first we didn't think we'd move into the family house, but soon we realized that it made the most sense. It was in a good school district and the kids loved it. In fact, they told us that they had always seen that house as their home base as we traveled around the world—something we had not fully understood. Also, of course, there were many fond memories and a few ghosts—most of them friendly, Casper-like.

CR: And it was a very special place to Daddy, so it was hard for Mamma to give it up. But it was also time for me to be mistress of my own house, with my own things around me. No matter how generous and wonderful my mother was, and she was incredibly generous, we didn't want to be camping out. If this was going to be our house, it had to be our house.

SR: Something had to give. And finally, our sister-in-law Barbara intervened just the way my brother had intervened years before and helped my parents accept our determination to get married. She went out and found Lindy an apartment.

CR: Which my mother never liked.

SR: And basically handed her the keys and said, "You're moving!"

CR: It wasn't quite that bad, but almost.

SR: Almost. For us, though, it was a great relief to finally be settled, particularly in a place that meant so much to us. It was springtime, and I realized there was an unwritten clause in the deed of sale that I would take over the gardens. Hale had focused on the vegetables, while Lindy had put in lovely perennial beds. The vegetable gardens had not been planted for years and I felt a powerful obligation, and even more a desire, to revive them. But I didn't have a clue about how to start, and I remember that first spring walking out and looking at the bare ground and thinking, "What the heck do I do now?" Fortunately, there was a man named William Barnes who had worked for my in-laws for many years, and essentially I apprenticed myself to him. Slowly and patiently he would teach me about this piece of land, and that gave me a great sense of continuity. He had worked with my father-in-law, he knew and loved the place, and we still had a lot of my father-in-law's tools, which had rested idle in the shed for years. I learned from William, but in many ways I was also learning from Hale. I felt a very strong connection to him when I worked in the garden, and I still feel that way all these years later. That's where his spirit is most alive, and in a way I feel that it's still his land. I'm just a caretaker.

CR: Well, I think you qualify! You've been at it twenty-two years.

SR: Some of my fondest memories of Bradley Boulevard involve Hale and his garden. I asked him for Cokie's hand in the tomato patch. Many of the earliest dinners I had there were in the summer and included his vegetables. Half the talk was about politics, the other half about vegetables, and that's still true. That first spring I planted tomatoes for the first time but I had no idea how big they would grow. Like a pupil seeking approval from the teacher, I went running over to William: "Come look, come look." One glance and he burst out laughing: "You've got to take every other one and dig them up because they get much bigger than you think. You've got to plant them much farther apart." Every Saturday, William and I had our rituals. During the morning we'd work together, and he would teach me things, and then we'd come in for lunch. Every Saturday I would offer him a beer and every Saturday he would say no. But I offered him one every week. He died much too young. But he stayed alive long enough to pass on his wisdom to me. I even have a few, just a few, of my father-in-law's tools. There are two old watering cans of his that I still use. Galvanized steel, they'll last forever.

CR: The kids were delighted that we had finally settled in and they had their things around them again, though Becca missed snuggling at night with her MawMaw. Lee had been sleeping in an antique four-poster with brocade spread and dust ruffle. He couldn't wait for his bunk beds to arrive, and for me to cover the brocade valances with NFL football fabric. Aside from missing their stuff, though, the kids had had a good adjustment to America. Since they didn't know anybody, I thought it was important to send them to the same school, one in the neighborhood where they could meet other kids. At the time we had no decent child care. A high-school boy named Anthony came for a few hours in the afternoon until we got home. But he needed to leave at a certain hour and I was always frantically trying to cover in case we were late, which we often were. Fortunately, my niece and nephew, Tee and Hale, were in high school and able to drive, so they were a big help. But sometimes everybody's signals got crossed, and the changing of the guard that was supposed to happen didn't happen. Lee once ended up standing on the curb for hours waiting for Hale to pick him up from soccer. At one point we were broadcasting the Senate debate on the Panama Treaty live on NPR, where I was still very much proving myself. I asked Steve, who was also working on the Hill, "Could you please call Tee and ask her to get over to the house and relieve Anthony." Steve said he'd do it but he didn't. He was working and just forgot. I was furious. Anthony stayed but was all bent out of shape. The hassle was constant. Finally, after about a year, Rosie Nowak, a Scottish woman who had been the kids' last baby-sitter in Greece, came over from Europe and saved my life.

SR: It was taking me some time to realize that for the first time in our marriage our jobs were comparable. We had moved three times for my work, really four times. To New York in the beginning when Cokie gave up her TV show. Then of course to California and Greece and then back to Washington, with my work dictating every decision. Through those years Cokie always worked, but we were not equal. Now that was changing. It was changing because we needed her income. It was changing because she was working full-time. It was changing because she had responsibilities. That caused a big adjustment.

CR: Huge adjustment, for the whole family. And the whole family also had to adjust to the fact that Steve was now home, not traveling a sizable percentage of his time. I was used to making very simple meals when he was away. The kids loved Spaghetti-Os. I would sit down and visit with them and pick at something to eat and then get everybody to bed early. It was a much more organized life when Steve wasn't there. His coming home was almost a holiday. So it was a big change to have a full-time man in the house. It meant a big meal on the table every night. I was incapable of doing something really simple with Steven home.

SR: Which was partly your problem. Often you'd insist on doing something complicated when I wasn't expecting it.

CR: I would come in from work and start making these time-consuming dinners and we'd finally all sit down exhausted at the dinner table at eight-thirty or nine o'clock. The kids were pretty good about it. When they got older they told us that they hated it when we'd call assuring them, "We'll be home in a half an hour," and then call back: "Actually, it will be an hour." They were expected to adjust their schedules to us. They thought that wasn't fair and they were right.

SR: Yes, they were right. We didn't mean to be negligent or thoughtless, but we were both covering news stories and couldn't always predict what was going to happen.

CR: And we wanted to be with them, we wanted our family dinner, so we'd ask them to wait for us to get home rather than eat early without us. Years later they told us that they sometimes shared an early meal at a friend's house and then had another dinner with us. Our motives were good, but we sometimes made their lives more difficult.

SR: Often we were commuting together and that meant operating on the latest common denominator. If one of us was done early, often the other was not. And it got worse when NPR started *Morning Edition,* which meant that after Cokie filed for the evening show, *All Things Considered,* she had to start all over again for the morning. Even so, we enjoyed commuting together, and it helped our relationship. On the ride to work in the mornings we'd make plans and coordinate schedules. On the way home at night we'd have half an hour in the car to catch up on the day before we walked in the door.

CR: A couple does that anyway even with the kids around; I've watched it with other people, too. At the end of the day the husband and wife catch up with each other. If the kids are there, they want to be part of the conversation, but the couple tends to exclude the children until they've finished exchanging the news of the day. By the time we finally got home, the kids had our undivided attention.

SR: Fortunately, I was fairly well established at *The New York Times* by this point. So while Cokie was in a position of proving herself, I had a little more security and a little more control. I wasn't great about it, Lord knows, but being at different stages in our careers helped a bit, I think.

CR: Well, it helped and it hurt. As you started to see how hard the home/work juggling act was for me, you started picking up more of the balls. On the other hand, I was in the uncomfortable position of being a junior employee, which meant I only had a two-week vacation and I sometimes had to work on weekends, which was terribly disruptive to the family.

SR: The best example of my increased flexibility came when the accident happened at the nuclear power plant at Three Mile Island. It was in early 1979, a little over a year after Cokie had been hired onto the NPR staff. There was a threat of an enormous nuclear disaster. That morning Cokie's editor sent her to Pennsylvania to cover the story and she was eager to go; it was one of her first really big stories. Just a few hours later my desk told me to go, too, and I said no. It might have been the only time that I ever said no to *The New York Times*. But I had no expertise, they were just looking for a warm body, and I didn't think it was fair for the kids to have both parents away, particularly when they were worried we might be in danger.

CR: And they were scared. It was big news here and they were old enough to understand.

SR: That was the first time in our marriage where your work took precedence over mine. Don't you think?

CR: Other than finishing up the paperwork for *Serendipity* back in California, yes. I had been away on stories before that and you had helped some at home. I traveled some during the '78 campaign, doing stories on gubernatorial and congressional elections. I had been determined not to cover politics and Congress. I thought that would mean totally enmeshing myself in my childhood. Not only was I back in my house, but I'd also be back in my second childhood home, the Capitol. NO! In truth, because of the stage of life I was in, I was more interested in stories about school and children. But when the '78 campaign heated up, my good friend Linda Wertheimer said to the editors at NPR, "Don't you think that Cokie, who was raised in a political boiler room, should do some of these stories?" So I did cover the campaign and liked it. I went out and talked to voters and found out what was important to people. In my view, that still didn't make me a full-time Washington type. I would help Linda out on Capitol Hill from time to time, but I was not assigned there. That happened after the '80 campaign. That year Linda and I divided up the coverage: she reported on candidates and I wrote about voters. After the election, public television started a program on Congress called *The Lawmakers,* and Linda, Paul Duke, and I were the anchors. In order to do that program well, I really did have to be on the Hill full-time.

SR: It was the same for me. I had been covering politics and the Hill part-time and I was having fun doing stories about other things. I had spent nine years running my own bureau, and one of the great things about covering a region of America or a foreign country is that you can write about anything. Culture, economics, sports, family life. To do your job right you had to cover the whole society, not just the government.

As much as I wanted to come back to Washington, it was hard to shift gears and write about a very small slice of the world, politics, and public policy.

But we learned something important during the '80 campaign, something many families with two working parents come to realize. What's important is not just the number of hours worked, but who decides the hours. I learned that controlling my schedule could make the difference between chaos and sanity. During the '80 campaign we both came to understand that if we were covering voters as opposed to politicians, it was a lot easier on the family. If a kid had a soccer game and I was covering Jimmy Carter and Jimmy Carter was in Iowa, I'd have to be in Iowa with him and miss the soccer game. But if I had to do a story on farmers in Iowa, I could stay for the game and then go to Iowa the next day. It was a small compromise but a critical one, and it gave me a measure of control over my life.

CR: We also preferred covering voters to candidates. The stories were more varied and it didn't involve sitting through the same speech six times a day, but occasionally we paid a price, in the sense that we saw each other less. There were times we traveled together, but obviously it was better for the kids if one parent was at home.

SR: Most of the time we would leapfrog. Cokie might do a story on Southern whites in Birmingham early in the week, then after she got home I'd go write about rubber workers in Akron. At other times we met up with each other on the road. We spent our fourteenth wedding anniversary together in Sioux Falls, South Dakota, covering George McGovern's 1980 Senate campaign.

CR: I had been in Texas and you were in Ohio or someplace. I got on your plane in St. Louis going to Sioux Falls. I knew you were going to be on that flight, but you didn't know that I was getting on it, too. You had all your work spread out on the tray table and I said, "Excuse me, could I please get in there?" You were so irritated to be interrupted! Then you looked up and said, "It's you!"

At the end of the 1980 campaign we wrote a big Sunday *New York Times* magazine article together, pooling the anecdotes and observations we had collected during the fall. When the galleys came back for the final edit, the piece needed substantial cutting. Steve had the galleys physically in his possession at home in Washington. I was on the West Coast in a hotel room and he would read me a section and say, "Well, this could go." And I would scream, "No, it can't, it's my section! I wrote that!" This was before faxes and e-mails, so just because he had possession of the actual piece of paper, he had too much say over the cutting of that piece.

SR: But it was an example of the evolution of our lives. This was a double byline. We had contributed equally, it was a totally joint effort. A lot of the things we had written earlier had not been. Cokie had done the research and I had done the writing. But now we were both full-time professionals, covering the same assignments, and the piece ran on the cover of the magazine the Sunday before the 1980 elections.

We enjoyed working on the same stories but we talked shop an awful lot. The kids would complain about it and say, "We've heard enough about politics for tonight, thank you very much!" Fortunately, we weren't direct competitors. Cokie was working for radio and I was working for print, so she was always going to get on the air first.

CR: I could be the world's most generous colleague, I had the earliest deadline in town. That was before twenty-four-hour channels and constant news on the Internet.

SR: We helped each other an enormous amount. Covering the Hill, you could never be all the places you needed to be at one time, so we constantly traded information.

CR: An added bonus to covering Congress was my mother. It was lovely to be able to just drop in and see her during the day.

SR: I'm sure I was the only reporter covering the Hill who lived in constant fear of being kissed by his mother-in-law. There I'd be, trying to act like a grown-up, interviewing somebody important, and she'd swoop down and nail me. But it was great to have family around, after so long away from home. Being with good friends for rituals and holidays and birthdays was always very important to us, and one of the things we missed most during our travels was the connection to our actual families and to very old friends. Now we were able to rebuild those connections.

CR: During our years away we missed being around our brothers' and sisters' kids, and it was a treat to become full-time uncles and aunts, really for the first time. We have a big family Christmas, with turkey and goose and all the fixings, and it was wonderful to be back celebrating it with everyone I truly cared about. Now that my job was settled and interesting, and the kids were happy, I realized Steven had been right to come home.

SR: And my parents in New Jersey weren't too far away. We always spent the long Thanksgiving weekend at their house with all of my siblings. One year we rented a van and organized a big family field trip to Philadelphia. It was the first time I realized I was now a member of the sandwich generation. My father and my nephew Zak, the oldest and youngest members of our group, got lost at the same time, and of course, those of us in the middle had to find them.

The family connections grew even tighter when my younger brother moved to Washington. When he had been living in San Francisco during our days in L.A., he had been a wonderful uncle to our children, and after a stint in Boston he'd decided to look for a job in Washington. He stayed with us for a while, which was great fun for all of us, especially the kids, and after he found work on Capitol Hill and a place to live, Cokie and her lady friends declared him prime marriage material. He was a single, funny, bright guy who had never been married and very much wanted to be. Men that sane are in short supply in Washington, so Cokie decided that he was not going to go to a stranger. She had a younger friend at NPR who also happened to be from New Orleans—a perfect fit! We had a big party at home for recently married friends and we invited the two of them. It was in the garden, a pretty spring night. I came through the buffet line last and the only open seat was next to the person we had picked out for my brother. He was sitting at another table and I thought, "What's wrong with him, hasn't he figured out he's supposed to meet this beautiful woman?" I sat down. She and I had a nice chat, and then I got up to help serve dessert. When I came back to the table, my brother was sitting in my chair. It happens that this table was only a few feet from the spot where we'd been married, in the same corner of the yard where our *chuppah* had been. They soon started dating and just over a year later got married on the exact same spot. It's practically sacred ground. Since then, there have been two more marriages right there—friends of ours who Cokie introduced and our daughter, Becca. And that doesn't begin to count all the parties related to weddings, from engagements to anniversaries to receptions, we've celebrated in that garden. More than a dozen in all. My brother always loved the idea that we'd all gotten married under the same old apple tree, and after the tree eventually died, the friends who had used that same spot for their wedding gave us a new one. It's growing nicely, almost ready for the next couple.

In many ways, this was the married life we had always planned, back during that first spring in Boston when the possibility seemed so remote. Steve had his dream job, covering Congress for *The New York Times,* and Cokie had her dream house, the one she had grown up in. Our daughter slept in Cokie's girlhood room and Steve farmed her father's garden. As our circle of friends and relatives continued to expand, every passing year required new and creative ways to fit everybody in for Christmas and Passover, birthdays and book parties. What we didn't anticipate back in Boston—or in New York or Los Angeles or Athens for that matter—was that our jobs would be equal. In fact, that they would be the same. And that sameness had its drawbacks. If you're sitting up in bed at eleven o'clock discussing the intricacies of the federal budget, you're doing something wrong. But the pluses far outweighed the minuses. We walked in each other's shoes every day, faced the same problems, covered the same stories. One member of Congress even complained one day about "stereophonic Robertses" as we fired questions at him from different sides of the room. And there was one phrase neither one of us could ever say to the other, a phrase that has gnawed and nibbled away at the foundation of many good marriages— "you just don't understand, dear."

SR: This new equality in our work situations required me to take more responsibility at home, particularly when Cokie started hosting her show on public television, *The Lawmakers*. It was broadcast live, on Thursday nights. And it happened that the wife of the other *New York Times* reporter, covering the Hill, Martin Tolchin, taught at George Washington on

Thursday nights. Marty and I had kids exactly the same ages and both of us were on duty the same time. I used to say, only half in jest, that you could pass by the *New York Times* booth on Capitol Hill and overhear the high-powered correspondents saying into the phone, "Now, dear, set the oven at three hundred and fifty degrees . . ."

CR: Which of course happens with women correspondents constantly.

SR: That's true. We had one friend, a female reporter with two little boys at home, who was so tired all the time that she actually fell asleep one day in the front row of the press gallery, her arms draped over the balcony. The kids and I worked out a routine that we all looked forward to. Lee was already interested in the law, and a show called *The Paper Chase,* set at Harvard Law School, was on just after Cokie's show. So we'd have supper, and then watch our two favorite programs.

CR: Then I would get home and we'd watch *Hill Street Blues.* It's the only time we've ever organized a family night around television. But I took on that job without any idea of how much work it would be. I had the family, NPR, and then *The Lawmakers,* and the schools didn't help much. Even in a neighborhood like ours, I was surprised how few mothers worked and how the schools were completely geared to at-home moms. I think it's still true. The schools don't take responsibility for the fact that the world has changed. At the first hint of a snowflake, they close at one o'clock in the afternoon and send children home to empty houses and there's no way for parents to know unless they've listened to the radio all day in the office. And how was a mother on a factory line supposed to get the information? For the few serious snowstorms we have in the Washington area, the schools could come up with a better system of communication. I had long conversations with the principal and teachers and tried to be infinitely reasonable, but I never felt the people on the other end were equally reasonable. The teachers would always try to schedule conferences at one o'clock in the afternoon. I'd say, "Could we possibly have it at eight o'clock in the morning?" Well, no.

SR: I think that's changing, now that so many mothers are working.

CR: Maybe, but I doubt it's changed enough. When summertime rolled around and the kids went to day camp, I'd have to try to figure out how to get them home in the afternoons. At the beginning of a session I'd get up all my nerve to ask the other mothers for help. I'm so bad at this, I can't even ask a good friend for a ride home, but I'd plead with these other mothers, "I'll drive your children every single solitary morning for the rest of their lives if you, you, you, you, and you will drive my children home in the afternoons." Living in the suburbs and working downtown, dealing with the logistics of getting children from school to camp to piano lessons to theater lessons is worthy of the most well-staged military campaigns. The ideal, of course, is having enough money to hire a nanny who drives, but we didn't have that. In fact, we gave our baby-sitter driving lessons and her first day out she wrecked a car.

SR: At one point you actually hired a cab.

CR: I hired a cab to take Rebecca and another little girl whose mother worked to piano lessons. We had the same driver every week. That worked out quite well. But with all the stress of balancing work and family, one incident made me feel better. I went to Becca's school one day to talk to the kids about the coming election. I tried to bring a few things along to make it more interesting, so I had my tape recorder with me and my press credentials, and I happened to be wearing a navy-blue suit. Halloween came soon after that visit, and I wanted to see this fabulous parade where the whole elementary school marched around the neighborhood in their costumes. I was at the Capitol and I went tearing out to Bethesda to see the parade in the middle of the day. Flabbergasted, Becca demanded, "What are you doing here? I don't care about you coming to see the parade." And I said, "Well, I care." It was her last one, her last year in that school. Then, as I looked at the parade, there were all these sixth-grade girls in blue suits with tape recorders! They were dressing up as reporters!

SR: Our own kids were less enthusiastic about journalism. They were used to my writing about them but they never really liked it. At one point, not long after we moved back from Greece, there was an oil crisis and the *New York Times* travel section assigned me to write about taking a family trip without using a car. Good idea. So we took a train to Philadelphia and went to all the historical sites. We were walking along and Becca, who was probably about seven or eight, said something cute. I pulled out my notebook to write it down when she turned on me and pronounced, "That's off-the-record, Dad!" I take some satisfaction in the fact that she is now a reporter herself!

But, as for so many people, family life was a constant juggling act. People often ask us, "How did you do it?" And the answer is pretty simple. Our first priority was always trying to be with the kids. We didn't make every important event but we made most of them—at least after I missed Lee's first birthday—because that's what we wanted to do. Sometimes it was quite a feat. One night I was at the Capitol and Lee was singing in a concert at junior high school; I was eager to go but the Congress was staying late.

CR: The members have that habit.

SR: The newspaper's rule was that if you were covering the Congress, you had to stay as late as the session lasted, no matter what. And this was one of the few times I broke that rule. I filed my story for the first edition, got in the car, drove thirty minutes to the school, heard the concert, and raced back to the Capitol, praying all the time, "Please, God, let nothing have happened."

CR: Which is a pretty safe bet.

SR: I got away with it. My desk never knew. I didn't do it very often. It was just so important that we try to make those events, and that one was memorable. The kids were singing songs from *Fiddler on the Roof,* and one of the soloists turned up sick, and at the last minute Lee took over all of his parts. That happened once. If I'd missed it, no second chances.

Lee traded singing for debating when he went to high school, but Becca loved performing, and one year she had the lead in the production of *Bye Bye Birdie*. The second act starts with the character that Becca was playing somewhat un-dressed. The character's just broken up with her boyfriend and she sings this torch song about how I'm a free woman now as she's getting dressed to go out on the town.

CR: This is a big high-school auditorium.

SR: With a thousand kids. The curtain went up and there stood my darling daughter in her underwear singing this torch song!

CR: It was modest underwear!

SR: All of these teenage boys were hooting and hollering and there sat poor Dad in the audience. I was within seconds of leaping to my feet and screaming, "I know what you're thinking!" The dangers of having children who perform in public.

CR: We also learned something else that proved useful—it wasn't necessary, contrary to popular belief, to participate in Washington social life. There's a theory that in order to get the story and make the contacts, a reporter has to be out every night, but it's not true. Now, we were fortunate because we both worked for national news organizations members of Congress cared about, so they would usually return our calls. But we learned we didn't have to abandon the family to get the story.

SR: I've always remembered a story Scotty Reston used to tell, about his early days in town, after the war, when he and Sally were going out practically every night to a different embassy reception or dinner party. One night one of his three boys was watching him get dressed and complaining that he wasn't going to be home. And Scotty had a conversion. He told himself, this doesn't make sense. And that was a story I never forgot.

CR: We also thought it mattered to be involved in the kids' education, and we had a serious problem—the county was trying to close down our little neighborhood elementary school. I was on the committee to keep the school open, which involved a great deal of work and time spent together as a committee. That produced one of those funny Washington situations outsiders don't ever understand. One of the other committee parents was a staff member on the Hill who later went to work for the White House, which made him a great source for stories I was covering. Nobody could ever understand where I was getting my information and no one would've ever been able to track it. He would take my calls because of the time we spent together and the friendship we formed working to keep the school open. Much more effective than trying to schmooze someone at a crowded cocktail party!

SR: There's a lot about Washington that has nothing at all to do with politics. It's a town like any other, with all of the usual activities. One of my favorites was basketball, which I played with a group of guys on Sunday mornings. Several of our kids decided to join a basketball league, but they needed a coach and I agreed to help. But most of the kids were terrible and so were the coaches. The team included a number of foreign kids, and basketball was not their first sport. This little kid from Bolivia was about three feet tall. A demon soccer player but he didn't know the first thing about basketball.

CR: At one point our kids marched off the court chanting, "We're number ten! We're number ten!" And it was only a nine-team league.

SR: The kids appreciated the time I would spend separately with each of them, and sports was a great way to do that. When we first came back to Washington, Lee figured he could pass as a native if he fanatically rooted for the Redskins, along with all the other crazed football fans. He dressed himself in every piece of Redskins paraphernalia available— sweatshirt, hat, socks. And the vicissitudes of another couple's marriage gave us the chance to go to some games, which was almost impossible because season tickets had sold out in the 1960s. This couple, good friends of ours, had bought season tickets when they were available, then later moved to New York. They kept their Redskins tickets and bought New York Giants tickets as well. Their divorce settlement gave the wife custody of the Washington tickets and the guy the New

York tickets. Every year, as a great act of generosity, our friend would give me at least two sets of tickets as birthday presents for the kids. I'd take each kid separately to a game. We loved having a whole afternoon just to ourselves, though they always joked that it was embarrassing to go with me because I would cheer so loudly. At certain ages, as all families know, kids are not exactly proud of their parents. In fact, in this period, I got one of the best birthday cards ever from Becca. It had this sweet, simpering front that read, "Dear Daddy, on your special day, I want to tell you three little words that I don't tell you often enough." Then inside in bold letters: "Don't embarrass me!"

CR: We tried to spend as much free time as possible with the kids, but as they got older we had to adjust more and more to their schedules and their sensitivities, and we didn't always get it right.

SR: During this period, I did have one memorable experience with Lee. He decided for his thirteenth birthday that he wanted to go to a rock concert with a bunch of his friends.

CR: There was no way on earth I was going to do this.

SR: So I took the kids to the concert. The group was called Foreigner, and the six of them were probably the youngest people in the building and I was probably the oldest. We were the oddest group there. It also happened to be the first game of the World Series that night, the Yankees were playing the Dodgers, and I went to the concert with a headphone radio so I could listen to the game.

CR: The kids were actually pretty tolerant of us. We went regularly to the theater and the movies together until they outgrew us and started going out with their friends instead.

And they usually attended church with me every Sunday. Steven didn't go to weekly services but we always made it to Jewish High Holy Day services; we found a comfortable, low-key congregation that met in a Korean church. And we continued to follow all of the rituals at home. When Becca was in high school, the church I usually attended asked for volunteers to sing in a little folk choir at the noon Mass. The two of us joined up and enjoyed singing together, especially since Becca taught me most of the music. It also meant she learned the Gospels, the Epistles, and the liturgical cycle. Later she took courses in college and is now quite knowledgeable about religion. Lee spent two years at a Jesuit high school, so he had plenty of exposure as well.

SR: We did a little freelancing with the rituals—one of Cokie's innovations was the children's Seder.

CR: I actually had two children's Seders, one for little bitty kids and another for those who were just beginning to read. Once they started reading, they graduated to the grown-ups' table.

SR: The copies of the Haggadah Cokie had put together back in California became increasingly dog-eared and splattered with wine over the years, so from time to time we'd Xerox new versions, wine stains and all, and they became great family heirlooms. For our twenty-fifth annual Seder one friend, who was trying to do something nice, put the Haggadah on a computer and printed out fresh copies. Everybody was distressed! Where were the wine stains?

CR: But when we updated the Haggadah we did make it gender neutral, a definite improvement. The God of Abraham and Isaac became the God of Sarah and Rebecca as well. But the complicated rabbis' names are still there, and every year without fail some non-Jewish first-timer gets that section to read! At our other holiday dinners, we set up tables all over the house, but for a Seder everyone needs to be in the same room, to follow the service. Eventually, our crowd outgrew the dining room and our only solution was to move to the porch, take out all the furniture, and rent tables. Despite all my efforts with linens and flowers, it still has the air of a banquet in a VFW hall. Our maximum capacity is thirty-six, and last year the guests ranged in age from three weeks to eighty. A bit larger than the "cheesecake" Seder back in Greece.

SR: When we came back to America we added an annual Hanukkah party to the calendar, a wonderful event that is still important to us, even if our own kids are well past playing the dreidel game. A dreidel is a small four-sided top, and which side it lands on tells you whether you've won or lost. When we started our annual party, little kids covered the floor spinning dreidels, and then one year I looked up and saw four teenage girls in black cocktail dresses and thought, "Goodness, something has changed."

We invite a lot of mixed religious families to Hanukkah, just as we do at Passover, and one year I looked around and commented that of the eleven couples there, in only two cases were both partners Jewish. A gay friend, who was there with his partner, quickly raised his hand and said, "Three." We all laughed, but he was right. You have to adapt ancient rituals to modern times.

CR: The only time in our married life where there was a real potential for discord over religion came when Lee wanted to change schools. He hated the big impersonal public high school he went to in ninth grade. He was lost and he wanted out.

SR: One thing we learned during this period is how crucial a parent's role is during the teenage years. It's natural to think kids need Mom and Dad most when they're small, but they need parents even more during adolescence. And there's no way to make appointments for soul-searching conversations. The trick is to be around enough so that when they want to talk, at whatever hour and in whatever place, they have a parent available. I interviewed the mother of two teenage girls recently and she said her biggest job was "hanging out" with them long enough so that they felt free to confide in her.

CR: During the fall of Lee's freshman year, we both covered the 1982 campaign. When I was on the road, Lee would call me late at night in hotel rooms and pour out his soul. He said to me years later, "I would've never had those conversations with you if you had been in front of me." That's certainly true; it's much easier to have talks like that at a distance. Of course, after we hung up I'd be left aching to hug him and he'd be fine and go back to sleep.

SR: Our own experiences caused us each to react differently to Lee's. Cokie had never gone to public schools, but I always had, and my rather irrational prejudice in favor of public education made me resistant to Lee's proposal that he change schools. The spring of his first year in high school, some family friends were visiting, and I told them what Lee wanted to do, but I kept insisting that staying in public school would be best. One woman, who was a trained therapist and knew what she was talking about, turned on me and warned, "You are not listening to your child." Stop imposing your own prejudices, she said, and start hearing what he has to say.

CR: It was one of those situations where an outsider makes all the difference. I had been trying to make the same point, but cautiously, because I didn't want to start a fight. Our friend finally caught Steve's attention.

SR: I was taken aback at first, even a bit offended. I was a great dad, how could I be making such a mistake? But I thought about it again and realized she was right. It was a hard lesson for me to learn, and then I had to learn another one when the school he settled on was Georgetown Prep, a Catholic school run by Jesuit priests. Usually, families threaten kids with the Jesuits, but this was his choice. His uncle Tommy had gone there, and it was just down the road from Stone Ridge, where Cokie had gone, and she'd known and dated many guys from Prep. But Catholic school was not part of our deal. Cokie and I had always said that we would train the kids ourselves. This was the first and only time in our whole marriage that we were faced with this kind of decision. Did I want Lee taught, and perhaps indoctrinated, by the Jesuits? I was extremely dubious, but he definitely wanted to go there, so I agreed to go see it.

CR: It's a spectacularly beautiful facility.

SR: That's true. It's surrounded by a golf course. But that didn't sell me on the place; the people I met there did. The director of admissions understood my concerns, all my uncertainty and ambivalence. I was hearing in my own mind an echo of my father saying, "I'll never be comfortable in your house if you marry a Catholic." This guy was terrific in terms of reassuring me that I would feel comfortable with my son in a Catholic school. I went through a struggle with my own feelings and I had to relearn and remember what I had come to understand earlier in our marriage, that the Church had helped instill in Cokie many of the qualities that I most admired. I had said to my parents over and over again that the important thing here is not the labels, not the stereotypes, but the reality. So finally I took my own advice, and when Lee got in I agreed to let him go, and Prep turned out to be the perfect place for him.

And I learned something important: when kids make a decision for themselves, they have a vested interest in showing they were right. So all the incentives are pointing in one direction. Lee wanted to prove to me that he had made the right choice, so he worked hard and did well. If we'd forced him to go somewhere else or stay in the public high school, all the incentives would've been different. Then he would have had a motive to prove that we were wrong. It was such a simple, profound lesson, but it took me a while to grasp it.

Lee flourished at Prep and then decided the only college he cared about was Duke. I'd be the first to admit that I was an Ivy League snob. My first reaction was, Duke? South? Fraternities? Why? The rest of the conversation with Lee went like this: "Remember when I wanted to go to Prep?" I said yes. "You didn't want me to go, did you?" No, I didn't. "I was right, wasn't I?" Yes, absolutely. "So why won't you trust me now?" I had no answer. His logic was airtight. He applied early decision to Duke and it, too, was the right place for him. The lesson I learned, at considerable cost, is clear: listen to your children. And I've always been grateful to that old friend of ours who first taught it to me.

CR: It's also true that what works for one kid doesn't necessarily work for another. Friends of mine who have large families tell me they have to constantly remind themselves to treat each child differently. Becca thrived at the public school. But Steve's right, it involves listening to children to know what they need. From a mother's perspective, I think it's easier to listen to girls than boys. They talk more. Also, girls tend to be more forthcoming. Becca and I would go to the mall and shop and have lunch and visit. We would cook together, which makes conversation easy. Still, at times listening isn't enough, talking's required. There were times when I would find myself saying, "We give all this lip service to values and morals that need to be taught in the home; what have I done lately?" In general, I believe in teaching by example as my mother did for me, but sometimes words are needed as well. You assume they know what you think about things, but how would they if you don't tell them?

SR: The kids needed their independence and we did, too, but we had to make sure that we didn't just become strangers living in the same household. We had dinners together most nights, but everyone was tired and not particularly eager to linger. On Sundays we had a pretty rigid rule that everybody showed up for a long, leisurely dinner with lots of good food and lots of conversation.

CR: We often spent all of Sunday together, but definitely Sunday dinner.

SR: It sounds odd to say you have to make appointments with your own children, but you do. To some extent it's out of consideration for them, because they have their own lives. But if everybody understands that everybody else is going to make the effort to be home, it becomes a habit, and that carried over. Years later, when Lee was in law school here in Washington and then working at a law firm, he still came home most Sundays for dinner.

CR: And he didn't even bring his laundry, which I thought was awfully nice!

SR: It's not only important to make appointments with the kids, it's important to make appointments with each other. It helped that we worked together, that we had the drive downtown and back together, that we would go on reporting trips and conventions and things like that together. But that was

more work than romance. We had to keep reminding ourselves of our old adage, "Have an affair with your wife!"

CR: We never traveled by ourselves at that stage of our life,
except for work, because we felt so strongly that we'd be
taking time away from the kids. When they started going to
summer camp, we would have a little more time together.
We were still working but it was a more relaxed atmosphere.
We would stay downtown for dinner without worrying about
rushing home. One year Lee was at a summer program at
Wellesley and we had planned to collect him there and go on
to Maine for a family vacation where Becca would meet us.
But for three or four days before that, we went by ourselves
to Quebec City. I remember looking at each other and saying,
"Do you remember how this used to be? This is fun." To
wander through a city and eat good meals and do some shopping and learn the history and go to museums. It had been a
long time since we'd done something like that, and we didn't
start doing it regularly again until they were in college.

SR: One place that became very important to all of us, and
still is, is the beach house we rent every year at Pawleys Island,
in South Carolina. When we were abroad, we had rented
houses on a number of Greek islands, and it was a type of
vacation we all loved. We'd unpack and unwind, sit there for
a week or two, and get into the rhythm of island life. When
we came back to America, we asked a friend, what's the closest we can come to a Greek island? And she suggested Pawleys. The first year we rented a house, sight unseen, for a
week. Soon we were up to two weeks, and last year was our
twenty-second year in the same house.

CR: We really are creatures of habit. Many Saturday nights
we go to the movies with the same couple and then to the
same restaurant afterward, and we get cranky if we have to

do something else. It's so pleasant, and so much easier than thinking. Once, after Becca was grown, she came home on a Saturday night and checked to see if our car was parked at its usual spot near the restaurant. Yep. She knew where to find us. It's comfortable—that thing Steve said he'd never become.

SR: Pawleys is like that. Lee was saying just the other night, "Gosh, I was thinking about Pawleys, how much fun it would be to be there with you."

CR: Another place that was always special to me was the Capitol. I'd practically grown up there, my seventh birthday party was in the House restaurant, I knew all the old waiters and doorkeepers and cops. I still get a thrill when I see the dome lit up at night, and Steve came to love it as much as I did.

SR: One of the things that I loved about the Hill was the opportunity to hear stories about Hale, which I made a point of asking about. Then I would come home and tell them to the kids. I felt that I was almost keeping an oral history for them about their grandfather. One day I was interviewing Danny Rostenkowski, the chairman of the Ways and Means Committee, in one of his many back offices. That man controlled more real estate than anybody in Congress. On his wall was this Plexiglas box, and inside was a gavel that had shattered in several pieces. He saw me looking at it and said, "You want to know how I broke that gavel?" When I said sure, he roared: "Getting your father-in-law to shut up!"

CR: The kids came to love the Capitol as well. When Lee was sixteen he was a page in the House, and he had a summertime romance with this darling girl page. Poor guy, every time they would be on the elevator together, trying to steal a minute alone, the door would open and there would be a parent or an uncle or a grandmother! He was surrounded. Miraculously, he still married the girl.

SR: We'd see him in the Speaker's lobby off the House chamber and he'd love to say, "Well, I've got to go to work," and march onto the House floor, where his parents, the big-deal reporters, couldn't go.

Becca worked a couple of summers at the Capitol as well, one of them in the office of California congressman Norman Mineta, where my brother Glenn worked. Norm was determined to rename an air force base in his district in honor of the Japanese-American astronaut killed in the *Challenger* accident, and an already scheduled ceremony provided a deadline for Pentagon action. Becca was assigned the job of making it all happen. She browbeat the military brass so mercilessly that when the air force guy arrived at Norm's office with the proper papers for the name change, he asked to meet Miss Rebecca Roberts. She deemed it the better part of wisdom to hide out in a back office so he wouldn't learn that his taskmaster was fifteen years old.

CR: When the children started to contemplate college, traveling around with them to look at different schools was a true eye-opener.

SR: They were seeing so much and absorbing so much every day that it concentrated their own thoughts about who they were and what they wanted. At dinner, those thoughts would come spilling out, and we had to be there to hear them. If we weren't, the moment would be gone. But Lee wasn't really interested in most of the places we'd visited; he had set his heart on Duke, and when he got in, there was no question where he'd go.

I think that the day your kids go off to college is one of the most indelible moments of parenthood. In Lee's case, we drove him down to Durham, and went to dinner at our hotel near the campus. It's the only time I've ever been in a restaurant where most of the tables were groups of three. I looked around the room and there were all these nervous, anxious kids and their nervous, anxious parents. The kids were allowed to get into their rooms in the early evening, and starting in late afternoon, they started gathering on the lawns outside their dorms with all their paraphernalia. It was like a lost tribe that had some mystical connection to each other, and they had been told to gather from all over the country and meet on this spot in Durham, North Carolina. The hour came and the tribe flooded into their dorms. By the next morning, less than twenty-four hours later, these bare empty buildings had been converted into hives of liveliness and color and sound. The tribe had occupied its turf, and our son had joined it. But we still had one left at home.

CR: We were looking forward to time with just the three of us and so was Becca. Two years as an only child sounded pretty good to her.

SR: We went back to Duke that fall for parents' weekend. Each college has its own traditions, of course, and at Duke, the rooters in the stands rattle their keys, to cheer on the pathetic football team. I looked around at our fellow parents and of course we all had rent-a-cars with a single key on a plastic ring that didn't make any noise! We all wanted to be loyal parents, but what is the sound of one key shaking?

CR: Neither one of our kids would apply to the schools we went to. Steve had gone out of the business of pushing Lee, but he pushed Becca a bit to apply to Harvard; she absolutely refused.

SR: I wanted her to take advantage of the preference for alumni children, but she wanted her own place, and she was right. In the end it came down to Michigan and Princeton, and after she made a visit to Princeton in the spring, she came home, announced she was going, and said, "Dad, I have a present for you." It was a Princeton sweatshirt. Now, it happened to be a Sunday night, and I was wearing a Harvard sweatshirt at the time. I ceremoniously took it off and put on my new one. Becca was so pleased she said, "Dad, we have a date for the Harvard–Princeton game," a date we kept. Later Cokie said to me, "See, do you get it now? You have lots of Harvard sweatshirts but no Princeton sweatshirt." It's always been a good metaphor—kids need to find their own place, their own identity. And like Lee choosing Prep and Duke, Becca was much better off—and so was I—if she made the decision for herself, and then had a stake in proving she was right.

CR: So we drove her to Princeton. We took two cars because she was keeping one at school. Steve and I would take turns getting in the car with her. She was in total costume. She had her hair up in a ponytail and her sunroof open and she was bopping her way off to college. I was trying to have a conversation with her about what lay ahead, how it could be complicated and she could find herself in situations that were emotionally difficult and intellectually challenging. I warned her that the work was going to be harder than any she had ever done before and I wanted her to feel like she shouldn't take on too much, shouldn't get caught in the myth that the women in our family could do everything all the time. She was insulted by that conversation; so much for maternal advice. We spent that night at my sister and brother-in-law's and then the next day moved her into her college room.

SR: We made a mistake. We stayed too long. We got her moved in and we should have left then, but we didn't, we stuck around for lunch. Lunch took a long time because the restaurants were all crowded, and Becca grew more and more agitated. She was ready to get settled with her roommates and start unpacking her stuff.

CR: And this is a kid who's essentially never given us any lip.

SR: Finally, after lunch, we went back to her dorm and she waved us a hurried good-bye. Now, colleges often have rules that parents have to leave by ten o'clock in the morning. They know this syndrome. They've seen enough fights on the lawns of dorms!

CR: She wanted us to go. She wanted to get started with college life.

SR: We walked off campus feeling a little bruised. She simply dismissed us, with no signs of regret or emotion of any kind. Then we saw a young woman weeping copiously into her parents' arms, beside herself with grief that they were leaving. Cokie turned to me with a smile: "Now, there's a satisfying child."

When we left Becca at Princeton our lives changed. We had always defined ourselves as parents first, and now that was no longer true. Our days became both easier and emptier. We could stay downtown and have dinner with friends, but when we got home the house was dark and cold. Except, of course, for Abner, the droop-eared, drool-stained basset hound Becca found for us as she left for college. Steve's first reaction when she brought him home was, "Why did God make a dog who looks like that?" But it's remarkable what a difference it makes to be greeted by a friendly face at the window, even one as goofy looking as Abner's. Becca understood, perhaps better than we did, that the old folks at home would need some companionship when Bradley Boulevard became an empty nest again, twenty-eight years after Cokie left for Wellesley.

CR: With Becca going away, I was not only losing my child but my friend. The idea that suddenly this friend wasn't there was shocking. I had prepared for it, but still I was bereft. I couldn't imagine what I would've done if I weren't working as hard as I was. I kept wondering, what did women do when they didn't work and their kids left home? I couldn't wrap my mind around it. I wasn't only missing my kids and seeing big changes in my daily life, I also had to redefine myself. From the moment I had a baby, my first responsibility was to those children. I saw my life first and foremost as that of a mother, and suddenly that wasn't my role anymore. At least not in a daily fashion the way it had been for twenty years. I felt almost uprooted.

SR: That was true for me, too. While I didn't define my-self as a father in quite the same way that Cokie defined herself as a mother, it was a very important part of what I did and who I was. So the kids' leaving left a big hole in our lives. But I also think it had a positive effect on our friendships.

CR: That's absolutely true.

SR: We've talked a lot about the importance of friends when we had young children, particularly since our own families were far away. But at that stage, with kids always around, our attention was distracted by dealing with them; we'd leave a party early because the kids were cranky or we'd jump up to make sure they didn't break something. Then, as the kids got older, we devoted most of our free time to being with them. Once they left home, we were able to spend more time and energy on friendships, and other members of our family.

CR: And not feel guilty about not being home.

SR: We also got more sleep, frankly. When the children were still living at home, we never quite fell asleep until we'd hear the back door slamming, announcing they were safely home. Cokie calls it the "praying them into the driveway" syndrome. When they went off to college, and we were no longer waiting up, the anxiety level went way down.

CR: The time with each other has been very nice, too. I think it could be rough to wake up with the children gone from home and look across the table and think, "Who are you?" Fortunately, we never asked that question. Working together all those years helped. We were around each other more than many couples with kids are.

SR: Kids going off to college is a real danger point in many marriages. I can't tell you how many students have sat in my office, with tears streaming down their faces, saying, "I just got a call that my parents are separating" or "I can't stand to think about going home for Thanksgiving because I can't please everybody." One incident really caught me up short. When Becca was getting married, I wrote a column about it, and gave it to the students in my writing course to criticize.

CR: This is a little dangerous for these students.

SR: Once they realize that God will not strike them dead when they criticize me, they actually enjoy it. Sometimes too much. But after they read the column, three or four young women told me essentially the same story: my parents have broken up and I think of a wedding as such a horrible time of rivalry and jealousy and tension that I can't relate to your story about your daughter.

CR: Just breaks your heart.

SR: It was a happy accident that I started teaching as an adjunct professor at George Washington University just a few years after Becca left. I always enjoyed teaching my own kids and reading what they had written, because that was what my father had always done with me. So my students have filled a real gap in my life, and it pleases me when one of them describes me as "our dad away from home." It's a reflection of how I feel that for the last few years we've celebrated Father's Day by inviting over several dozen of my favorite former students. One couple already has two daughters, who they've dubbed my first "grand-students." I love the term.

CR: The mantelpiece in the kitchen is reserved for pictures of our surrogate grandchildren—nieces, grand-nieces and

-nephews, godchildren—there are a lot of them running around.

SR: We were also lucky that our kids were in college not more than about three or four hours away from home—the ideal distance. Far enough away so we couldn't just drop in on them but close enough to come home for a weekend. Even though the kids were away at school, they were still very much a part of our lives, and they usually came home for the summer.

One summer Becca worked at the Caucus on Women's Issues, and one day they were holding a press conference. Talk about family values. Our daughter had helped arrange the event, Cokie's mother was one of the speakers, and Cokie and I were both covering it. If that wasn't enough, after I wrote my story for *U.S. News,* a researcher at the magazine called the caucus to verify some facts and the person who answered the phone was Becca! Of course she told them not to believe a word I had written!

CR: I spent a lot of time in Princeton during Becca's sophomore and junior years because my sister, who was mayor of the town, was dying of cancer. And Becca was unbelievably wonderful with Barbara. She'd drive her places, amuse her, fill in for her at public events, and at the end, physically carry her from room to room.

SR: I was worried about Becca. Caring for a dying aunt is not usually part of a college experience, and I didn't want her to feel burdened. But she absolutely insisted on doing it, and I was very proud of her.

CR: That was a tense time between us, though, because I think it took you a while to understand how devastated I was and how much I needed to be there.

SR: True, but I knew how devoted you were to Barbara, and that was part of what I loved about you, that you would be that loyal.

CR: We had one fairly unpleasant conversation about it, but then you finally said, "Look, if you need to be there, then be there. Don't worry about it."

SR: We also had some very happy times visiting Becca at Princeton, where she joined an all-women's singing group, the Tigressions. Listening to them gave me a great sense of déjà vu, since I had sat through so many of Cokie's concerts during our college days. But one song was my favorite. It was called "Dedicated to the One I Love." Becca sang the solo, and she would always haul some guy out of the audience . . .

CR: . . . generally an old guy . . .

SR: . . . and sing the song to him, vamping and flirting the whole time. More than once she picked me out . . .

CR: . . . he loved it . . .

SR: . . . and it became a bit with all of her friends cheering her on! Then, at her wedding, many of her friends from the singing group were here as bridesmaids or guests and they cooked up a scheme.

CR: Without telling her, the band started playing "Dedicated" as the friends crooned the background vocals and pulled her up on the bandstand for her solo.

SR: So she sang our old song to her new husband. Not to Dad. A fitting gesture.

CR: You took it well.

SR: After Lee graduated, he decided to take a year off between college and law school, and went to work for CBS in New York on their election coverage. He rented a nice little apartment, but he needed furniture, and he and Cokie rented a U-Haul truck and drove it down to Ikea, the furniture store, which has a big branch about forty-five minutes away from us in Virginia.

CR: Lee said, "We're going to pull up in this U-Haul and the manager's going to come out and welcome us personally." Wrong! There were about forty U-Hauls in the parking lot with mothers going shopping with their kids.

SR: I remembered so vividly going to New York at age twenty-two for my first job at the *Times*. I had gone by bus from my parents' home in New Jersey the night before my first day, and here was Lee driving to New York for his first job and first apartment. There was a great sense of continuity.

CR: He had carefully counted out all of his money for his trip to New York. But he didn't realize that a U-Haul cost more than a car in tolls, so when he reached the Lincoln Tunnel he didn't have enough money. Somehow he convinced them to take a check!
    After the '90 election CBS kept him on because it was clear we were going to war in the Persian Gulf and they needed more hands here in Washington. He was going to law school in the fall, so it was silly not to move in with us until then, and we wound up having a great time together. Once the war started, all three of us were working around the clock—there were times where we would bump into each other at four o'clock in the morning, the first sighting of the day. We

were all engaged in the same endeavor and we all had strong opinions and we enjoyed talking it out.

SR: It was the first time we dealt with a child as a professional colleague. During this period I occasionally hosted a show on CBS called *Nightwatch*. It went on the air in the middle of the night, but we'd tape interviews during the day, and one Sunday during the war I went to the bureau and dropped by the control room and there was Lee. He was answering the phones and everyone else was schmoozing. I went over to say hello, and right in front of him was a bank of monitors tuned to the other networks. As I was standing behind him, patting him on the shoulder, up popped a picture of Mom on ABC! After I left the room, he told us later, a silence descended and everyone looked at Lee. He rolled his eyes toward the ceiling: "Now you know why I want to go to law school!"

Two years later Becca went off to her first apartment in Chicago. It took all day to rent the size U-Haul truck we wanted, it was driving me nuts! By the time we got the truck home, it was late in the afternoon. I called the Pier One store in the neighborhood and found it was open for about another twenty minutes. So we raced over and it was like a TV game show where contestants have three minutes to fill their shopping carts. Becca would say, "These are nice glasses, I'd like four." And I'd say, "No, you would need twelve!" It was on that shopping trip that she dubbed me Daddy Blank Check. When we reached the checkout counter, the young woman at the cash register looked at Becca and looked at me: "First apartment?" I kept thinking of our honeymoon, when the clerk at the hotel gift shop spied my shiny new wedding ring and teased, "Just married?"

As the children moved on to other places and other lives, we enjoyed going to visit them. Those trips were part of the readjustment in our relationship. When parents are on the kids' turf, the younger generation becomes the hosts, the experts. I remembered when our parents came to visit us, how we felt more like grown-ups, and the tables were now turned in Chicago or New York or wherever they were living. *They* were the tour guides. They showed off *their* favorite places. Becca lived within walking distance of Wrigley Field, and she took me to my first and only ball game there.

CR: After a year in Chicago, Becca moved to Philadelphia and started working for a political consultant, so I regularly used her as a source! It was a treat to have her just a short train ride away.

SR: Lee was even closer. He went to law school here and then worked as a lawyer in Washington for three years. His apartment was just a few blocks from my office at *U.S. News* and on his way to work he would walk right past my parking lot. Some mornings I'd see him on the street and we'd stop and chat, but he was usually at work much earlier than me! He offered to give me a key to his apartment, saying I might like a place to drop by during the day. Cokie demanded, "What for?" and nixed that idea fast.

I had moved from *The New York Times* to *U.S. News* while the kids were in college. Our professional lives changed at the same time our personal ones did. During that period I came to understand why "midlife crisis" is such a common phenomenon. The kids left home, and like a lot of other people, I took stock of my career, wondering about the future. It all happens at once. I think of it as the forty-five-year-old disease, because that's when it happened to me, but people hit a crunch point at different ages.

CR: This midlife crisis stuff is much more a male thing—I haven't seen it happen to many women I know. I'll be curious to see how it evolves in future generations, but the expectations of many women my age were so different from what our lives turned out to be, both for good and for bad. Since we grew up at a time when the ultimate goal in life was marrying well, most of us measured our success by whether in fact we had succeeded in doing that. What we're doing professionally is like icing on the cake. It never occurred to most of us that we'd be in this place at this age. Whereas the men we knew always had great expectations, unrealistic expectations. Half of them expected to be president or editors in chief of newspapers. Then they come face-to-face with life in their late forties, or early fifties. They realize what didn't happen and what's never going to happen and they have a tough adjustment to make. Whereas for women, of my age and acquaintance anyway, we look at what we're doing professionally with some surprise: "Hey, that's pretty cool."

SR: Well, it was cool. As National Public Radio became more popular, so did Cokie. After *The Lawmakers* went off the air, she contributed pieces to *The MacNeil-Lehrer NewsHour* and then started making occasional appearances on *This Week with David Brinkley*. In 1988, when she signed a contract with ABC, she was better known and better paid than I was. I don't pretend the transition was an easy one, but from the beginning I don't think our core relationship ever depended on who made more money or appeared more often on television. That was still true even after the balance shifted, and I give Cokie a lot of the credit; she never tried to use her new position to change the relationship.

CR: Oh, please, what would I do?

SR: I think a lot of marriages founder on this. The person who makes more money, the person who is more visible, can easily use that as leverage. It happens all the time.

CR: I do remember saying to you, there were years and years and years when not only did you make more money than I did, but I made hardly any money at all, and you didn't resent that. I know there's a difference between attitudes about men and women on this question, I'm not stupid, but I think you heard me.

SR: Cokie's success in many ways has been liberating for me. I was able to make some decisions, like teaching college, not based on money because I was no longer the chief bread-winner.

CR: Which is a terrible burden. I had never really thought about it because I was a girl. We have this expectation of men that they are supposed to be out there making it right for the whole family and it's an unfair expectation.

SR: Things had come to a head for me at the *Times*. I had left the Hill to cover the last two years of the Reagan White House, but as the Bush Administration was coming in, a new bureau chief came in as well and decided to shift reporters' assignments. And I realized that I was running out of options for advancement.

CR: He had always talked about this problem, even when we were very young. He would say, a guy joins the *Times*, goes to New York, goes to Washington, goes abroad, and then he's thirty-six years old and where is he? Well, Steven was older than that, but still, the pyramid was narrow at the top and he could do one of three things: keep doing what he'd always done, become an editor, or leave.

SR: I had seen several generations of people above me go through that process and I knew it was inevitable. One of the options that the *Times* suggested was becoming an editor and in some ways it made sense. I had always produced a lot of ideas and helped plan our political coverage and tried to be a mentor to young people in the bureau. But I had become a reporter because I loved being out every day and learning something new, and I feared that by coming inside I'd stop learning and deal only with recycled information. More important, I had to be honest with myself—would I be happy losing my visibility, my byline, at the same time that Cokie's career was taking off? When I asked that question the answer was no, I would not be happy, and in fact I thought it would be risky for our relationship. So I decided to accept an offer as a senior writer from *U.S. News and World Report,* where I would have a chance to move beyond straight reporting and establish myself as an analyst and commentator.

CR: I couldn't imagine him ever leaving the *Times,* and I worried that would put us in a bind at some point because his loyalty was so great. Look, I'm the beneficiary of his loyalty to me. I think it's wonderful. But I worried that his loyalty to the *Times* meant he could never leave. For many years, if you woke Steve up in the middle of the night and said, "Who are you?" he would say, "A *New York Times* reporter."

SR: After I made the decision Cokie joked that it was a question of my leaving the *Times* or leaving her. A gross exaggeration, but the experience reminded me of that series I had done about divorce back in California. I remember one therapist saying to me, listen, marriages are forced to carry so many burdens. People want to change their lives, but there's not much they *can* actually change. They can't change the way they look, at least beyond a certain point. They can't change their skin color or ethnic origin or who their parents are. They can't even change their basic talents and abilities. What they can change is their spouse, and marriages can easily crack apart under that pressure. So I was much better off trading in a twenty-five-year job instead of a twenty-three-year marriage. And I actually think that leaving the *Times* was very healthy for our relationship.

CR: Partly because that last year had grown so unpleasant. You were no fun. After you had been gone from the *Times* for a few months, the sunny you returned. I suddenly looked around one day and realized, "I've got my husband back." Neither one of us was fully aware of how destructive that period had been until it was over.

Steven felt unappreciated at the *Times;* everything about that relationship had gone stale. So starting a new job where people wanted him and flattered him made him feel good as a person. We've been saying that in any marriage, it's important to appreciate each other and do the things that work for each other. We can't make bosses do that, no matter how hard we try. And no matter how hard we try to leave work problems at the office, they're bound to affect life at home as well.

SR: But even after I left the paper I had to come to terms with Cokie's growing celebrity. In those last months of turmoil at the *Times,* one possibility was returning to Capitol Hill. It probably was not a good idea anyway, but the bureau chief said no and appointed a woman to the job instead. At one point my frustrations came spurting out and I said to Cokie, "This woman only got the job because she was a woman." I was hurt and angry about it, and my feelings spilled over onto Cokie. It was one of the few times that I expressed any resentment or rivalry toward her, and I didn't like the way I felt or sounded. At that point I decided that the only way to manage this was to stop being competitive. Our relationship was too important to put in jeopardy over professional jealousy.

CR: There were some fairly dramatic conversations where I would announce, "I'm quitting. This is not worth it." There has never been any question in my mind about what the priority is here. Let's make that clear.

SR: Every time you said that . . .

CR: . . . you always said, "That's crazy."

SR: I never expected you or wanted you to give up your career. I knew what made you happy. This goes back to our first days in New York, with you parading around in your nightgown in the middle of the afternoon.

CR: I had a coat on.

SR: What made it easier is that I've always been Cokie's biggest supporter. People come up to me all the time and say, "I'm a great fan of your wife's," and my answer is, "So am I." I knew her talents long before the wider world did.

CR: And had confidence in me long before I did.

SR: But people don't always believe me. In fact, there was even a magazine piece written by a woman who was absolutely determined to portray me as this fragile male who simply could not handle being married to a famous woman.

CR: She didn't like you. That's all I can tell you. I don't know why, but she plain didn't like you.

SR: Apparently not. But it seems to me that the key to sanity is a sense of proportion. One day a TV interviewer asked Cokie to retape a conversation because she had talked a little too long and kept him from saying more. Here's a guy who appears on national TV all the time and he was bickering about a few seconds. The thought occurred to me: "How much is enough?" Somebody else will always be richer, better looking, appear on TV more often. Since then, that phrase has become a maxim we say to each other when things are getting a little nutty. How much is enough?

That time we hit on something important on our own, but often we've needed someone looking in from outside to make us realize that there's some lesson we needed to learn. Familiarity is a great gift, but over a long period of time we've occasionally fallen into patterns of behavior where we've irritated each other and not listened. And sometimes it's valuable to have someone else point that out.

CR: I have a sense from my friends that good marriage counselors do that. They're voices from outside saying, "Listen to yourselves." Steven had this experience after reading a book by the linguist Deborah Tannen.

SR: She's a shrewd observer of speech patterns and the way people relate to each other, and a few years ago I interviewed her for a program on public television. One thing that would drive me crazy about Cokie, and occasionally still does, is her tendency to interrupt me. It caused some real tensions. There were evenings after parties with very unhappy recriminations. But I had to study Deborah Tannen's work to do this TV show, and she says in one of her books that this is a common problem between men and women because they approach conversations differently. Men see them as competitions . . .

CR: . . . as speechmaking . . .

SR: . . . as occasions to score points . . .

CR: . . . to show off . . .

SR: Women see conversations as a more cooperative endeavor, and when women chime in, or interrupt, they think they're helping.

CR: That's the way we talk. And the truth is, when Steven listens to a conversation between women, he can't stand it. We're constantly interrupting and going off on a path and coming back. We all know what we're doing. It's a completely different language from the one men speak. I can't abide going to a meeting with men because they rattle on trying to impress someone, and who cares? I feel like they're wasting my time. I could be doing something important like folding the laundry! By and large, women don't behave like that. So when Steven read this book, it hit him in the face— hey, this is what we've been arguing about all these years. She's just acting like a girl.

SR: I can't say we've never had a disagreement on this subject since. But that insight sanded down a particularly sharp edge in our relationship. And even though it's true that the way women talk can be irritating, it's also true that I generally prefer the company of women to men. I don't go out and pal around with a lot of guys who are insensitive or uninterested in what women say. I find that by and large women talk about relationships and men talk about . . .

CR: . . . sports . . .

SR: . . . issues. I'm more interested in relationships. I like having conversations with women at parties. I've always liked listening to talk about people and families. I remember as a little boy sopping up the stories my grandfathers and grandmother used to tell. My father's father in particular fascinated me with tales of life as a youth in Eastern Europe, a place that seemed so strange and foreign to an American boy in the 1950s. As I grew older I wished I had some way to connect to those stories, but it never seemed possible—I always felt walled off from my past. Cokie's direct ancestor first landed in America in 1620, and there's a good record of her family going back quite a long time. In some ways, I've always envied her that. For me, as for most American Jews, those records don't exist. Our ancestors often fled the old country in panic and fear and didn't want to look back. Whoever stayed behind was slaughtered during the Holocaust. And for most of us, our homelands were locked behind the Iron Curtain; we couldn't visit them even if we wanted to. And when those places did open up, after the fall of communism, there was no one left to preserve the records or the graves or the memories.

I was very fortunate, because I knew my grandfather well, he lived only three blocks away, and his storytelling provided me with a rich oral heritage about his hometown of Bialystok, which is now in eastern Poland. My family name was Rogowsky, the "sky" was dropped at Ellis Island, and my birth certificate says Rogow, not Roberts. My father changed our name when I was two, but my grandparents and all my cousins on that side were Rogow and still are.

Living in Europe had brought me closer to my heritage, and after the fall of the Berlin wall, we planned a trip to Eastern Europe, starting in Vienna, where our niece was living. I badly wanted to see Bialystok and Cokie agreed, but I had no idea how to start. So I literally looked up Bialystok in the New York City phone book, and found an old-age home on the Lower East Side with that name. I called the number, described what I wanted to do, and asked if anybody there knew the town. I was in luck, the director of the home hailed from Bialystok, and after we talked awhile he told me to write to his friend Anatole who lives in Warsaw and studies the Jewish history of eastern Poland. I wrote to him and heard nothing back, but I had his phone number, so when we got to Warsaw, I called. Anatole said, well, I'm getting old, it's a long trip, but when I heard your family name I decided I had to help because Artur and Shmuel Rogowsky were two of my father's best friends when I was growing up and they must be your great-uncles. It turns out they're not my uncles. But Anatole agreed to guide us, we hired a car and driver, and we set out the next day for Bialystok, about two and a half hours due east of Warsaw. On the way we stopped at Anatole's home village, and while we're walking around he talked about how fondly he remembered Artur Rogowsky singing the prayers on Friday night in a beautiful voice.

CR: I said that settles it, he can't be a relative of yours, nobody in your family can sing a note.

SR: So much for sentiment. Anyway, we were standing in the main square when I said, I've always heard my family name comes from a village around here. And Anatole answered, I know the place, but I need directions. I was stunned. I'd come wanting to find some sign—a birth record, a gravestone—that my family had been there.

CR: We both thought our best bet was a graveyard.

SR: So we drove down this dusty country road in rural Poland . . .

CR: . . . it could have been the nineteenth century, there were oxen pulling carts . . .

SR: . . . and we came to a roadside sign that reads ROGOWO. There was my name!

CR: It was a sign all right.

SR: I said I was looking for a sign. I didn't bargain for a real road sign! There were, of course, no Jews left in the village; still, we took a lot of pictures under the sign. Then we went on to Bialystok, which turned out to be thoroughly depressing. The town is one monument to devastation after another.

On that corner, a synagogue was set on fire, killing five thousand Jews. In this field, the Nazis slaughtered six thousand Jews. We went to the graveyard, but most of it was overgrown, except for a small plot that Anatole tended himself. There was an obelisk on the plot, a memorial to about seventy-five Jews killed in a pogrom in 1906. My grandfather would have been about sixteen in 1906 and I realized that this was probably the pogrom that had helped drive him out of Bialystok. I approached the obelisk, where the names were written in Hebrew or Yiddish. When Anatole slowly started reading the names, I realized that, in effect, we were saying "Kaddish," the Jewish prayer for the dead, and I remembered enough from my Hebrew-school training to point to each name as Anatole read it.

CR: You could actually read a good many of them once you started.

SR: I could follow it. When he said "Katz," I knew which one was Katz. I'm sure some of them knew my family, my grandfather. His name could have easily been on that obelisk. Then I said to Anatole, you know the one place I always remember my grandfather talking about was the railroad station. My great-grandfather was a cloth merchant and Grandpa Abe would always go down to the railroad station and pick up packages for him. It was from that railroad station that he left for Palestine. Anatole's face lit up; you're in luck, he said, because the railroad station is still the way it was a hundred years ago. It's practically the only building left in Bialystok your grandfather might have seen. We went to the station, I walked out onto the platform, and then I knew I was standing in his footsteps. I could almost feel his presence. I said to myself, "Pop, we survived, and I've come back to prove it." Then I broke down and sobbed for twenty minutes, totally without warning.

It was a moment of profound meaning. It connected me

to my whole past. I wrote about it for *U.S. News* and was flooded with letters from people saying, "How can I do what you did? How can I get in touch with my ancestry?" Many wanted to share the stories of their own families and one of them wrote, this is where my family's from, this is what the name was, maybe it has some meaning for you. I realized that that's what all those letters were about; people were searching for meaning, for connection, for some sign of their own that their families had been a part of history.

CR: There is a coda to the story. Steve's grandmother was from a small village outside of Bialystok called Eishishok and we had heard the story many times about how his grandfather and grandmother had met—how he fell in love with a picture of her in a photographer's window. But we couldn't find Eishishok. It wasn't on any map. We knew it couldn't be too far from Bialystok, they didn't have cars, but no one we asked knew what we were talking about. There was a town with a similar name, and when we got home we said to Steve's dad, "We couldn't find Eishishok anywhere; it simply doesn't exist. Is it maybe this other town?" He said, "No, no, no, I don't have this wrong, it is Eishishok." We let that pass. Then Steve's sister and I went one day to the Holocaust Museum and lining the central tower of the museum are photographs from the town of Eishishok. We couldn't find it because it no longer exists. It was completely wiped out.

SR: Also, it was in Lithuania and it had a different name in Lithuanian.

CR: I grabbed Laura and whispered, "This is your grand-mother's town! We couldn't find it but here it is!" They were studio portraits of ordinary life, weddings and birthdays and anniversaries, pictures that would have hung in photographers' windows. They were taken perhaps fifteen or twenty years after Steve's grandmother had left the town, but of course there had to be relatives in those pictures.

SR: I got a phone call after my article appeared from a cousin of mine who was sobbing: "I read your article and I'm so grateful. We have all of these scrapbooks and mementos of my husband's family, but I never had anything about our family to show our children. And now I do." And I said, "Pam, that's why I went, I went for all of us."

CR: We were particularly pleased to be able to come home and tell Steve's dad about our trip; after all, it was his father whose story we were trying to trace.

SR: I always had a wonderful relationship with my father. Early in his professional life he had written and published children's books, so he was a man of words. His younger brother, for whom our son, Lee, is named, had also been a writer, and after my uncle was killed in a plane crash, I felt strongly that I was carrying on a family tradition by becoming a journalist. Dad was always my best editor and biggest supporter, and the day my first professional article was published in *The Nation* magazine—I was eighteen at the time—he drove me into New York and we scoured every newsstand in lower Manhattan looking for a copy. When we finally found one, with my name on the cover, I think he was more excited than I was. In later years, when I started appearing on television, I would call home every time I was on, and I still do. Since Cokie had lost her father so young, I knew how blessed I was and tried not to take that blessing for granted. I would look around at my friends and realize that I was one of the very few people at my age to have both parents alive and healthy, and we made a big effort to see them every chance we could. When Dad turned eighty in December of 1996, we had a party for him at our house.

CR: It was a great party. He loved it.

SR: Some of the most touching speeches were made by his children-in-law, who talked about what a loving figure he had been in their lives. We tried to think of something special to mark his birthday, something more permanent than a set of golf clubs, and we decided to honor his lifelong interest in books and libraries. Right near my parents' winter home in Palm City, Florida, was a branch of the county library that they would visit several times a week.

CR: They were still in the library habit. They had been active supporters of public libraries.

SR: We decided to raise some money within the family and name the children's reading room at this local library in honor of my parents, but we were having trouble finding a date when everybody could come to a dedication ceremony. I didn't have a premonition, but I did say to my sister, who was doing most of the planning, "Let's not wait." So we picked a date that worked for most of us, and about a hundred people came, including some of my parents' oldest friends. Dad was deeply touched. My mother even joked that it was a pleasure to unveil a plaque honoring people who were still alive. A few weeks later they came to Passover on their way back to New Jersey for the summer and in early May I called my parents late one afternoon . . .

CR: To say you were going to be on TV.

SR: Actually, to say I wasn't going to be on TV, as I had expected to be. I reached my mother, and before I could speak she said in a rush, "Steven, I have something to tell you, your father has had a stroke." He had had a stroke the night before but she hadn't called me.

CR: Any of us. She hadn't called any of us.

SR: If you didn't call, it wasn't serious, it wasn't real.

CR: He was in intensive care but the doctors led us to believe that he wasn't in a life-threatening situation.

SR: I consulted with my siblings and we agreed that Mom would need help over a period of time.

CR: Everyone would take turns visiting her.

SR: It so happened Cokie and I were free the next day, so we took the first shift.

CR: We walked in the hospital and I tried to prepare Steven for a terrible shock because I'd spent a good deal of time with people in intensive care units. I thought, we're going to get in there and Steve's going to be undone by this. His father's not going to be communicating, there are going to be wires and monitors everywhere, he's not going to look like himself, and it's going to be so unsettling and disorienting and sad. But when we walked in the room, we found his father joking and talking, asking about the stock market and the ball scores. Totally 100 percent with it. His speech was slurred but that was about it.

SR: Also, he was having trouble swallowing. Throughout the day he actually seemed to be recovering, and it was heartening for everybody. Late in the afternoon I went to a pay phone down the hall from his room and got my messages, and one was from the president of George Washington University, calling to follow up on conversations we had been having about my taking a full-time faculty chair. When I returned the call he said that everything was set, my appointment would be approved the next day. I went back to Dad's room and relayed the news and he was very pleased and excited. It turned out to be the last thing I ever told him.

CR: He had been talking nonstop and he needed some rest, so we took Steve's mother out to dinner, leaving instructions for the nurse: "We're only two minutes away, call us if there's any reason at all." At three o'clock in the morning the phone rang. Nobody heard it at first. Finally, I shook Steven awake: "The phone's ringing." I think his mother didn't want to hear it, because it couldn't be good.

SR: I raced into the kitchen and picked up the phone and it was the intensive care nurse saying, "Your father has coded." I didn't know immediately what that meant . . .

CR: . . . he had had another stroke . . .

SR: . . . it meant that the code had gone out for emergency personnel. She wanted to know whether he had a living will and I said, "Is he still alive?" She said, "Yes, but it doesn't look good." And then her voice caught: "Oh dear, they've just come out of his room. He's gone."

CR: It was very sudden, almost like a traffic accident. From Monday morning till Tuesday night . . .

SR: He was still so vigorous that he was planning to captain his boat in a race on Wednesday.

CR: In fact, his crew called on Wednesday morning to ask what time to pick him up.

SR: I had to turn to my mother and tell her that my father was dead. I just thank God we were there. Cokie was holding

Mom. I can't imagine her getting that phone call all alone. Then I had to call my siblings. I felt very bad that by the luck of the draw, I had had that last day with Dad and they had not.

CR: And they did, too.

SR: It was very unfair. I have memories they don't have. We were allowed to go to the hospital and see him for the last time that morning. I'm still haunted by the sight of him.

CR: Well, it's such a strong visual image. For a long time after Barbara died, I couldn't remember her alive. I could only see her dead. My sister died at home and it took a while for the funeral home to arrive to collect her. I thought she looked lonely all by herself in the bed while everyone else was rushing around making preparations, so I got in bed and sang to her. It's almost impossible to erase that image. Steve's parents had been married fifty-seven years. His mother had to somehow find the strength to tell her husband good-bye. When she did, the nurse in the intensive care unit who must have seen this countless times broke down in tears herself. She was a kind, sensitive soul.

SR: That was, without a doubt, the worst day of my life.

CR: In cases like your dad, people always say, "Well, he lived a long and full life and he died without being disabled." And all of that is true. But it doesn't help. That's the part that people never understand. It's still very painful. Would you prefer for him not to be disabled? Of course. Or would you prefer for him to have lived to eighty instead of fifty-eight? Of course. Does it make it any easier? Of course not. It's a cliché, but it's a cliché because it's true. In your parents' eyes, you become an adult when you have children. In your own eyes, I think you fully become an adult and fully aware of your own mortality when you lose a parent.

SR: Even now I expect to hear from him when I've done some television show or written something that he would enjoy. It was so much a part of me to know that he was there and cheering me on.

CR: This was May of 1997, and both kids were about to get married, Lee in June and Becca in August. He would have loved that so much, watching Becca walk down that aisle. That's all I could think of the minute I heard the news. He missed seeing it. He didn't miss much. He did see his children and grandchildren grow up and know they were well launched. But, boy, he would've loved those weddings.

SR: When my father talked about my mother he would say, "You know, separately we're very flawed people, but together we make a good team." Over fifty-seven years they were like two trees holding each other up, or vines that were so intertwined it was impossible to tell where one ended and the other began.

CR: Some women, even when they've had wonderful marriages, blossom somewhat when they're given a sense of freedom. But it's been very very tough for your mother.

SR: There's a hole in the center of her life that will never be filled. It is the price you pay for a long, happy marriage—when one partner dies, the survivor is very lonely. In my view, it's a bargain worth making, but my father would openly muse about this in the last year or two of his life. He'd say to my mother, "Wouldn't it be fitting if we could go together?" And my mother would reply, "Will, just give me enough notice so I'll have time to pack." But he gave her no time, no warning at all.

As Cokie mentioned, my dad died just weeks before our summer of weddings. We only had two kids and they decided to get married eight weeks apart. Great planning.

CR: Lee and Liza met when they were teenagers; they were both pages at the Capitol and they had a sweet puppy-love summer.

SR: I remembered Liza vividly. One evening she and Lee and Cokie drove home together from the Capitol and found a note in the kitchen from Rosie, the kids' old baby-sitter, who had been there to feed the dog. It read simply, "There's a bat in the living room." Lee and Cokie were ready to run right out of there; Liza grabbed a broom and drove the creature out—a take-charge woman even at sixteen.

CR: Liza lived in California, so it was not easy to keep up a relationship once the school year started. They wrote each other for a while. But then they lost touch. They went to colleges in different parts of the country and didn't get back together until they were grown.

SR: After graduation she was working on Wall Street and he was in law school. She had a business meeting here in Washington and called him up out of the blue. Obviously, there was a spark between them that had never quite gone out, and when they saw each other again it heated up instantly.

CR: Liza went on to journalism school at Columbia and then moved to Washington. Lee would bring her over for Sunday-night dinner and we became great friends. She even worked for me as a research assistant during the 1994 campaign. I kept hoping Lee would do the smart thing and ask her to marry him, then one day he invited to me to lunch, and I sensed something was up. In the middle of this stuffy dining room, he solemnly said, "I need your advice about diamonds." I wanted to whoop and hug him and make a big hoopla, but he would have killed me. I didn't know anything about diamonds, but told him where we could go to learn, and then we had to sit through this insufferable food service. Finally, lunch ended and I was able to grab him. Then we went jewelry shopping.

SR: It was supposed to be this big secret. That night, when I asked Cokie what she talked to Lee about, she got this strange look and mumbled, "Nothing much." So immediately I guessed what was up. No one in the family believes I can keep a secret, but I kept that one.

The wedding was in Southern California, Lisa's home. A priest was presiding, but Lee wanted to do what we had done, have part of the ceremony recognize his Jewish heritage, and he asked me to perform the role of tribal elder that Justice Goldberg had for us. As the wedding approached, and I was thinking of what to say, out of the blue one day we received a letter from Arthur Goldberg's son Bobby. He had been going over his father's papers, and found the original hand-written notes the justice had used at our wedding. In fact, they were written on little pieces of notepaper . . .

CR: . . . it was a telephone pad . . .

SR: . . . from the Waldorf-Astoria, where the UN ambassador has a residence. The symbolism was perfect. I was able to use Goldberg's words as the text for my own remarks, almost thirty-one years later. And I made sure to repeat my favorite phrase, "Never cause a woman to weep, because God counts her tears." The priest got so caught in the ecumenical spirit of things that he expressed the hope, off the cuff, that Lee would read the same words at the marriages of *his* children.

CR: Meanwhile, Becca was living in Philadelphia and dating Dan Hartman, a young man who grew up in Tennessee and was working for a financial consulting firm.

SR: I hold only one thing against Dan—I root avidly for the Duke basketball team and he went to the University of North Carolina, their arch rivals. But I knew Dan would make a good son-in-law one day when he left me a phone message: "Dan Hartman here. Just in case you missed it on the news, North Carolina beat Duke last night by one point in the last six seconds. I knew you'd want to know." Click. The guy had guts, and a sense of humor, a pretty good combination. But it took at least another year after that call before he phoned to set up an appointment.

CR: Oh, that was funny because Steve didn't catch on.

SR: Yes, I did.

CR: No, you didn't, but I didn't either at first. I told you one night when you came home, "Dan's looking for you. He's left a message." Then suddenly I realized, why did he have to talk to you and not me? "Oh, my goodness, he's probably calling to ask for your blessing to marry Rebecca." Then you wouldn't call him back.

SR: I did the next day, but I needed time to collect my thoughts. On my way down to the office, I was rehearsing my lines in my head. I only had one daughter, and this was only going to happen once in my life. When I reached him, and he said that he wanted to come talk to me, I replied, "Dan, I think I know what this is about. It's very honorable of you to want to come see me, but if you're busy, we can do this on the phone." And he said, "No, no, no, there's only one proper way to do this and that's in person." A well-brought-up young man. So we agreed that he would come down on the train from Philadelphia and I would meet him in a restaurant at the train station for a drink, and then Cokie would join us for dinner. Now, Dan's consulting firm does a lot of work with the D.C. government, and when we walked into the restaurant, sitting at the next table was half of his office, having dinner with several city officials. Poor Dan; his face turned white! When he told me what was going on, I asked if he wanted to go somewhere else, but when he said no, I suggested, "Well, before we start talking, why don't you go over there and say hello and then you won't feel uncomfortable." Which he did.

CR: Of course all his office buddies knew what was going on, or figured it out pretty quickly.

SR: He was so dear, he didn't have the ring with him . . .

CR: . . . it was being made . . .

SR: . . . but he had a photograph that he brought to show us.

CR: Becca didn't know he was coming, she was still in the dark, but we knew what day he was going to propose, so we stayed by the phone waiting for a call.

SR: When she did call, her voice just sparkled with excitement. "I'm getting married," she said, and I don't think there are three happier words in the language. People kept asking me whether I felt sad about "losing" my daughter, but that question never made any sense to me. First of all, I wasn't "losing" her, I was gaining a football-watching buddy. More importantly, if you've been lucky enough to have a good marriage, isn't that what you want for your own children? How could you possibly have any regrets? After the wedding one friend said to me, "I've seen beaming brides before, but I never saw a father of the bride beam so much."

CR: From the time she was born, Becca knew she wanted to get married at home. In fact, she often joked that she could only pick out two things for her wedding, the groom and the dress. But actually there were many choices to make, and she was determined that everybody be seated at a table for dinner, a logistical nightmare with seven hundred guests. I didn't know what we were going to do if the weather turned bad. I had tents ordered to cover the entire yard if I needed them, but they only protect against drizzle, not a blowing, whipping wind. I kept fretting, "What am I going to do if a hurricane comes?" I finally decided that there was only one thing I could do—move the entire event to the gym of my old high school, Stone Ridge. It's not far away, people could get there, we could still use the caterer. I called the headmistress, a nun who is a good friend of mine, and informed her, "If there's a hurricane, I need the gym." I love the school and I've been quite involved with it, but the headmistress had a problem with my plan: the annual book fair was going on in the gym the same day. I was so panic-stricken that I shamelessly pressured her: "Well, then, that's a good reason to pray really hard that there's no hurricane."

Even with all that heavenly intervention, with about two weeks to go, my degree of terror hit fever pitch. At some point I was going to have to make decisions, not keep everything on hold. So I became best friends with the long-term weather forecaster for NOAA, the National Oceanic and Atmospheric Administration. His name was Ed Olenic, and after a while he didn't bother to wait for my call. He was so sweet about it. He would call me first thing in the morning and tell me the forecast. But he could never voice the only words I wanted to hear, which were, "There's absolutely no chance of rain." Of course he couldn't say that. He had to hedge his bets, telling me there was a statistical chance of precipitation. But it didn't rain. It was a beautiful night, a little warm, but nice.

SR: We did run into one problem because our son-in-law is six feet six, and at the rehearsal, he couldn't fit under the *chuppah*. We had to raise it with bricks in order to fit Dan under it.

CR: Becca wanted a colorful wedding, nothing pale or prissy, and the *chuppah* was covered with flowers and vegetables.

SR: I remember most the huge yellow sunflowers. On the day of the wedding, the woman who was decorating the *chuppah* noticed my vegetable garden, part of which is right out by the road. And she told me to pick something that could hang right in the center of the canopy. Immediately, I knew what I wanted, and picked the two reddest, hottest peppers I could find. In all the pictures you can see the peppers right over their heads as they're getting married! I thought that was a pretty good symbol.

CR: I had thrown a lot of parties and I thought I knew what I was getting into. The tent guy's number is in my Rolodex, so are some band numbers . . .

SR: . . . the hooks to hold up the tent have been in the walls of the house since our wedding . . .

CR: But this was different. Fortunately, I had the best in the business helping me: my sister-in-law Barbara, who is a professional events planner, and her best friend Susie Hoskins, who is a caterer. They knew what to do and bossed me around to make sure I followed orders. In fact, Becca couldn't get over it. Along with my sister, the two of them had been bossing me around since I was born, so I automatically did what they said, which was wise.

SR: Since Dan's a Protestant, Becca's wedding was even more complicated than ours. Both a priest and a minister officiated. The priest had been a great friend of Cokie's sister and had married our nephew a year or two before, and he repeated a line that has become a favorite of mine: "Marriage is our last best hope for growing up." He also noted, with engaging modesty, that before he performed his first wedding, his mother had told him bluntly, "You're a celibate priest, you don't know the first thing about marriage!"

Like Lee, Becca wanted a Jewish element to her wedding, but she wanted the tribal elder to be a woman. So she asked our friend Millie Harmon Meyers, who's known Becca since birth. In Jewish ritual, the groom breaks a glass right at the end of the ceremony, and after Millie placed the glass in front of Dan, she was about to launch into an explanation of the custom. Dan thought it was his cue, so he immediately mashed the glass and everybody yelled out "Mazel tov," cutting off Millie's speech. To this day she stands ready to give the rest of it with the slightest encouragement. Later, at the reception, Dan's great-aunt approached me to tell me why her husband and his brother, Dan's grandfather, had left Germany together in the mid-thirties. They were actually one-quarter Jewish, she confided, and while they were not raised Jewish, they were considered Jewish under Nazi law, and their father encouraged them to leave and start a new life in America. (No wonder Dan was so good at breaking the glass!) On their way to America, the two young German brothers stopped over for a while in England. On the night they finally set sail, they stayed out late drinking with friends and had to make a mad dash for the boat train. On the platform, a very proper English couple was saying good-bye to their daughters, who were taking the same ship for a holiday. As the Germans came barreling down the platform, the parents warned the girls, "Stay away from those boys, they're up to no good." So of course one of them married one of the boys. That was Dan's grandmother. She had died before Becca and Dan met, but Grandfather Frank was there, at age ninety-four. He's one of the few men I didn't enlist to help me hold up Dan on a chair while the wedding guests danced the hora, the traditional Jewish dance. From the moment I realized he and Becca were serious, I started worrying about how we would ever hold this big guy up above our heads!

CR: After all of the planning, all of the panic, the wedding came off beautifully. Everything was absolutely perfect. The bride and groom left. All of the guests eventually went home. And I felt I had much to be grateful for. At about two o'clock in the morning, when the last of the help was packing away the tables and other equipment . . .

SR: . . . I was already in bed . . .

CR: I sat down under the *chuppah* to say a prayer of thanksgiving. At that moment the sky opened up and it poured. Rain came gushing out of the sky! It had to be God saying, "Just remember, I could've done this anytime!"

Chapter Six

———∞∞∞———

OTHER LIVES

BROKEN MARRIAGES

GETTING DIVORCED

Divorce is now so common in America that a national publication is devoted entirely to the subject; *Divorce* magazine was recently started by two former editors at *Wedding Bells* magazine. How's that for symbolism? Since almost twenty million people, or one out of ten adults, are now described as "currently divorced" by the Census Bureau, the divorce business is booming. The World Wide Web has more than fifty sites aimed at "generation ex," from DivorceNet and SmartDivorce to more specialized markets such as California Divorce Guide and Kayama, solely for couples seeking "a Jewish divorce." An on-line newsletter, *Divorce Hot Tips,* features "A Teen's Message to Divorcing Parents" and an article on "When Business Owners Divorce." Divorcinfo.com promises to help you survive "one of the cruddiest experiences you'll ever face."

They're right—divorce is almost always brutal—but for all of our devotion to marriage, we understand that not every match is made in heaven, and not every couple can or should stay together "till death do you part." In fact, according to the National Marriage Project at Rutgers University, modern American marriages "are more likely to be broken by divorce than by death." That was not always true. Census figures show that before the Civil War, only one married woman out of a thousand was divorced every year. That rate grew to 8.8 women per thousand in 1940, and while divorce spiked during World War II, when so many men were gone for so long, the rate was still only 9.2 in 1960, on the eve of the country's cultural upheaval. The divorce rate more than doubled over the next two decades, reaching a high point of 22.8 per thousand women in 1979. Since then it has declined slightly and leveled off, and demographers estimate that if current rates stay steady, 45 percent of the marriages taking place today will end in divorce.

One reason for this trend is that divorce breeds divorce. As the National Marriage Project puts it: "Divorce is an ever-present theme in the books, music and movies of the youth culture. And real life experience is hardly reassuring; today's young adults have grown up in the midst of the divorce revolution, and they've witnessed marital failure and breakdown first-hand in their own families and in the families of friends, relatives and neighbors." There are many explanations for the "divorce revolution," but the principal motive was summed up in an article Steve wrote for *The New York Times* twenty-five years ago: "Marriage has been caught up in a revolution of rising expectations. People want more out of their marriages than their parents ever did, and in the words of one counselor, 'They're not willing to make do, or slide by anymore.' They also have the time, and the money, to worry about their personal needs in a way that was seldom possible a generation ago. Divorce, in one sense, has become a great leisure time activity."

This can be a positive development, particularly for women. In all three cases we write about, wives jettisoned marriages they felt were restricting their growth and individuality. Their words echo the feelings of a woman Steve wrote about in California who said of her husband, "When I went to a shrink I began to break out of the old things. He was one of the old things I broke out of." At the same time marriage is by definition a partnership, and nothing can poison a relationship faster than selfishness—from either partner.

For most of our history, society discouraged divorce, but in many ways the reverse is now true. New laws in many states make divorce easier, and legal-service programs make divorce more affordable for poor families. The stigma once associated with divorce is now totally gone, to the point where people are almost too eager to discuss their most intimate experiences. We received a two-page Christmas letter from a woman we barely knew who wrote in great detail about her husband's infidelities and concluded: "I am grieving the end of a twenty-five-year marriage that has [put me] in a pit of deception and disrespect. Thank you for allowing me to use you as a release and to move on." If the divorce business is booming, the singles business is even bigger, offering clubs and cruises, menus and mortgages, for people without partners.

Religious strictures against divorce have also lost authority, and Roman Catholics split up almost as often as the rest of the population. Then there is simply the pressure of constant adjustment and anxiety. When couples find themselves living in new neighborhoods, performing new jobs, learning new technologies, marriages can shatter under the weight of uncertainty. In his book *Future Shock,* published back in the 1970s, Alvin Toffler predicted that rapid change would create "temporary marriages," different relationships for different stages of life. We've altered some names and places in this chapter, but the stories are real, and they show that for many Americans, Toffler's prediction has come true.

Carol Tobin can pinpoint the day that her marriage collapsed. It was in the early spring of 1994. After work she went out and got her hair dyed, and when she arrived home at seven-thirty, she was greeted by a famished and furious husband. "I was treated like a child," she recalls. "He was mad, he was yelling at me, and I said, 'This is it, screw you.' " She got in her car and started driving with "no idea, none" about where to go. She thought about getting a room for the night, but worried that her husband would see the bill and get angry all over again: "I had the feeling as I was driving, how am I going to pay for this without him breathing down my neck? Isn't that weird?" But after a while, Carol remembers, "I had this big surge of freedom. Like wow! I did this! It was the greatest feeling on earth, just to get in the car and say, 'I don't have to take this crap anymore.' " With her courage cranked up, she finally stopped at a motel: "I was shocked, I felt everybody was looking at me because I was by myself." Once inside her room, she looked at herself in the mirror and asked: "Why me? Why couldn't I be treated the way I wanted to be?"

She returned home the next morning, but a week later Carol asked her husband, Bernie, to leave their house. "I felt like I had walked through a brick wall," he remembers. It's now more than five years later, both Tobins are in their early fifties, yet their divorce is still not final. They've both found other partners, but strands of memory and regret keep them tied together, almost against their will. "I admit it, I still love him, and probably I always will," says Carol. "When you meet someone and you're seventeen years old and he's number one in your life for many, many years . . ." After a pause, she adds: "I lived a very fifties marriage, I lived my parents' marriage. But it's the nineties."

Carol and Bernie met at a high-school graduation party in

the spring of 1966. Her father had died a few months before and her brother, being protective, had agreed to play escort. She saw a guy with big dimples and a bright smile across the room and turned to her brother and said, "I'm going to marry him." Her brother, according to family lore, suggested that meeting him first might be a good idea. "I made the first move," Carol recalls. "I sat down on his lap and said, 'Hiya, cutie.'"

Bernie was two years older, an accounting student who had spent his childhood living above the family hardware store in a poor section of Queens. But as the business prospered, the Tobins had moved to a better neighborhood. "We had a backyard," says Bernie, "and I made friends who had a lot more than I had at the time." He left the party with a tall blond *shiksa*. But Carol and Bernie lived only a mile apart, and when they met again at a bus stop a few weeks later, they talked on the ride home. He asked her out to a Ray Charles concert and they were married two years later. "He was everything I wanted in a man," says Carol, "and that carried over for most of my life."

Carol wanted kids quickly—"she was very adamant about it," says Bernie—and through her twenties she was happy to stay home with Peter and Nicole. Bernie's accounting career flourished and they moved to a comfortable Long Island suburb. But when she hit her thirties, Carol's attitude changed: "I was a mommy pretty early in life and I got to the point where I said, 'What about me?'" She'd dropped out of college after a few months and now her lack of education started bothering her: "I had a very high IQ and I said, 'This is ridiculous, do something with your life.'" Bernie agreed that Carol had "a terrible image of herself" and supported her plans to go back to school. "I paid for the whole thing," he notes. "I even paid for Nicole to be in the preschool program at the college." When he asked her where she wanted to go, Carol said jokingly, "Berkeley." But the answer revealed her growing sense that she had missed out on something important: "In the sixties when I should have been swinging, instead I was married."

Carol settled for a local college. At first, she'd take Nicole with her, and after her daughter started school, she remembers that "we'd all sit at the table and do homework—I miss those times." Then she fell under the influence of her sociology professor, a gay black man from the Deep South: "He took this white Jewish girl and opened my eyes to a world I knew nothing about." She read feminist writers like the novelist Toni Morrison and recalls: "I really thrived in college, and I couldn't go back to being Bernie's little girl anymore."

The normal domestic battles grew louder, the atmosphere in the house turned frigid, but somehow Bernie missed the signals. "I really didn't see a change in her," he says, but he does remember adjusting to his wife's new schedule: "I got a girl in to clean house for her every week and we'd eat out more often so she didn't have to cook." After graduating with honors in only four years—"I was very proud of myself"—Carol tried law school. She never finished but took jobs in and around the court system. One involved counseling women involved in divorce cases and she thinks now that the job contributed to her growing restlessness. She wondered how she could advise women who "had the ability to leave when I didn't."

Bernie insists that "all the things she wanted, I was all for," including her work: "I felt it would be tremendous if she had a career and brought in some bucks. That meant more dollars we could save." In Carol's view, Bernie was too much the accountant, always focused on saving for retirement, and that he used money to dominate their relationship. She wanted to move to a new house at the beach, to put "life back in our marriage," but the guy who grew up living above the store said they couldn't afford it. "It really killed me, I felt locked out of the marriage," she says. "What I tried to do was reverse the roles. I begged him, let's do something different, and when he said no, I couldn't forgive that. He put me on the same level as my children."

Yes, Bernie now agrees, he did use money at times to control his wife. But there were also times when "she was really controlling herself," asking him permission to spend money when she always had "the same access I did" to their joint accounts. When Carol's father died, he had left her mother impoverished, and Bernie believes the experience scarred his wife and turned *her* into a "tightwad." Whatever the cause, one thing is clear: money was at the root of the Tobins' problem. "We had a very big misunderstanding in that area," says Bernie. Carol adds: "His thing was power and money. He had both over me and he still does." But she also thinks she bears some of the blame: "I had twenty-five years of anger, and I let it happen. If I had stood up to him earlier, I probably would have saved the marriage."

Money was one issue, sex another. Carol says that she had a "purely platonic" relationship with a man in the neighborhood, a fellow who fixed the family cars. But she insists that she "didn't see him romantically" until after Bernie left the house. Bernie is convinced she's lying, that the affair started before he was tossed out. "When I married her, she was a virgin," he says, "and part of the reason we broke up is that she wanted to sow her oats." He recalls a conversation they had a few months before he moved out: "We were getting into bed one night and she said to me, 'Bernie, I think you should have an affair.' I was startled. I asked her, 'Carol, what are you saying?' But now my shrink says that she was actually asking my permission for *her* affair." Bernie has it wrong, his wife retorts: "I didn't leave my husband for another man, I left my husband to find myself." In fact, she says, she's only been with two men in her entire life, her husband and her current lover, and her words carry a trace of regret: "I'm still the little girl who wants to go to Berkeley. Now, when I *could* swing, I can't do it."

By the time Bernie moved out, their son, Peter, was long

gone from home, but their daughter, Nicole, was still in high school. "I definitely wasn't a happy camper," she says of her father's departure, "but at the time I thought that if it stops the fighting and the screaming, then why not? You can only escape so far. No matter how much time you spend outside the house, you still have to come back in at some point and sit down at a dinner table where there's tension and nobody's looking at each other and that's not pleasant."

But if his daughter was relieved, Bernie was devastated. He wanted to keep the life he knew: "We had two sports cars, a nice home in a nice area, we had clothes, we went on two cruises a year. We lived right and we still saved." Then he adds about Carol: "I was crazy about her, I didn't want to leave, I wanted to stay." He sank into an "awful depression" and explains: "I couldn't understand what was happening."

Neither could Nicole: "My dad moved out and my parents dated each other for a while. He'd come over, he'd sleep over. It was pretty weird, but I just tried to go about my daily life and pretend it wasn't happening. They were always in this on-and-off relationship." Bernie says Carol "had me on this merry-go-round emotionally. I would come back for a day or two, I'd be on an up, and then I'd be down again, down and depressed." The tranquilizers he was taking made the depression worse, and thoughts of suicide slowly began building up over a period of months. He started hoarding pills.

One morning Carol woke up in a pool of blood and needed an emergency medical procedure. Bernie was on a cruise at the time with his new girlfriend, a woman Nicole will only refer to as "that horse-faced bitch," but when he returned, he called his wife to express his concern. They hadn't seen each other in months, but they agreed to meet at a local diner for dinner. The talk, as it always did, turned toward a possible reconciliation. Bernie's apartment lease was up and he wanted to come home. Carol recalls her reaction: "He pushed it before I was ready, and I panicked. I liked being able to decide what to eat and where to go without somebody else." When they parted that night, Carol says, they had agreed on a plan: "You talk to your therapist and I'll talk to mine." But when Bernie got home, he felt himself spinning "out of control." He wrote several notes, sent his daughter a check for her college tuition, and gulped down the pills he had been collecting. "I just wanted to be off the merry-go-round," he says. "It was killing me slowly." Apparently he had second thoughts, and tried to go for help. He didn't make it, and collapsed near the door.

When Nicole got the check, she couldn't figure out what it was for, but when she called her father, she got no answer. People at work hadn't seen him for two days. Finally Bernie's girlfriend and brother went to his house and found him unconscious, lying where he had fallen. Accounts vary, but Nicole says that while the brother and the girlfriend were waiting for the ambulance, they stole money from her father's wallet and confiscated his suicide notes, which she has never seen. They also blocked Nicole and her brother, Peter, from entering their father's house, but the children got a key from the cleaning lady, retrieved the cash and jewelry he kept hidden in a secret place, and changed the locks. "It was a big mess we didn't need on top of the first mess," says Nicole. Meanwhile, Carol "almost had a stroke" when she heard the news of Bernie's overdose, but she denies that her conversation with him about a possible reconciliation helped provoke his suicide attempt. "Why was I made to feel guilty?" she asks.

After he recovered, Bernie bought a Corvette and moved in with the girlfriend Nicole suspected of robbing him. In fact, he chose the same beach community Carol had wanted to move to several years before. Nicole was furious. The girlfriend, she feels, was a "gold digger" who resented every dollar Bernie spent on his kids. The girlfriend, in turn, called Nicole a "spoiled bitch," right to her face. Bernie put in a separate phone line just to talk to his children and get their messages.

As the legal proceedings dragged on—Carol calls it "the longest divorce on record"—she tried to confide in her daughter and enlist her support against her father, but Nicole would have none of it. "She was just trying to tell me all the bad things," Nicole says. "She'd feed me information to piss me off about him, or attempt to." Bernie took a different tack, buying his kids presents and taking them to nice places— things Carol could not afford to do. Says Nicole: "They use me as a tool, each in their own way."

Holidays are the worst times. Bernie and Carol both try to bribe their children by buying them plane tickets home, and then pressuring them not to visit the other parent. "I don't like to share my children, no mother does," admits Carol. But the result is that both kids avoid going home as much as possible. "I don't want to shuffle and fight and be stressed," says Nicole. "That's what it ends up being." On Thanksgiving two years ago, the kids had dinner with their mother and dessert with their dad, so last year Nicole tried to reverse the deal. But Carol moved first, paying for Peter and his wife to come north from their home in Florida, so he felt obliged to eat with his mother. "I was very upset with my son," says Bernie. "I wanted Thanksgiving at my house, so I called him up and said, 'I'm really very angry, you have to learn to say no to your mother, you were there last year.' " The solution: Peter ate with his mother and Nicole with her father. After dinner, Nicole picked up her brother and his wife at Carol's and drove them thirty miles back to Bernie's for dessert. Then she returned alone to her mother's for another dessert, "only I was too full." The next morning she had breakfast with her father. But now that she's twenty-two and out of college, Nicole has soured on those trips home. The next time Rosh Hashanah, the Jewish New Year, comes around, Nicole has decided to tell her parents: "Just forget it, I'll do it on my own. You just don't want to go home for the holidays—it's awful."

An aspiring writer, Nicole lives in an apartment outside of Washington with several friends of both sexes. She dates a lot and likes men but draws a clear lesson from her parents' experience: they made a mistake getting married while they were still so young and living at home. Like many women of her generation, she believes that "living with someone is really important" before marriage. "Even if there's not a ring on your finger," she explains, "you're still in a committed, living-together relationship and you get to see how people act and how people are. I still want to get married, I think. Sometimes I say I don't but that's not true. I want to have children, three of them. I know I'm going to get married if I find the right person. I just hope I've learned from them. Money's so stupid to fight over. It just makes me so mad and I hope I never have that mentality." Nicole and Peter talk about their parents and share a common view: in their own marriages, they'll avoid divorce at all costs. "We don't want to become our parents," she says emphatically. "We always say we'll kill each other before there is another divorce, even though we both don't like guns."

But the divorce continues to ripple through the family. After Bernie's overdose, he went on a variety of drugs to help him "cope with stress," but they hurt his performance at work: "I wasn't able to spend the time and attention the job required, I let things slide." Recently he was fired. "That's why guys tend to lose their jobs after a divorce," notes Bernie. "It's very common."

Carol is still with the car mechanic, but she insists she'll never marry again. "I don't want anyone to have legal ties on me," she says. Bernie has met a new woman, a distant relative of Carol's through marriage, and he's planning to wed again when the divorce is final. He says he no longer loves Carol, that "too much has happened" to poison their relationship and it's time "to start a whole new life." Yet he can't quite leave his old life, and his old wife, behind. "We could have lived and laughed and had a ball," he says. "It would have been great."

Cathy and Richard Bishop: "I Don't Know If That's What You Call Love"

His kids were just a few years old when Richard Bishop and four of his buddies took a sailing trip to the Virgin Islands. The others went ashore one night and came back to the boat with five friendly female schoolteachers—including one for Richard. He insists "nothing happened" in the way of sex that night. His ex-wife, Cathy, has a different view: "Yeah, right." Whatever the details, a lot did happen to Richard's outlook on life and marriage. "All of a sudden it was fun being together with a young lady," he recalls. "We were laughing and enjoying ourselves and having a good time. I had not spent a lot of time with Cathy doing that—it was quite an eye-opener."

Back home, Cathy was nursing her sick mother through an Illinois winter, digging out from two feet of snow, and keeping the wood fire in their rustic house burning. When Richard came home, he was "out of sorts" and "acting weird," she says, and a month or so later he announced he was going back to the Caribbean—a trip he did in fact take. As Cathy remembers the conversation, they were getting into bed when her husband told her, "I've met somebody and I think I love her." Then she says: "He wants to have sex, so I did it. I was in shock. Of course, he falls asleep and I sit up all night."

It took many more years for the Bishops to get legally divorced, but their emotional divorce began that night, or perhaps a month earlier, when those five schoolteachers first set foot on Richard's boat. But in another sense, the Bishops' marriage had been flawed from the outset, full of cracks and crevices that they covered over in their early years but never permanently patched. Looking back, Richard says: "We always had our own interests, but in the beginning, that part got overlooked. You can't expect to change anybody, you have to accept what's there."

They met in college, at a small church school in the Midwest. She was an eighteen-year-old freshman, he a twenty-year-old junior, when they started eyeing each other one night in the library. "I was a big flirt," Cathy says proudly, and she agreed to go to a barn dance with him. "He tried to kiss me all night and I wouldn't let him," but the dates continued and soon they were sleeping together. "A lot of the other guys wanted to tie me down and he didn't do that. There were a lot of things I wanted to do with my life, and getting married and having children was not one of them."

The view of marriage Cathy absorbed from her parents was hardly a healthy one. Her father "ran around" for years, her mother started "drinking a little bit too much," and they separated when Cathy was in high school. "People didn't do that back then," she says, referring to the mid-sixties. "I was embarrassed when my parents split up." That experience, Richard believes, helped make Cathy so fearful of being tied down: "She didn't have a good taste for men of any sort."

In Cathy's view, her upbringing left another mark as well. Since her parents had no sons, she says, "I wasn't raised to be a typical female, I was raised to be an individual. I was a tomboy, I used to fight when I was a kid, I was a rough-and-tumble person who could do anything a boy could do."

Richard graduated and went off to dental school in Chicago. They were still attached but dating others, and Cathy had a fling with another man when she was student teaching. "He was an artist, we really clicked," she says. And what she saw in her lover was missing in her regular boyfriend: "Richard was not very intellectual, we couldn't really discuss deep issues." But she viewed him as "honest, a person of integrity," and they moved in together after he graduated from dental school, with Cathy insisting that she pay half the rent. Richard kept pressing for marriage and Cathy explains: "I think he was afraid he'd lose me. I was getting hit on all the time by other guys." But in Richard's view, they basically drifted into marriage: "We had a long history together, and once you meet someone, and meet all their friends and family, it's a lot easier to go on with that person than imagine not being with that person. I don't know if that's what you call love."

She was twenty-three, he was twenty-five, and soon he was lobbying for a child. So were Richard's parents, and Cathy got so irritated with their questions that she finally told them to stop asking. When he threatened her by saying, "If you won't have a kid, I'll find somebody who will," she stopped using birth control. After the doctor confirmed she was pregnant, her reaction was a pithy "Oh, shit." Then she went home and cried: "Deep down, I thought it was an end to my freedom."

Richard now thinks he made a mistake: "I thought that her attitude would change with time, but that was probably an error on my part. She feels she sacrificed everything to have kids for me." That *is* how Cathy feels, but those misgivings did not stop her from marinating in motherhood, from becoming "the housewife and mother my mother was." This woman who prided herself on being "a feminist before feminism was popular" was canning tomatoes and peaches and baking pies twice a week.

Two years after their daughter, Shannon, was born, they had a son, Joseph. Both Bishops think the other spouse adjusted badly to parenthood. Says Cathy: "Richard would come home from work and go play tennis for a couple of hours, and that really ticked me off. I wanted company, and he'd take off for the neighbors' court. Sex was his answer to everything. After he played tennis, he'd want to eat and then have sex, without any real connection between us. I didn't feel he was very responsive to what I was going through. I was exhausted and I wasn't getting much understanding. Sex doesn't start in the bedroom, it starts in other places, and I wasn't getting much anyplace else." Says Richard: "It's probably a common feeling among husbands, now maybe you're the third most important thing around. Kids obviously take over a woman's primary focus and it seemed like we just drifted apart." Cathy answers: "When you have a baby, it's time to say, 'Okay, buddy, you're an adult.' He really wanted children, but he didn't want to alter his lifestyle to accommodate children. He expected me to do all of it." So when those schoolteachers showed up on Richard's boat, he was ready for a change, a change that avoided his kids' diapers, his wife's demands, and his own aging.

Cathy was ready for a change, too. As she points out, both Bishops had been buffeted by the untimely deaths of several friends: one choked on an orange, a second died in an accident, two had aneurysms. "I started reassessing," she recalls. "What's really important to me? Where should I put my focus?" Richard's reaction was "I only have a short amount of time, I better not miss anything."

After Richard returned from his second sojourn to the Virgin Islands, Cathy recalls, "I was so disgusted with him, anytime he came into a room I'd go out." She borrowed two thousand dollars from her parents and went to visit her best friend, who lived in London. The trip was a big ego boost: "I met like three guys on the plane and they all wanted to go out with me. I thought I was a slug, and they were all hitting on me. So I was thinking, 'I'm okay, I'm still sexy.' " She did go out with one of the men—"he was really good-looking"—and while she insists their relationship never went beyond a few kisses, the experience had a profound impact. "I was very changed," she remembers. "Other men thought I was attractive. So I told Richard, 'I want you out of the house.' "

But they could not afford two houses, so Cathy moved downstairs into a guest room, and they started living separate lives. Richard had an affair and told her about it. "I felt she should know, but she was infuriated and hurt," he says. Cathy thinks the deaths of their friends changed her husband: "The man I married never would have cheated on me. He was facing his mortality, I think he was running away from getting older." Meanwhile, Cathy kept contact with the man she met in England. She never slept with him, she says, although she regrets that decision: "If I could do it over again, I would." Still, she admits, it was an act of infidelity, "a psychological affair, a keeping-my-sanity affair." One day Cathy and Richard took a long walk in the woods near their house and Richard confided, "I don't know if I want to stay married."

They tried therapy, but the Bishops remember the experience very differently. Richard says that the sign outside the office read "Feminist Counseling," and he recalls thinking, "Oh, brother." Still, he says, "I spilled my guts out" during the sessions and it did no good: "I would get reamed up one side and down the other, by my wife and by the counselor, and I finally said, 'Why am I doing this to myself?' " Cathy's memory reveals how badly they were communicating: "The therapist tried to get him to face some things and he wouldn't admit to anything." At about this time Cathy also contracted a sexually transmitted disease, but even though Richard was her only partner, she was not sure how she got sick: "Dumb me—I was wondering, where did I get this?"

The relationship continued to unravel. When Cathy planned another trip to England, Richard asked her not to see her male friend, but she refused. As he remembers her retort: "I've got to do what I've got to do." His reaction: "That was it. Nothing mattered after that." For Cathy, the break point came when Richard started an affair with the assistant in his dental office. "She was incensed," he recalls. "She even tried to run the lady down with her car. It was like, wow, I can't believe that." Cathy's price for continuing the marriage was firing the assistant. When Richard refused, she went to a lawyer. "There was no turning back," she says. "If he couldn't make a commitment, it was over."

But divorce does not end a relationship, and the escalating war between the Bishops was fought on two fronts: children and money. Cathy and the kids moved to a condo near Chicago. Shannon and Joseph took their mother's side in the breakup, and their relations with their father turned poisonous. "All through high school we fought all the time," Shannon recalls. "There were times I'd call my mom crying from his house, and she'd come out and pick me up, and it's like a forty-five-minute drive. We just did not get along. And then whenever we'd argue he'd mistakenly call me by her name, Cathy. So I was like, 'Um, no.'"

Richard blames Cathy for his children's attitude toward him: "She wanted to drive the biggest wedge between me and the kids that she possibly could. Everything was made to make me look like the bad guy." But it didn't help when Richard dated a stream of young women that his children ridiculed. One was the secretary for a friend of Richard's, and when she joined them one night at the movies, Shannon remembers: "My brother and I were like, 'Who is this girl?' She was wearing cowboy boots, which we thought was ridiculous. Like, 'Who is this hick?'" When she went away to college, Shannon thought she was putting the mess behind her: "I was sick of dealing with it, I wanted to start a new life."

But her old life kept returning. Richard had taken up with his dental assistant, Vicki, who was almost twenty years his junior. They were planning to get married during a ski vacation in Canada and took Shannon and Joseph along. Richard remembers the trip as "a wonderful thing," but his daughter's memory is very different: "They just rented a suite in the hotel and there was a minister or whatever there and a photographer. We just stood in a row and my brother and I had to sign the marriage license or whatever as witnesses. They got married. Vicki had a picture in this frame when we got home. It was this black-and-white, and I look so pissed off, it's hilarious. She put it in a frame and I couldn't believe she was such a moron that she would do this. I'm sure there were other pictures where we weren't looking quite so annoyed. I thought it was kind of funny because she was such an idiot."

Now out of college, Shannon sees both of her parents "more as teenagers and I'm the adult." But she reserves most of her scorn for her father: "He's like been in a midlife crisis for the last twenty years and buying all these toys like kayaks and stupid stuff he's never going to use. He just wastes all this money, so I think of him more like a kid. My mom is also like that but not to the same extent. He's like one of those guys with the T-shirt that says, 'The one with the most toys when you die wins.' "

As in many divorces, money has become the continuing source of discord between the Bishops, a tangible way to act out their resentments. Cathy says she has taken Richard to court eight times over late child-support payments. She has also sued him over access to a complicated family trust established by Richard's parents, and he was devastated when his son, Joseph, joined the suit on Cathy's side: "I felt someone had just kicked me in the stomach. I couldn't believe it. I thought we were extremely close."

In Richard's view, Cathy has only one mission: "She's there to make my life miserable, and she doesn't want me to forget it. I can honestly say I hate her, and I never thought I'd say that." Cathy says he's wrong, she's not out to get him, but she does sound obsessed with their skirmishing. Shannon has advised her mother to back off, that she's losing too much in legal fees, but Cathy won't be deterred: "I want my day in court and I want my money and I'm going to get it."

Richard says their battles have become the "whole center" of Cathy's life, and adds: "The sad part about it is that she's aging tremendously with the hatred she has. She's gained thirty or forty pounds." Cathy admits she's been "a bit depressed," but her weight gain is more like twenty-five pounds and she's now on an exercise program to slim down: "I'm working on me now, doing things I enjoy." Now approaching fifty, back to teaching and supporting herself, Cathy says she has a "full life" with one exception: "I wouldn't mind a good sex life." But in the end, the "sad part" is about Richard, not her. At fifty-two, she says, "He's running after the impossible dream, because he *will* get older someday."

The breakup of Cathy's parents left her deeply suspicious of marriage, a suspicion that colored her relationship with Richard from the moment they met more than thirty-one years ago. And now her daughter has inherited the same attitude. "I think I'm very distrustful" of men and marriage, says Shannon, and her own experiences have made matters worse. The guy she dated for three years in college "cheated on me," she says. And now marriage looks less appealing than ever: "I had totally trusted him and he knew the whole situation with my parents and I was really really hurt that he could have done that. It's definitely made me like, whoa, who am I ever going to marry that I'm not going to get sick of? There's not really anyone I can see myself being married to at this point, so if I was some old lady with a cat, I'd probably be okay with that."

Peggy McDonald: "Marriage Is Probably Not the Best Option"

The first time Peggy McDonald got married she was twenty years old and four months pregnant. The setting did not exactly fit her childhood dreams—a county courthouse in suburban Maryland, outside of Washington. She wore a blue double-knit dress, not a white gown, and after the ceremony, her sister blew bubbles at her instead of throwing rice. The half-dozen wedding guests—a few of her relatives, two of her husband's fraternity brothers—then had dinner at Blackie's House of Beef.

The marriage did not last long, less than two years, and Peggy went on to marry and divorce twice more. Now, at age fifty-one, she is not interested in trying again. "For me," she says, "marriage is probably not the best option." Her daughter, Laura, born a few months after that first wedding, shares her mother's view of matrimony: "I don't want to get married, it makes me very skittish, because I don't want to get divorced. The idea of walking down an aisle or standing in front of a justice of the peace and saying words like 'till death do us part' and 'forever and ever' makes me want to vomit, because it just scares me. I don't want to go through that. I watched my mother go through that. All my friends say that because I so desperately don't want to get married, I'm going to end up married for like thirty years. I don't know about that. If I could get a relationship to last more than a year, I would be happy!"

At nineteen, Peggy was living in Italy, where her father, an air force pilot, was stationed. She was dating an Italian nobleman with a big title and small prospects—the "countless count" in family lore—and one day took a picnic into the mountains with a friend of hers, a young American soldier named Len, who was based in the area. Len was also dating someone else, and after lunch, Peggy remembers, the two of them were "just kind of lying around" on their blanket. She was still a virgin at the time, but "the next thing you know we have this spontaneous energy going, and we make love on this hillside in Italy." Afterward, they packed up the picnic and headed back, "a little bit embarrassed by what we had done." Her embarrassment would get worse. She was pregnant.

Peggy says that because she's a Roman Catholic, abortion was out of the question, and she never considered putting the child up for adoption. "Should I get married or not get married?" she recalls. "Those were my choices." She was "enamored" of Len and "fascinated" by him. She was not in love, but he was eager to marry her and "very persuasive." Add "a lot of family influence" and soon she found herself at the courthouse in Maryland, getting married and preparing to move to Atlanta, Len's hometown. "I was a little panicked," she says. "It was the first time I was starting a new life without my family to support me."

After Laura was born, Len worked at a bank during the day and went to school at night, "so we didn't see much of him," Peggy says. They were living in "this little tiny apartment with no furniture," and the newlyweds painted the walls "to make it look bigger and nicer than it really was." Peggy had always been good with numbers, and a few months after giving birth, she found work as an accountant with a big oil company. She moved ahead quickly, but needed a degree to advance further, so she suggested night school. The company would reimburse the cost, a hundred dollars for two courses, if she got good grades, but she needed to pay her tuition up front. When Len objected, the relationship splintered. "I didn't see why I couldn't have a hundred dollars for me to go to school," Peggy recalls, "when he could have a hundred to play poker or golf with his buddies."

Len then learned something about Peggy that many other men would learn over the years: don't try to push her around. Says Laura: "My mother is very much the kind of person you cannot put in a box. Anytime that anybody's tried, I feel sorry for them. She's a very generous giving person, she'll give up everything she has to help somebody. But you can't force her to do anything." Peggy borrowed the hundred dollars from her mother and enrolled in school. Len was "very upset I could do such a thing," she says, "and the marriage wasn't the same from that day forward." If her degree would add to the family income, why was he so angry? "He was afraid I would get ahead of him," Peggy maintains. "I might graduate ahead of him and earn more money than he did, and he felt threatened by that."

Peggy took Laura and moved in with her parents, who had transferred to Florida and lived near a large air force base. It's a period that mother and daughter both remember as a "magical time." As Laura describes it: "My grandfather was my father at that point. He would come home from the base and I had a little chair next to his chair and we would have happy hour. He would have a martini and I would have juice and we would have cheese and crackers and watch Walter Cronkite. I can see it in my head, because every night, that's what we did." Peggy was working and going to school and dating guys from the base, and she was more a big sister than a mother to Laura. "Sometimes I feel like my mother and I grew up together, because she was real young when she had me and we have been through a lot as a pair," says Laura. Peggy agrees: "My parents had two daughters; that's the way they looked at it."

Peggy and Laura spent many weekends at a beach club attached to the base, and one day a young flier named Jim, an Italian from New York, came over and introduced himself. They had mutual friends, he invited her to dinner, and "we enjoyed ourselves for the rest of the summer," Peggy remembers. They talked of marriage, "but we were going to wait until after he got back; he wanted me to get my degree out of the way." Jim left in the fall for Vietnam and talked about sending her an engagement ring, "but the ring never arrived." He was shot down and killed in the spring.

She had no official status, just the summer girlfriend left behind, so she got no official notice of Jim's death. Her father knew Jim's unit and where he was stationed, and when he heard a report on the news about the firefight, he was pretty sure Jim had been shot down, but he didn't tell his daughter. "He was going nuts," she learned later, "but he didn't want to believe it." After a week, Jim's best friend wrote to Peggy, confirming her father's fears. She called Jim's father in New York, whom she had never met, hoping for an invitation to the funeral. "I felt real strange; it was very difficult to talk to him on the telephone," she recalls. He never invited her, and she never went. Even today, more than twenty-five years later, Peggy tears up at the mention of Jim's name. Has she romanticized him over the years? That's certainly possible. But Jim's death, says Laura, "broke my mom's heart."

There were more breaks to come. Peggy had an affair with a married man, the owner of the accounting firm where she worked, but he never made good on his promises to leave his family. Then her father was diagnosed with lung cancer, and died within months. The tragedies sent her back to the Catholic Church and she remembers asking God: "What did I do wrong? Please, tell me." She thought the answer to her prayers was a pilot named Brian Kennedy, who came calling after her father's death. There were "a lot of 'life is too short' thoughts going through my head," Peggy remembers, and she agreed to meet his parents: "Everything seemed quite nice, he was a Catholic boy and all those things." Adds Laura: "He was somebody who was going to take care of everything."

But even before the wedding, Peggy started to sense that Brian had "a dark inside." Laura remembers her mother and Brian standing in a garden, made of seashells, and arguing over whether he could adopt her. "My mother basically told him to take a flying leap and took off the engagement ring and threw it at him and it landed in the shell garden," recalls Laura. They made up the next day, but it took hours to find the ring, with five or six people searching inch by inch through the seashells.

Peggy has another version: two weeks before the wedding, she and Brian were squabbling over the details, from the limousine for his parents to the dress for his sister. "He just got madder and madder and more intolerant," she says, and at that point she broke off the engagement. But she got no sympathy at home. Her mother said the fight was probably all *her* fault and Laura burst out: "If you don't marry him, you'll be hurting my chances to have a really good father." When Brian apologized the next day, Peggy took him back, and after the wedding they moved to Virginia, near Brian's new assignment at the Pentagon.

Like her first marriage, Peggy's second match was probably doomed from the outset. Brian was unhappy at work and drinking heavily, and by the time Peggy came home from her office, she had to "work around him and keep him placated." Laura recalls: "He was a little bit messed up about sex. My mom tells me this horrible story, that they were in bed and she wanted to try something and he called her a whore and all this kind of stuff. There were a lot of times she would just crawl into bed with me and sleep there."

After Peggy suffered a miscarriage, she decided the marriage was too shaky to risk having a child, so she asked her doctor to insert an IUD, a permanent birth-control device. Brian was furious, yelling at Peggy, "I'm a Catholic, and your job is to bear my children, that's what you're supposed to do." Laura remembers hiding behind a couch as Peggy and Brian were "throwing things at each other. She said something to him, I don't remember what it was, and he slapped her. I had never seen a man hit a woman. Never." Peggy snapped: "I couldn't believe my own rage. I was so mad I threw his clothes out of a second-story window and locked him out in a snowstorm."

They made up, but the damage was done, and then Brian made the same mistake Len had made: he tried to put Peggy in a box. He announced he was taking a new assignment in San Antonio and moving the whole family. Peggy by this time was working at an accounting firm and studying for her CPA certificate: "I was trying to establish myself in the area so I could start on my career, but that's not what he had in mind at all." Brian promised to look for an assignment near Washington but he never did, and one day a team of movers arrived at the house: they had orders to ship the family to San Antonio and were calculating the size van they would need.

Peggy decided she had to act. During her lunch hour, she scouted out possible apartments and arranged for a mover of her own to come one day when Brian was at work. She cashed her paycheck, opened a new account, wrote a "hot check" for the first month's rent at her new place, and cleaned out the old one. She left no note, no forwarding address. Once a week she would sneak back to the old house and see if she'd gotten any mail. "I had no idea if he would come looking for me with a gun," she says. "I lived in mortal terror he would show up eventually." Two months later Brian called, saying he wanted to see her. She said only in a public place, the local Laundromat. He was leaving for Texas and he wanted her to come along: "He wasn't even asking, it was more like he was demanding." She refused, and her marriage was over.

Now Peggy was the sole support of herself and her daughter, and times were tight. They lived in a shabby, third-story walk-up, trying to save enough to buy a town house, and Peggy baked bread and made clothes to stretch her salary. Laura remembers a showdown with her mother over a box of pencils: "The Snoopy pencils came six to a pack, and they were a dollar-fifty. Then there was a twenty-pack of plain yellow pencils for a dollar-fifty. My mother and I got in a screaming match in the middle of the supermarket because I could not fathom that we could not afford the Snoopy pencils." Christmas was also bleak that first year: a homemade tree, made of green cloth, with crocheted red ornaments. But, Laura recalls, "it was also the most amazing time because it was just the two of us. The two of us against everything."

Peggy was always ambitious, and she felt thwarted at her accounting firm: "I was the wrong sex and wrong religion." She sent out some résumés and was "flabbergasted" at the response. A computer-industry trade association offered her a job at thirty thousand dollars a year, a 50 percent raise, and she recalls: "I'm thinking thirty thousand is a fortune, but all I could think to say was 'Is that all?' So they upped the offer—I don't know how I kept a straight face." They bought the town house, and Peggy's social life, never slow, picked up speed. There was Marty the banker and Buddy the car repairman and Laura's flute teacher, ten years younger than Peggy. "My grandmother at that point threatened to take me away," Laura recalls. "She said my mother was behaving like a child. That was a really weird year." There were other bad influences on Laura as well: thirteen-year-old pot smokers in the neighborhood who had little adult supervision and spent their afternoons shoplifting at Kmart. "I was growing up too fast," says Laura, and Peggy agrees: "She did everything in her power to flunk out of school, she became a real problem child."

To make matters worse, Peggy went to a conference in Houston and met Bill Rinaldi. When they decided to get married after only a dozen dates, Laura was appalled: "He came to visit and I hated him, like instantaneously hated him. I think I was threatened. I know I was threatened. Here my mom and I have done all this on our own and I don't want to share her with anybody." Since Bill wouldn't move to Washington, Peggy agreed to move to Houston, and Laura boycotted the wedding in protest. She was just starting high school and wanted everybody to know how unhappy she was: "I was like, this sucks. You are taking me away from my friends. Why are you marrying him? He's gross." Then, when they got to Texas, Bill decided to quit his job and start a software company of his own, and Peggy felt compelled to help him out in the evenings, leaving Laura alone in a new city. "Laura was pretty much left out in the cold," Peggy now admits. "We really didn't explain to her in a reasonable way that Bill was starting his own business and it would be hard on all of us, especially her."

Bill's scheme was also hard on the marriage. The company never did very well, adding to the family's emotional and financial stress. After a few years, Peggy took a consulting contract in California that was supposed to last two weeks. The assignment stretched into months, then led to an offer of a permanent job. She saw it as a great career move, and Bill promised to join her in California, but he never did, and money continued to eat away at their relationship. She was supporting her own family financially and Bill objected fiercely: "He was totally against that, against our giving money to my mother and brothers, partly because he was still feeling quite needy himself." Under Texas law, a couple can divide their assets without getting divorced and Peggy proposed that as a solution: "I didn't want to feel guilty if I wrote my mother a check, but Bill had to be in control of all the finances, I couldn't make any decisions on my own."

Money was mixed up with issues of power and pride. Peggy went to China on business and Bill wanted to join her, but she said no: "I needed to concentrate and focus on business, and I didn't have time to be a travel agent for my husband." One weekend she canceled a trip to Houston and instead went to New York, to oversee her company's initial stock offering, and Bill exploded: "He was just going crazy, calling my hotel room every five minutes. I told him I was at the lawyers' office until three A.M., but he found that totally irresponsible." After he left her a series of "belligerent and horrible" messages, Peggy called a friend and asked him to recommend a good divorce lawyer in Texas. "Do you want the mild-mannered guy," he asked, "or the thermonuclear-war guy?" She hired the low-key fellow over the phone, and to this day, almost three years after the divorce, she's never met her own lawyer in person.

Peggy's involved with a new man now, but he's more

committed to the relationship than she is, and her daughter feels sorry for him, because she's seen what happens to men who think they can control her mother: "I'm like, you're about to get run over by a truck." Peggy sees no need to tie herself down: "At this stage I can enjoy the benefits of companionship and I don't have to have a marriage license." At the end of our conversation, we asked Peggy this question: after three marriages and countless affairs, have you ever been in love? "Probably once," she answered, her voice quavering, and it was clear she meant Jim, the pilot killed in Vietnam. Have you ever admitted that to yourself? "Maybe," she said. "It's not something I dwell on."

At age thirty, Laura says that when she talks to her girlfriends, they all agree that "as we grow up we feel that we are so much more like our mothers than we ever really wanted to be or expected to be." And after her last romance collapsed, she became convinced that like her mother, she'd be no good at marriage: "When David and I broke up, he said, 'I think I was wrong, I think I made a mistake when I told you that I loved you, because I don't.' I could not imagine hearing that after being married with kids. Imagine twenty years from now, my husband comes to me and says, 'I think we made a mistake, I don't love you.' I don't want to hear that again."

Afterword

Hearing these stories, we are struck by the legacy of divorce, the impact of broken marriages on how the next generation views love and commitment. Children of divorced parents are two or three times more likely to fail at marriage than young people from intact families. But nobody coming of age in the last twenty years can escape the divorce culture entirely. Even if your own parents are still together, odds are that you know many couples who are not: aunts and uncles, teachers and coaches, mothers and fathers of friends. The National Marriage Project says this culture "has made almost all young adults more cautious and even wary of marriage," and that's certainly true for the families we profile in this chapter. Nicole and Peter Tobin are so scarred by their parents' breakup that they threaten to "kill each other" before either one can end a marriage. Cathy Bishop feels that her parents' divorce made her suspicious of men and reluctant to have children—attitudes that helped undermine her own relationship. No wonder her daughter, Shannon, thinks growing old with her cat is an attractive option. After watching her mother's three failed marriages, Laura McDonald speaks for many children of divorce when she says of matrimony: "It just scares me."

Many Americans don't live out their married lives in Leave It to Beaverland, with Mom and Dad and their 2.5 biological kids all together all the time. Many forces—death and divorce, estrangement and adoption—can fragment traditional families and then fuse the pieces back together in new shapes, creating new family forms to carry on. This isn't a new phenomenon, but it's assumed new configurations. In earlier times, because so many women died in childbirth, it was quite common for children to grow up cared for by women who were not their real mothers: stepmothers and grandmothers, aunts and cousins, even family friends. And some of those arrangements could get quite confusing. Cokie's great-grandmother died giving birth to her fourth child, and her husband quickly married his late wife's sister. They proceeded to have four more children, who were both half siblings and first cousins to the first four. Steve's grandparents took in a niece for several years after her parents died. As complicated as these arrangements might seem, they were much simpler than what many modern families experience. Divorce can poison relationships, even when parents and stepparents have good intentions toward their children, and it's much worse when children become the focal point of their parents' unresolved animosities. In America today, more than five million children live with a stepparent as well as a parent. Life in these "blended" families can present special problems and provide special joys for married couples. Here are portraits of three families we've come to know. In some cases, names and other details have been changed to protect their privacy.

When Connie Morella's sister, Mary, was diagnosed with terminal cancer, she was thirty-eight, a divorced mother with six children. As Mary grew weaker, relations with her ex-husband grew worse, and her last months were shadowed by the question, what would become of her children? Connie and her husband, Tony, already had three of their own, but as she sat at her sister's bedside one day, Connie suggested, "Maybe Tony and I could take them." Twenty-three years later she remembers that day vividly: "I don't think I'd even consulted with him at the time. I had my fingers crossed, not really knowing what this would lead to." When Mary protested, Connie soothed her dying sister: "I think we could do that, so don't you worry about it."

But it was Connie who was worried. She remembers thinking about her husband: "It's my blood that goes through these children. I'm the one that pulled this together. Is he going to feel alienated? How about our children?" Connie recalls telling Tony of her offer: "Thank goodness I had a great guy, who said, 'All right, we'll all move over.' They did. And that's when the fun began."

Mary's oldest girl stayed behind in Massachusetts to finish high school, but two weeks after their mother died, the other five—four girls and a boy, ranging in age from nine to sixteen—moved in with the Morellas in Bethesda, Maryland, just outside of Washington. And Tony's two-door automobile started looking awfully small. "All of a sudden it dawned on me," he says, "and I called a friend of mine and got his huge station wagon and went out to the airport. And there were these waifs, coming off the plane, led by Connie. It was just an extraordinary experience." Ursula Munroe, the youngest child, who is now a nurse, recalls that "once we got there, the first thing we all did was pull out our stationery and write letters to our friends back home."

The Morellas' modest home bulged at every seam. A recreation room and a study on the lower level had been chopped up into three bedrooms, and the laundry room was now a bathroom. The oldest Morella boy, Paul, was away at college most of the time, so there were seven kids in full-time residence, five girls and two boys. "The boys had a bath and the girls had a bath," recalls Catherine Sanborn, the second oldest cousin along with her twin sister, Louise. "We wanted nothing to do with their bathroom, but when the girls' room was busy we had to use the boys', and it was horrible!"

"The transition was a lot smoother than I anticipated," recalls Paul Morella, "but it was tough for everybody. I'd be lying if I said otherwise." When he came home from college, he sometimes slept on a cushion underneath an air-conditioning unit. "I kind of liked it," he says, "because it had white noise, and I wouldn't hear all the ruckus that was going on. People got up at different times and had different patterns as far as breakfast was concerned. It was almost like shifts." Mark Morella and his only male cousin both worked as janitors at a nearby church: "It gave us a place to go sometimes when we had to get away."

Tony installed an industrial-strength washer and dryer in the garage, telling the salesman, "I want the longest warranty you can give me." But Connie's idea, assigning different kids to do the laundry each week, quickly broke down. Somebody was always complaining about shrunken jeans, lost socks, dirty blouses. So she bought each child a separate laundry basket, showed them how to operate the appliances, and put them on their own. "This meant"—she laughs—"that there were times in the middle of the night you'd hear 'clunk, clunk, clunk.' Those were the sneakers in the dryer."

The Morellas had always been "frugal," one of Connie's favorite words, a habit learned from her mother, an Italian immigrant who worked much of her life in a Laundromat for minimal wages. Connie was a schoolteacher who went into politics and now serves in the U.S. Congress, representing the Maryland suburbs of Washington; Tony teaches law at American University. So while the family was always comfortable, it was never rich, and Paul Morella remembers that long before his cousins arrived, his mother was a master money manager: "When I was young, I was amazed at how many sandwiches she could squeeze out of a can of tuna fish. She would sometimes make them ahead of time, and freeze them, and I remember taking out my lunch at school and the bread was sort of warped, because it had been in the freezer. And there was this thin layer of what I guess was tuna fish. Maybe sometimes she just whispered the word 'tuna' over the bread."

Ursula recalls a truck backing up to the house and unloading large quantities of frozen food, which the family bought wholesale: "It was the joke of the neighborhood." When Connie went shopping by herself, she'd load up three carts. One day, she says, "a woman said to me, 'You must be shopping for six months,' and I smiled and said, 'No, five days.' " How does one person handle three carts? "You push one ahead and park it," she replied with a chuckle, "and then you can pull the other two along."

Since one teenager can tie up a telephone single-handedly, a half dozen vying for a line can cause chaos. "Getting the phone on a Friday night was quite an assignment," says Mark. "Within seconds someone else would pick it up and say, 'Can you hurry?' So I used to get on my bike and ride up to the corner to make my phone calls."

Getting the car was harder than getting the phone. Connie thinks that nine trips to the Motor Vehicle Administration for driver's licenses qualifies any parent for hazardous duty pay. "It never ended, you're taking somebody every year," she recalls. "And it took one of the girls four times to get that license! She couldn't parallel-park, so each time we went, we took a smaller car. Finally she made it—in a Yugo we borrowed from a friend."

Tony bought the kids an old used car, an "army green" Dodge Dart, and laid down one rule—they paid for gas. Maryland license plates contain three letters, and just by accident, the Dart's tag said "IRV," and that of course became its name. "I was mortified to drive around in that thing," recalls Ursula, "but I grew to love it." No one loved buying gas, however. "I remember buying one gallon, that's all the money I had," says Catherine. All the kids earned their own spending money, and at one point, so many of them were working at the local Roy Rogers restaurant that they could have staffed an entire shift by themselves. Ursula, however, opted for a greeting-card shop because her older sisters smelled so badly of grease when they came home.

Gas money was one thing, college money was something else, and Connie likes to say that the family suffered for years from "maltuition." Tony tried to contact Mary's former husband and "get some help out of him for college—it was getting pretty rough." When persuasion didn't work, Tony sued, and hired a prominent Boston law firm to handle the case. As he tells the story, the law firm was too genteel for its own good, and couldn't find the guy to serve him with a subpoena. Finally Tony learned the father of his six wards was getting remarried and he told his lawyer, "He's having a reception at five o'clock at the Ritz-Carlton; get a process server over there to meet him." When the lawyer gulped in reply—"You really don't mean that"—Tony shot back, "I certainly do." But in the end, Tony says, the father fought the case "and never did contribute" to his children's education.

The real challenge was not food and phones and laundry, it was emotions. Asked if he felt cheated at times, deprived of his parents' attention, Paul replied, "To be brutally honest, I'd have to say yes. There were times when I felt like saying,

'Hey, look at me.' " One Father's Day, he adds, his sister Laura sent Tony a card signed, "Your only daughter." It was her way of reminding him that "there's blood and there's blood, so let's be aware." And Tony *was* aware: "I would find an opportunity to take her off, to hold her hand and say, 'You're my baby daughter, you're my girl.' I still say it to her because it was hard on her. She'd been our total focus among the girls and all of a sudden she's got five sisters."

The transition was even harder for the newcomers. "The biggest adjustment was realizing this was really home now, we weren't visitors," recalls Catherine. "We couldn't say, we're just here a little while, and go back home later. At times we felt like we were intruding on what they had. They never made us feel that way, but we just felt it anyway."

Things improved after Mark burned a hole in his pillow smoking, and his cousins covered for him when Tony got home, assuring their uncle that what he was smelling was overdone grilled cheese. "Later we told Mark, 'You owe us big time,' but it really bonded us together," laughs Catherine. There was always a line, however, between the cousins and the "real children." After Mark cracked up the family car while Connie and Tony were away on a trip, Catherine remembers thinking, "Thank God it was Mark and not one of us."

Perhaps the biggest source of tension was the cousins' father. The elder Morellas "never even discussed him" with their nieces and nephew. "We just lost him," says Tony. "I don't know to this day if the kids had any contact with him." The most angry family member was the mother of Connie and Mary, who harbored deep resentments against her ex-son-in-law and communicated them to her grandchildren. "My grandmother was very Italian, very old-fashioned," remembers Catherine, and she was convinced that her daughter's divorce had somehow contributed to her illness. "That added to the tension." Ursula understands why her father was never mentioned in the Morella household, but his absence left his children with a stain of insecurity. "I had this feeling that my situation was precarious in some ways," she remembers. "I didn't have anything to fall back on, so I always had to tread lightly on things."

As the girls went away to college and started getting married, each one in turn asked Tony—not her father—to give her away. "I really feel closer to him than my own dad," explains Catherine. "He cared about me when I really needed a dad." Her words reflect the critical role Tony played. As Connie points out, the six cousins were *her* family, not his, and she offered to take them in without consulting him. But he treated the newcomers with a warmhearted, low-keyed affection that filled a deep need in their lives. As Catherine puts it, "If we had problems, or celebrations, Uncle Tony was the one who was always there. For him to take us all in was an outstanding thing to do." Tony was particularly touched by his role in his nieces' weddings, and he can still remember how each young woman would clasp his arm as they stood together at the back of the church: "I could feel her trembling, and each time I said to myself, what a joy, and what a stupid idiot this guy was to give that up."

Catherine now says that she "used to be bitter" about her father's absence, but feels less that way now. "It really was his loss and his choice." By the time Ursula, the youngest girl, was getting married, her father had gotten back in touch with his children, but she asked him not to come to her wedding. "I didn't want to upset my aunt and uncle," she recalls. "He wasn't very happy about it but he respected my wishes."

Today, with a daughter of her own, Ursula feels closer to her father than ever before. "He's had to make an effort," she says, "to prove to us he's really serious about having a relationship with us. As he's been getting older, I think he regrets the way he handled some things."

The Morellas have few regrets. Tony likes to call his six

extra children a "gift from God" and Connie's experience has helped her become one of Congress's leading experts on family and women's issues. One lesson she has learned at some cost—blended families need help. "You need help from your spouse, you need help from other family members, and if you don't have any of that, you need help from special neighbors and friends that you can call on for peace of mind," she says. "People should realize that women sometimes carry tremendous burdens and knapsacks of guilt, because we want to be everyplace and do everything. And frankly my advice is, you can't be Wonder Woman. Don't expect that you're going to be the fashion expert and have the perfect office and the perfect home and entertain beautifully and take care of children and do a great job at your profession. You're going to have to establish priorities. And the family and the children come first. You can't do everything."

Those "waifs" who trooped off that plane twenty-three years ago are now all married with children of their own—twelve in all. And they've learned well the lesson that "you need help from family members." Four of the five sisters live in New England and stay in close touch, helping out with each other's kids and sharing a special bond forged by their unusual upbringing. After their grandmother, Connie and Mary's mother, died last year, her house was sold and the cousins inherited a slice of the small profit. The five women decided there was only one way to spend the money and honor their grandmother. So they left their husbands and kids at home and went to Italy together.

Ellen Terry: Only Child of Four Parents

Ellen Terry flew so often between Kansas City and Houston that she belonged to several frequent-flier programs and qualified regularly for first-class upgrades. But the free drinks and bigger seats didn't matter much. She was eight years old.

Like many kids in modern America, Ellen spent her weekends shuttling between divorced parents. There were so many regulars on the Friday-afternoon flights between the two cities that the airline dubbed them the "brat pack" and sat them all together in the first few rows. "Everyone would have their backpack of goodies, with their Rubik's Cubes and their coloring books and you would kind of trade off on what you were going to play," Ellen recalls. "Pretty much the same kids were on the pattern of every other weekend and you kind of got to be friends. I didn't like a lot of them, though. I thought they were rude to the flight attendants and would throw things, so I tried to have my father seat me by myself."

Ellen had other motives for sitting separately. She was very worried about her mother, Rita, raising a child by herself in a big lonely city, so on her way to Houston she would interview fellow passengers as possible dates. "I think deep down I selfishly wanted someone to settle her down and make her there more for me," says Ellen. "I would meet guys who I thought were good-looking on the plane and haul them out to meet my poor mother and just build her up the whole time. Of course, I had already slipped them our phone number on the plane, and once they saw my mother, they would always call and pester her." The Ellen Terry Dating Service was not very successful—Rita rejected most of her selections—but Ellen's Insurance Referral Service was another story. Her father, Stan, ran an agency outside of Kansas City, and when she spotted a likely prospect, she made her pitch: "I knew my father's address and phone number and I would just write it down on the napkins they give you with your Coke, and say, 'He's the best in town, you gotta call my dad to get insurance.' " And some of them did. "I made some money off some of them," Stan recalls with a laugh.

Rita was almost ten years younger than Stan when they got married, and it was never a good match. Ellen likes to quote an old country-and-western song to sum up her parents' marriage: "While the guy's kicking his shoes off, she's putting hers on to go dancing—she's got the 'Friday-night blues.' She wanted to do things and he'd already done that, he'd had that time in his life, and I think that's where they grew apart." The divorce came through when Ellen was four, and when the judge gave custody to her mother, she remembers "seeing my dad cry for the first time in my life." Stan kept fighting the judgment, and eighteen years later the scars have not fully healed. "It was a rough, rough few years," Ellen explains. "I learned most of the bad words that I still know now at that age, because they were being thrown back and forth between my parents. It was just a lot of hurt. I don't think either of them knew how to deal with it and to leave me out of it, so I was pretty much in the middle."

Three years after the divorce, Rita wanted a fresh start in a bigger city, so she got the court's permission to move to Houston, but she soon learned a harsh lesson: divorce often sends women spiraling toward poverty. Weekdays Rita worked two jobs, secretary and jewelry-store clerk. On Saturdays, says her daughter, she "was one of those perfume girls at the mall, bugging you as you went into stores." There were no relatives in town to help out, and Ellen spent her afternoons at the YMCA or with a baby-sitter. Rita was out every night, but her daughter was always "very standoffish" with the guys and figured, "You won't be here long." Usually she liked their dogs better than the dates themselves. Dogs wouldn't leave your mother or bruise your feelings: "One of her boyfriends had a dog named Buster, and he was my best friend. I would just curl up on the couch with this big Doberman and go to sleep when we were over there late."

Meanwhile, Stan's business was doing well and he was living a much more stable life. "He always had time for me and we always did stuff," Ellen recalls. Time and money, Rita says with a tinge of bitterness: "He was able to give her things I couldn't." And when Stan went to court a third time, seeking custody of Ellen, Rita gave up: "I just couldn't afford another fight."

Ellen was eager to live with her dad. Kansas City was home, and Stan was about to get married again, to a schoolteacher named Arlene. But the first time she met Ellen, Arlene almost failed a key test. The little girl, now nine, had a ritual with her dad: he'd buy her a chicken sandwich at Burger King, but she'd only eat half and save the rest for later. Arlene was cleaning up the kitchen and threw out the half-eaten sandwich. "She almost died," recalls Ellen, "because she knew that if I didn't like a person, my dad would quit dating them. But for some reason, I forgave her."

Arlene was in her mid-thirties, this was her first marriage, and she was determined to be a good stepmother: "Actually I was marrying Ellen, too. This was a double commitment for me." During our conversation, Arlene turned to Stan and said, "I don't think I've ever told you this, but the week before we got married, I got cold feet. All of a sudden it hit me—gee, do I know what I'm doing?" But her feet warmed up when Ellen moved in, just weeks before the wedding. "I felt like I was Ellen's parent," Arlene remembers, "but I was not her mom. She already had a mom." A mom who did not get along with her ex-husband, so Arlene had to walk a very fine line, staying loyal to Stan without criticizing Rita.

"I did not want to be the parent who put her mother down," explains Arlene. "I felt if I did that, it would backfire, and Ellen would grow to resent me." In fact, Arlene came to understand, "the better relations Ellen had with her mom, the better relations she had with us." It proved to be an important insight. Arlene started out as a friend and "just became my mom," Ellen remembers. "She would do the carpools with my friends and cook the meals and take care of me when I was sick. She was a mother to me." But it took seven or eight years before Ellen started giving Arlene a card on Mother's Day that did not say "stepmother" on it. "One year I just said to myself, this stands out so bad," she remembers. "It's kind of a slap in the face, after everything she's done for me, to say, 'You're a great stepmom.' " Did Arlene notice the change? "I'm sure she did, but she never said anything."

After Ellen moved in with her dad, she made her biweekly trips in reverse, flying to Houston for weekends with her mom. And while Rita "would cry for about a week" whenever her daughter left, the new arrangements changed her life. Without a child to care for regularly, she was able to fulfill a dream and become a flight attendant. Three months after meeting Tom Branson in an airport, they were married, and Tom took a different view of stepparenting than Arlene had: "Ellen wasn't lacking parenting, and basically, we became pals. I was more like a big brother than a father. We'd call ourselves 'the three musketeers,' and out of the three, Ellen was the most mature." But it took Ellen well over a year to give Tom a hug. She still preferred dogs to men.

It helped that no other children entered the picture, leaving Ellen, as she likes to put it, as "the only child of four parents." With more financial security, and free airline tickets, Rita was able to visit Kansas City more often. After Ellen made the high-school cheerleading squad, Rita would try to arrive in time for the Friday-night football games, and often she and Arlene would sit together in the stands, rooting on their favorite daughter. But having two mothers is never easy, particularly on Mother's Day, and one year Ellen forgot to send Rita a card. Rita had never really forgiven Stan for taking Ellen, or Ellen for wanting to go with her father, and years of resentment came spilling out. "Ellen was having this cheerleading thing, and I was going to go up there and be one of the sponsors," Rita recalls. "I called her up and said, 'If you can't find the time to send me a card, I won't spend the time to be with you.' It was very childish of me, but my feelings were hurt."

It was Tom, Rita's new husband, who stepped in and

smoothed things over. "I told Rita that kids get very self-absorbed, and it was just part of Ellen's growing up," he recalls. "She shouldn't take it personally." In fact, Ellen's stepparents have often been the peacemakers. As outsiders, unburdened by buried guilt or bad memories, they can usually calm things down when tempers start to flare. When Ellen was applying to college, Stan favored a state school, but Tom thought his stepdaughter had the brains for the Ivy League and said so. When Stan continued to resist, Tom cashed in enough frequent-flier miles for two tickets, sending father and daughter to see colleges together. And when Ellen got accepted by Dartmouth, she decided to go. At her high-school graduation, she managed to seat an aunt and uncle between her two sets of parents. And then she went back east to college, hoping to leave the tensions of her childhood behind.

For the most part she did, but not completely. During a summer internship at a congressional office in Washington, she made such an impression that she was offered a full-time job. So she transferred to a new school and finished her college degree at night. On her twenty-first birthday she told the secretary that if her father called to put him right through. But when he did call, he was complaining about money and never mentioned her birthday. Ellen was devastated: "I was bawling. My dad's just business-oriented; feelings are the side attachment you sometimes get. So my best friend takes me out into the hall and someone comes out and says, 'You have to come back into the office, there's someone to see you.' I said, 'Tell them to go away, I don't want to see anyone.' And she's like, 'No, you really need to come in.' So I dry my face, and my mother had hired this gorilla in a tuxedo to come sing 'Happy Birthday' to me and give me balloons. And I'm hitting this gorilla because my father hadn't wished me happy birthday. At that point I realized, you've got to talk about this stuff! You've got to get it out. So after that I called my dad and celebrated my birthday on his credit card that night with my friends."

Once Ellen left for college, her parents had no reason to see each other or even talk very often. When they did, it was usually over arrangements, for tuition or holidays, and since old resentments still simmered, Ellen found it easier not to mention one parent to the other. The tussling left a mark, though, and she jokes that she'd never marry a man whose parents were divorced, because then they'd only spend every fourth Christmas with each of their parents.

As her college graduation approached, panic set in: "These two separate lives that I had managed to lead for about five years were suddenly colliding." The big problem was Ellen's father, Stan, who still resented his ex-wife and was the one most likely to make a scene. So Ellen called her stepmother, Arlene, who assured her that everyone would behave. "I said, 'Well, I just need you to know that if you don't, I'm not having a wedding,' " Ellen recalls. "Since I'm the only child, this is huge to my parents. This was my last threat to them. I was just so nervous."

Arlene had a request as well. Years before, in a fit of annoyance, Ellen had said that maybe she'd have both Stan and Tom, her father and stepfather, walk her down the aisle at her wedding. "It had bothered me ever since," said Arlene, "and I'd always looked for an opportunity to bring it up with her." This was the chance. "I'll make your dad behave," she told her stepdaughter, "if you promise him that he'll be the only one to give you away." Ellen was amazed, she'd forgotten the incident entirely, so it was a small price to pay for a peace treaty.

Graduation time came. Ellen was waiting with Stan and Arlene in front of a campus building where a reception was being held. They spotted Tom and Rita, coming down the street to meet them, and Stan leaned over and whispered to his daughter, "What happens now?" Nothing bad, it turned out. Everybody behaved. At one point during the weekend, Ellen and her roommates were hosting a small party, and Ellen looked over to see Rita and Arlene, her two mothers, side by side, decorating the table and putting out the food. Tom and Stan fixed stiff drinks for themselves and stood together talking. Ellen savored the moment: "I just kind of stopped and looked around and said, 'What's going on here?'"

Progress, apparently. Ellen has withdrawn her threat to avoid a big wedding, but her painful past has left her deeply cautious about marriage: "I will not get married until I can be at least 99 percent sure. Saying 'I do' will have a different meaning for me. I will never put my children through a divorce. I wasn't like the rest of my girlfriends, having these casual fun boyfriends. It just wasn't me—I think because I was so afraid of getting hurt. It definitely has affected my relationships. The one thing I've always told myself is that I will not get married until I know I will not get divorced."

Marriage might not be forever, but kids are. And blended families have to learn to live with imperfect solutions. "The bad thing about divorce is that it's not going to end," says Rita. "When Ellen gets married, and has children, and they have a birthday party, we'll all want to be there. So we'll have to make the best of it."

Frank, Perry, Inez, Sari, Abigail, and Mark Owens:
A Mother Without the Honor

Inez Owens wanted a small simple wedding, but she didn't have a small simple family. A dark-skinned woman of West Indian origin, she was adopted by a white couple who then divorced and remarried other people. But since her mother and stepmother detest each other, a joint bridal shower was out. So her groom's mother stepped in and organized the party.

As for the wedding itself, her stepfather sent out the invitations, with all six "parental persons," including her in-laws, listed as hosts. Her mother made the tablecloths for the reception. Her father brought the champagne, and her stepmother's father, a retired judge, presided. Says Inez: "I was trying to navigate very carefully. I divvied up the jobs so everyone got something to play with."

Still, the anxiety level was sky-high. When the florist suggested different-colored corsages for the stepparents, Inez nearly panicked: "I said, 'No, no, no, we can't do too many line drawings here.'" She even thought about having two aisles instead of one, so the bride's side could be divided in half and her parents wouldn't have to sit together. "Where do you put everybody," she mused, "when they don't want to talk to each other?"

No event tests a divorced couple like a wedding. That's the moment when old rivalries and resentments are most likely to surface. Even the smallest detail is weighted with symbolism. People who don't want to talk to each other have to share the same child and the same room. And the child is caught in the middle, trying to keep everybody happy and wondering whether she can succeed where her parents have failed, and stay married.

Frank Owens, Nancy Clark, and Perry Friedman all knew each other in college, and Frank jokes that his two wives hated each other before he married either one of them. Frank and Nancy's marriage was troubled from the outset, and a series of miscarriages added to the tension. In Frank's view, they adopted Inez and Sari—another infant with a West Indian background—in large part to "save the marriage," but "it didn't work," and they divorced when the girls were seven and nine. As Inez recalls, "We were relieved when our parents divorced; they had been fussing for years."

When Perry heard about the breakup, she invited Frank to dinner with other friends. Perry remembers what happened next: "Someone called me up after the dinner party and said, 'Are you out of your mind? Why did you invite other people? He's very interested in you and he's terrific.'" When Perry told Frank the next move was up to him, he asked her out.

"He took me to dinner and I said, 'It seems to me that you are flirting with me and that you have been for maybe fifteen years.' He thought about that and said, 'Well, if that's true, why don't you let me continue?' "

Perry was thirty-six at the time, a "ticking clock," in her own words, who had always wanted children of her own. She moved in with Frank, got pregnant, lost the baby, and then got pregnant again. The day after their daughter Abigail was born, Frank decided to finish a long-delayed project, painting the stairs. He stripped to his underwear, and was about half done, when Sari appeared on the landing wearing a coat and carrying a suitcase. "She looked up with these very large eyes and said good-bye," Frank remembers. With a new baby coming, she didn't think she was wanted anymore.

But she was. Perry defines herself as a caretaker and she welcomed her stepchildren. "I love being a mommy, and they were very appealing," she recalls. "Mostly it was like baby kittens. They were so needy. And the fact that they didn't look like either of their parents made it possible for me to adore them for themselves, all by themselves, with no complications. I never saw Nancy's face in them."

For Inez and Sari, however, the situation was not always easy. During the week they lived with their mother, Nancy, a lax housekeeper and disciplinarian who allowed them to eat dinner on the living-room floor in front of the TV. When they got to Perry's on Friday night, the table was set with good china and lighted candles and they were expected to report on their week's activities. "The ideas and wishes were so different at either end," recalls Inez.

Perry felt she was providing a refuge of stability for the girls, and she worried that the new baby had introduced a damaging note of uncertainty in their lives. "They were really afraid that I would take that baby and go," she remembers. So when Abigail was about a year old, Frank and Perry got married with Inez and Sari in attendance.

A year after the wedding a second child, Mark, was born, and from the beginning, the four youngsters got along very well. When Abigail was in the third grade, she had to assemble a photo collage of her family. Without thinking twice, she included pictures of her two stepsisters. Classmates at her fancy private school were disbelieving. "They can't be your sisters," Abigail was told, "they're black!" To this day, ten years later, Abigail remembers her anger. "But they *are* my sisters," she insisted. "Who are you to say they're not related, just because of their skin color!" On another occasion, one of Frank's business partners came to the house, and when Sari answered the door, he thought she was a maid. The kids were amused and outraged at the same time, and took to calling the hapless partner "butler boy."

The real tension was between mother and stepmother. Their different views of parenting caused constant conflict. "Sari would come on Friday afternoon in her red-and-white polka-dot dress and she hadn't bathed or had her hair brushed since she'd left on Sunday night," recalls Perry. "So I'd put Sari in the tub and wash her and brush her hair and wash her clothes and send her back with clean clothes every Sunday night." Perry remembers those years with fury and frustration: "I was the mother without the honor. And still am."

Nancy, not Perry, went with Frank to PTA meetings and teacher conferences for Inez and Sari, and those evenings often ended in recrimination. "Perry could smell Nancy on my clothes and go crazy," Frank remembers. Perry agrees that being excluded from those school events made her "hysterical," and she feels that Nancy did not expect her daughters to do well in school and did not push them hard enough. Nancy always referred to the girls as "free spirits" who shouldn't be shackled by conventional expectations, but others thought she was expressing a latent racism, holding the girls to lower standards because they were not white. When Sari had an asthma attack and was in danger of falling behind her class, it was Perry who taught her third-grade math. And when Sari wanted to apply to a special school for artistic children, it was Perry who encouraged her, while Nancy remained skeptical. "I went nuts, I was in such a rage," Perry remembers. "She was going to undercut that kid in every way she possibly could."

The girls sometimes felt like pawns in their parents' power struggle. "They would schedule holidays and parties on the same night, and make us choose to prove our loyalty," recalls Inez. Since Perry is Jewish, Passover became a particular problem, and she still gets agitated remembering the year that Nancy, "with typical insensitivity," sent the girls back from vacation too late to attend the Seder. The Owens household had "the longest Christmas Day in the whole wide world," because Inez and Sari spent Christmas Eve with their mother, and Abigail and Mark couldn't open their stockings until the girls arrived around noon. Then all four kids waited for Perry's father before opening the rest of their presents. Christmas, sighs Perry, "just goes on forever."

Perry has a complicated relationship with her stepdaughters. At times the girls threw "terrible, terrible tantrums," and occasionally they still do. Not long ago, Sari marched into Perry's office at a publishing company and shouted that she hated her stepmother "more than life itself." With grim humor Perry recalls the day: "Thank God I'd been promoted and had a door to my office." On other days, Sari, who works in a social-service agency, will call her stepmother at seven in the morning and ask for advice on how to handle a particular problem. On Mother's Day, she called Perry and reminded her, "I have three mothers to choose from"—her adopted mother, her stepmother, and her biological mother, who has recently reappeared in her life. Perry treasures the fact that Sari called *her*.

"There were periods that were just incredibly tough, where the girls were acting out big time," Perry says. "I remember being incredibly upset, but I never didn't want them. I never didn't love them." She takes comfort in the advice of several therapists who explain the dynamic this way: "Oftentimes the stepmother, especially a good stepmother, is the focus of all sorts of anger and tension because I'm the only one it's safe to be angry with. To be adopted and have your parents divorce is to be very fragile in a lot of ways. And to be terribly afraid of the anger of both of your parents. But your stepmother is fair game."

It was not just the kids who were caught between their mother and stepmother. Frank felt squeezed as well. Perry maintains that her husband favored his adopted children over his natural ones because he was "terrified of being disloyal" to Inez and Sari. And she accuses Frank of not standing up to Nancy on questions of child rearing: "I was furious with Frank because he really couldn't cope. I would be frantic and upset and we would get into rows, but it never occurred to me to walk away from the kids. Frank maybe, but not them." Frank has a slightly different take on the conflict: "Perry was angry for a long time, because I cared more for the older ones than the newer ones, but it was mainly a question of age. I care more for jokes than I do for bottles."

Handling Inez and Sari has been a major source of friction between Frank and Perry, a recurring spark of discord that at times has threatened the stability of their marriage. Perry wanted her husband to share her hatred of his first wife, but he never did, and they could not get the conflict behind them because the girls were still around, forcing their parents and stepparents to deal with them and each other. It's easier now, with Inez and Sari gone from home, but the girls can still stir up trouble in the Owens household. Frank and Perry were planning a reception in New York for Inez and her new husband a few weeks after the wedding and Perry wanted something "spectacular," complains Frank, at least in part to show up her old rival Nancy. But Frank, who still sees himself as a small-town midwesterner, found the thought of a "spectacular" New York party deeply nerve-racking. "I was depressed for a week," he says.

In blended families, graduation days can be almost as hard as weddings. When Inez graduated from college, Perry arranged a lunch and Nancy and her new husband, Ralph, both attended. Perry describes the event: "It's perfectly pleasant and celebratory and Ralph leans across to me and says, 'Well, I guess we don't have to do anything like this again until Sari graduates.'"

But when Sari graduated from college in Ohio a few years later, there was no second attempt at togetherness. Frank and Perry were talking to Sari after the ceremony, and as Perry remembers: "Nancy comes up and says, 'Oh, are you ready? Let's go, we're going to have lunch and go to these antique shows,' and takes Sari and walks away. I cried all the way to West Virginia. I just cried and cried and cried. I was just so upset and angry. There's nothing you can do."

No one in Perry's family questions her devotion, but they do question her judgment. Frank says his second wife always felt competitive with his first wife and "it was very important to her" to tell the girls "what a lousy mother Nancy was." But in Frank's view, "the girls didn't want to hear that" from Perry, and her animosity toward Nancy "gets in the way of the adult relationship she wants with the girls." Abigail agrees with her father: "It's got to be hard to be a stepparent, but there are times when you have to shut up and deal. You have to remember that you aren't the only parent and some occasions are not meant for you. There are times when you should back off." Inez agrees that her stepparents should not feel so competitive: "I keep wishing they wouldn't try to supplant my original parents. It doesn't have to be one over the other."

Despite considerable professional success, Perry says, "I'm pretty much defined by my family and I wouldn't have it any other way." She is proud of her children, all four of them, and happy that they all see each other as siblings. And she knows that being a stepparent means making mistakes and accepting compromises: "But you have to play with what's there. Do I regret any of it? No. Do I wish I'd kept my temper better? Do I wish I weren't so tired so much of the time? Do I wish I hadn't been on overload so much of the time? Yes, very much. Very much. I worry that they will think of me being so strung out and tense, when I was juggling, juggling, juggling all of the time. But are they all terrific? Yes, absolutely. They're really super."

Afterword

After talking to us, and comparing notes with each other, these three families had some fascinating reactions. In just about every case, people told us they'd learned things about each other and their relationships they hadn't known before. Ellen Terry says it was like "therapy" for her two sets of parents to express themselves about some long-simmering grievances and hear her version: "This was an excuse for me to bring some things up and make my parents think about them, because obviously these are conversations you try to steer clear of." In particular, her mother, Rita, was struck by the insight of her stepmother, Arlene: there shouldn't be a competition for Ellen's affection. If she had a good relationship with one woman, her relations with the other improved as well. "Now my mother *wants* me to have a better relationship with Arlene," Ellen notes. Tony Morella learned, for the first time, that when he came home one day and smelled something burning, it was not overcooked grilled cheese—as he had been told at the time—but the incendiary effects of his son's cigarettes. It was also news to Tony and Connie that their six wards are now in touch with their biological father, a subject they still don't discuss. And one of their nieces, Ursula, had this reaction when she read that Tony considered his six surrogate children a "gift from God": "I wish we had heard that sooner." Frank and Perry Owens read our conversations with their daughters before attending Inez's wedding and it helped them survive the weekend. "I really understood what was going on a lot better," says Perry. She also realized that her husband and her daughter Abigail were using us to send her a message: be less critical and more tolerant of others in the family. All this reinforces a simple point. Communication is to a marriage what sunlight is to a plant: a basic necessity.

Chapter Seven

OUR LIVES

FROM THIS DAY

FORWARD

Becca's wedding completed a cycle that had started thirty-one years before, almost to the day, on the exact same spot. For both children, their primary responsibility was now to somebody else, not to us. When they arrived safely somewhere, they would call their spouses, not their parents. But seeing them married, to people we liked so much, gave us a wonderful sense of completion. Parenthood is easily the hardest job either of us has ever taken on, but also the most rewarding. Now we could say, "We've done it." Sure there was a sense of loss, but that's what life is about, letting go. The words of the wedding ceremony, "from this day forward," had new meaning. Our travels together still had a long way to go, and now our children were starting on their own journeys, joining their own partners, writing their own stories.

CR: At this stage of life, with the children grown and gone, think how sad it would be not to have each other. We're still able to look at each other in the morning and say, "Gee, I'm glad you're here."

SR: Or at least most mornings! Let's not get too sappy here.

CR: Fair enough. Most mornings. I think the word is devotion. There's a special level of affection that is based on longevity, on knowing each other well over a period of time and going through many things together, happy and sad.

SR: I think of the day my dad died. Cokie was supporting my mother as we walked down the corridor in the hospital to see my father for the last time. Those moments are as meaningful as walking a daughter down the aisle to be married. I think that there is a great joy in familiarity, and the most obvious sign of that is the way we finish each other's sentences.

CR: Or don't even have to begin them. The kids think we're quite loony. They picture us as these doddering old people, barely managing to make it through the day!

SR: Well, we do give them reason to believe that! We are creatures of great habit.

CR: Humans, you mean.

SR: Humans in general but us in particular. At times in our lives we've lived in exotic places and done adventuresome things, and with any luck we're still able to do that. One of the things I've learned in midlife is the importance of accepting new challenges, and the first day I walked into a college classroom at age forty-seven I was taking a long leap off a high board. But I also think at this stage you come to cherish what's comfortable and ordinary, sometimes in very little things. I plant white geraniums in the same pots every summer so we can see them from the kitchen table, and I've told Cokie one of my aims is to fill her life with flowers . . .

CR: . . . I'm afraid we've become fogies . . .

SR: We've lived in the same house for twenty-two years.

CR: I've lived here for forty-seven myself.

SR: We vacation in the same house for the same two weeks in South Carolina every year. The shape of the beach, the smell of the sea. It's all the same.

CR: We don't like to make choices. We have to do that all day, every day. We have to decide what stories to write, what people to interview, what's important, what's the lead, what words convey the meaning. We also have to be "on" a good bit of the time, to perform. But at the end of the day we want to shut down, have our own time . . .

SR: . . . to unplug from all the sockets . . .

CR: In fact, when a rumor spread recently that our favorite neighborhood restaurant planned to close, I stormed in there and attacked the owner! Don't you dare do this! We are incapable of change!

SR: And, we've learned after all these years, we're not going to change each other. For all the ways we've adapted and the quirks we've accepted, we remain different people with different backgrounds. For instance, I will never share Cokie's experience as a woman, or her education as a Catholic, and occasionally we've disagreed so strongly on an issue that we've split our newspaper column in half, with each of us writing a different opinion. But the differences show up in personal ways, too.

CR: I was raised in a situation where family members and close friends stayed with us for weeks and even months at a time. I would move into my sister's room with her and the guests would take my room. It never occurred to me that I wouldn't inconvenience myself for other people. My aunt Tootsie, who had seven children and not much money, had a saying that summed up the family attitude: "If there's room in the heart, there's room in the home." And sure enough, I would sometimes move into her home for the whole summer. That was very different from the way Steven was raised. I don't think you ever had people spend the night, right?

SR: That was partly because we lived in very cramped conditions. By the time my sister was born, almost every room in our house that wasn't the kitchen or a bathroom became a bedroom. But basically I agree with you, we grew up with a very different sense of privacy, and it's taken more than a little adjusting on both sides. I had to learn to be more flexible and Cokie had to learn to be more protective.

CR: But it's still a source of tension, in fact the greatest source of tension in our marriage. There are times when I feel Steven is being selfish, when he doesn't want to put himself out. Other times I know he is absolutely right, that if we operated the way I would instinctively operate, we would never have a minute to ourselves, we would be completely overtaken by other people's demands. But there are still times when I think he's wrong.

SR: I think at times she allows our lives to be dictated too much by other people. She can push herself to exhaustion with the demands of work and entertaining and caretaking. I love having our home be the center of family events. The portrait of Cokie's father hangs right there over the dining-room table, a table that has been the setting for so many ceremonies and celebrations. But Cokie has finally learned that our house can't always be the center. Other people in the family and other friends want the chance to be the host, and not always come to us.

CR: That's true.

SR: Sometimes there aren't enough holidays to go around. Our niece Elizabeth, who's very special to us, is married to a Danish man, Michael Davidsen, and in Danish culture, Christmas Eve is a special time. So they've made a big point in the last few years of making Christmas Eve *their* holiday. Michael cooks a Danish meal and we go through the Danish customs, like finding the nut in the rice pudding. It's a good example of the next generation saying, "We don't always want to be the kids, we want to be the grown-ups," and it's important to give them that chance.

I've discovered that with my students as well. I have a deal with them—when they're undergraduates and don't have any money, I always pay when we go out to some campus beer joint. Once they graduate and have jobs and want to take me out to lunch, I will happily accept.

CR: It's a passage.

SR: I now have students calling up all the time saying, "I can buy you lunch!" Which means, I have a job. One young man, during his first week at his first law firm, took me to lunch and paid with a credit card that was so new, it was glistening. It was a great moment for him. I've learned that it would be insulting for me to say, "No, I'll pick up the check."

CR: It's also nice for kids to have adult friends who are not their parents. To have someone who is interested in you and cares about you but does not have the emotional baggage of a parent-child relationship. But it's good the other way around, too—for us to have young friends who are not our children.

SR: Then there are the four-legged friends. I had never grown up with animals, but our kids let it be known at a young age that they would not be similarly deprived. When Lee and Becca were little, we had the usual assortment of guinea pigs and hamsters; then, even though Cokie is wildly allergic to them, we collected a few cats as well. The move back to America meant the younger generation's demand for a dog was no longer something we could ignore.

CR: Sebastian, a cute little poodle-terrier mixture from the pound, had hair just like Steve's. In fact, one night when Steven was away on a trip, he got home earlier than expected and crawled quietly into bed so as not to disturb me. When I turned over and felt this mop of curly hair, I started fussing, "Get out of this bed, you know you're not supposed to be here." Steven was somewhat taken aback, to put it mildly. When I realized my bedmate was my husband, not my dog, I thought it was pretty funny.

SR: That dog, Sebastian, was my first animal buddy; he lived with us for seven years and then was killed by a car in front of our house. We waited a little while and then got another dog from the pound, a beautiful female something-or-other who turned out to be completely wild and dreadfully disruptive in the household.

CR: Even so, it was plenty upsetting when a car got her, too, after she'd only been with us for about a month. I said, that's it. No more dogs. Becca was going to college the next year, and I'd be the one left to train and walk a dog. I absolutely put my foot down. Steven and Becca both walked around for months with long faces calling me the Wicked Witch of the West. So finally I relented: "Okay, you can have a dog if you find one that's house-trained, likes cats, and can't jump on our bed."

SR: Becca scoured the pounds and pet shops and ads in the newspapers and finally found Abner, a three-year-old basset hound no one could describe as cute or beautiful, or smart either. Except he possessed one brilliant trait: he could open the refrigerator door. Cokie hadn't put that on her list of don'ts. One Thanksgiving he ate an entire ten-pound ham and had to be rushed to the doggie emergency room.

CR: At Becca's wedding, where he wore a black bow tie with sparkles, I had to surround the cake with a fence of pretty boxes so the dog couldn't get to it.

SR: Abner always slept on a favorite chair in our bedroom, but as he grew older he couldn't make the leap up, so he settled for a smelly old bedspread on the floor. After a while he couldn't make it to the second floor anymore, but he hated to be alone, so he sat at the bottom of the steps and howled until the guilt got too great or the noise too loud and I'd go down and carry him, courting permanent back injury. He had never been the most scrupulous dog about house training, but at the end he was hopeless. Cokie finally put him in Depends, but we spent a good deal of time on our hands and knees doing doggie cleanup. Still, he had such a sweet, dumb disposition and he loved us so unconditionally that we were heartbroken when he died.

CR: Steven was so dear to that dog. You know the old joke, life begins when the kids leave home and the dog dies. But we missed Abner, and Steve wrote a column about caring for the old fella that got the attention of the Basset Rescue folks. They gave us a suitable mourning period and showed up one fine day with Rupert in tow. So here we are again with an unruly hound in our midst, chasing the cat and chewing up books and pillows. At least he can't open the icebox door. Yet.

SR: Cokie and the kids taught me to love animals; as she said, I had never grown up with them. Another thing that I've learned from Cokie is the spirit of charity. Growing up in a more private setting meant that we were more inward looking as a family. My parents were public-spirited, and my father was very involved in local politics and civic organizations and he gave money to causes he cared about. But for Cokie, charity is a part of her everyday life. She practically has a florist on retainer and visits so many hospital rooms she could probably qualify for degrees in several medical specialties. Or at least she thinks she could. I take so much time with my students because of three people: my dad, who was my first mentor; Scotty Reston, who took so much care and time with me; and Cokie, who keeps reminding me of the virtues of serving others.

CR: Steven, who's a naturally generous and gregarious person, likes to schedule his time. But sometimes things happen which demand attention, regardless of the schedule. It's not what you planned to do that day—too bad.

SR: On a recent Sunday our newest great-nephew was born. At about eight or nine o'clock we'd just finished dinner, and Cokie announced, "Come on. Let's go to the hospital, we have to meet William."

CR: He was only a couple of hours old.

SR: So we did.

CR: It's easy to convince Steven to throw plans to the winds where our own kids are involved. We miss them so much that we'll take any opportunity to see them. But we've had to adjust to the fact that they have other families who want to see them as well, particularly at holiday times.

SR: Like every couple, when we first got married, we had to work out a holiday schedule. Cokie felt strongly about celebrating the religious holidays with her family, so the Robertses got Thanksgiving. We made it into an annual reunion and tried to spend several days together. After Becca got married, she decided to spend Thanksgiving with Dan's family, and the first year she was missing was tough for us. In fact, I wrote a column about it called "The Empty Chair at the Table." It was a sign that they now had obligations to other families. They didn't belong only with us anymore.

CR: Distance also creates problems. When Lee and Liza moved to London, and couldn't get home for Christmas, they spent it with my mother in Rome instead. And for the millennium we had this extended family, Liza's and ours, in Rome together. What could be better?

SR: The year after Lee got married I opened a Christmas card from his in-laws, and there was a picture of their whole family—including Lee! It was a bit of a shock to see my son peering out from another family's Christmas card!

CR: Our children are also at an age where they can take responsibility for their grandparents, and they're happy to oblige, as are their spouses. When my mother broke her foot in Rome, Liza and Lee were practically on the next plane from London.

SR: One of the things that made us all feel better about Lindy moving to Rome was that Lee and Liza were only an hour away.

CR: Liza has no living grandparents and after a recent visit with my mother, my daughter-in-law said of her husband's grandmother, "It's so special for me to spend time around someone who's lived that long, to receive her wisdom and have a sense of what her life's been like."

SR: It's also fascinating to watch their careers evolve. In some ways, each of them has gone into the family business. They have remained interested in public policy and politics. But they've each grown branches off the family tree. Lee plans and strategizes for an investment bank—which means he analyzes economic and political trends. Becca reports for public radio and television, hardly an odd notion in this family, but she covers technology, a subject neither one of us knows anything about. So both of them are in positions to teach us about what they're doing, and that's good for everybody.

CR: But it's still recognizable. It's not like they're scientists or artists, where we'd admire their work but struggle to understand it. And their spouses have sprouted their own branches. Liza's in the reporting business, for a rival network, and Dan advises cities and states on their finances, so he's deeply into the political scene.

SR: I remember well our parents traveling to be with us as we moved around the world. And now we're the ones who travel to see our children. Last summer we met Lee and Liza in Italy, and had one of those lovely Italian lunches in a garden in Tuscany where we sat down at about one-thirty and didn't get up until four-thirty. We had a similar lunch with Dan and Becca in the Napa Valley wine country. Those are the rare moments in life when you say, "There is no place in the world I'd rather be and nobody I'd rather be with than this group, in this place, right now."

CR: The trick is making time for those moments. When my father disappeared, I was so young that I didn't immediately draw a life's lesson from the experience—too much of life was ahead of me. But my sister's death at age fifty-one had a profound effect on me. I'm now older than she was then, almost as old as my father was when I last saw him. Their losses at such young ages have taught me the hard way that we mustn't put off time together, hoping to have more of it in later years. Those years may never come. On the other hand, the fact that my mother took on an interesting new job at the age of eighty-one tells me that the world of work will always be there, if that's what I want. I know those truths well, but acting on them is not always easy given our demanding world. I need Steven to remind me, to help me live the way I want to.

SR: Some years ago the priest at our nephew Paul's wedding described marriage as "an unlimited commitment to an unknowable partner," and that's true. Marriage is an act of faith, as well as hope. Not every marriage endures, and not every marriage should, we know that. But marriage will never work without that "unlimited commitment" to the future.

CR: When we go to weddings, at least ones where the couple recites traditional vows, we find ourselves becoming awfully sentimental and teary. I've noticed that's true of other long-married couples, who nod their way through the ceremony, squeezing each other's hand as the bride and groom pledge "to have and to hold, from this day forward." Those newlyweds can't possibly know what that promise will mean. We didn't either, when we said those words under the *chuppah* that beautiful September night when we were so young. We've been incredibly blessed. So far, we've lived for better, not worse, richer, not poorer, in health, not sickness. Still, after thirty-three years, we can't anticipate what will happen from this day forward. But we're eager to find out.

Afterword

Since we finished this book, some interesting things have happened to the people you've just read about. We write that four couples had gotten married in our yard—us, our daughter, Steve's brother, family friends. Now there is a fifth. Our niece Jenna Roberts married Andy Mammen (they met as medical students at Johns Hopkins) on the same spot in May 2000, and that evening marked several firsts. It was the first Quaker wedding at Bradley Boulevard, with guests standing as the spirit moved them to speak during the ceremony. And it was the first time that it rained. But the tent held up and all was well.

After we described how Justice Arthur Goldberg spoke at our wedding as an "elder" of the Jewish tribe, we got a call from his great-great niece. She was marrying a non-Jew and wanted to use "Uncle Arthur's" words in her ceremony. So we sent them along, and just recently received several photographs of the happy couple. Our nephew Steve Sigmund is planning to marry a Jewish woman and has asked his Uncle Steve to play the "elder" role at their ceremony. The two Steves often attend Yankee baseball games together and a ceremonial first pitch might be added to the traditional glass breaking.

During our book tour Steve often told the story of the "book of poems" that made its way from Europe to America and wound up uniting Sam and Norma Weiss in a sixty-three-year-marriage. One night C-SPAN covered our appearance at the Politics and Prose bookstore in Washington, and the morning after the talk was broadcast our phone rang. "My name is Mel Weiss," said the fellow on the line, "and the book of poems story is about my parents." Steve had never met Mel, who was very gracious. When Cokie spoke at a synagogue near their beach home in New Jersey, Mel and his wife attended her talk.

We got another call from a woman named Yaffa Eliach, who has written a book, *There Once Was a World*, about Eishyshok, the home village of Steve's grandmother, where the book of poems story took place. "Your family is in my book," she told Steve, but he insisted they weren't. He'd already looked them up. You're spelling your grandmother's name wrong, she said, it's "Vasilishki" not "Wasilsky." Sure enough, there is a Berl Vasilishki in the book, described as a "shtetl medicine man and horse expert."

Then there is Lilly Friedman, who wore the white wedding dress made from a German silk parachute in a displaced persons camp in early 1946. The dress went on display at the Holocaust museum in December 1999, and just before the event Steve called her. Lilly told him that her father, Rabbi Yitzak Lax, who died at Auschwitz, was born on the fifth day of Chanukah, a joyous Jewish holiday that lasts eight days. So even though the holiday falls on a different date each year, the Friedman family always remembers the rabbi on the fifth night with special prayers. Steve was taken aback. "Don't you realize," he told Lilly, "that the ceremony opening the exhibit falls on the fifth night?" Lilly was shocked and pleased. Several dozen of her relatives came to Washington for the event, filling a bus by themselves. With twenty-one grandchildren, and a new great-grandchild, Lilly has fulfilled the biblical admonition to "be fruitful and multiply." We wrote in our column that week: "As we light our candles on the fifth night of Chanukah, we will add an extra one for Rabbi Yitzak Lax, for his sons who died with him, for his daughters who survived, and for the generations he never lived to see."

Many people who read the book or heard us talk about it wanted to share their own stories of love and marriage, including the young couple who approached us one Saturday night as we were coming out of the movies in our neighborhood. The woman was shaking, on the edge of tears. "It's incredible," she blurted out. "We just finished reading your book and decided this afternoon to get married." Steve was touched, but Cokie was less sentimental. "I don't want to take responsibility for their marriage," she muttered.

We're particularly pleased when readers want to give this book to others. One man at a book signing in Charlottesville, Virginia, was buying four copies, one for each of his children. A TV producer told us that her mother in San Francisco couldn't get her father to read it. Mom solved the problem by buying the taped version and playing it for Dad while he was trapped in the car on a long trip.

A Jewish woman gave the book to her brother, who was about to marry a Catholic, and then sent us a note saying: "The priest who they talked to *told* them to read it because it was a good source on mixed couples." A rabbi in Florida wrote that he was giving the book to young couples who came to him for advice: "It really forces people to deal with the seriousness of commitment and the potential rewards of union." A friend attended a wedding in Boston, where the celebrant read from the book as part of the service. A minister from Los Angeles told us that he and his wife read portions aloud to each other. That sounds a little weird, frankly, but we're glad they enjoyed it.

One of the reasons we wrote the book was to shore up young people who are surrounded by failed marriages but still have an elemental yearning for their own mates and matches. So we were heartened by the letter from David Popenoe and Barbara Dafoe Whitehead, codirectors of the National Marriage Project at Rutgers: "We talk to so many young people who are searching for good models and inspirational stories of marriage to encourage and instruct them but who find only bad models and cautionary stories of divorce. *From This Day Forward* makes a tremendous contribution to changing all that."

Not all the reactions have been so favorable. A woman from Staten Island wrote about our children: "To say you brought them up in both religions does not make sense. True, tradition is a part of religion. But if the children are baptized Catholic, then they are not Jewish. Likewise, if they are not baptized, then they are not Catholic." Some Jewish readers expressed similar views, that mixed couples have to choose one tradition or another, and can't be both. We respectfully disagree, but we also recognize that our way of doing things is not the only way. Every couple has to find their own answers.

In writing the book we came to realize that all marriages are mixed marriages, starting with those between a man and a woman. The whole notion that differences between religions are greater than the differences between genders is ridiculous. All relationships make the same journey and meet the same obstacles. They just take different paths to the same place. As one old friend of Cokie's, a mother of three living in Pittsburgh, wrote of the book: "Its message is so simple: we married people are human, we fall down on the job occasionally, we pick ourselves up, and keep on trying to love each other."

That's it exactly. A typical letter came from a man who's been married fourteen years: "Like you we have a mixed marriage (she is Jewish and I'm Lutheran). We are the only ones in our circle of friends who are married longer than five years. A few are into their second and third marriages. A few years ago I heard a great quote (unfortunately I cannot remember the author). It went something like this: 'The problem with divorce in this country is that it is not an effective deterrent to marriage.' A lot of folks in long marriages feel a bit under siege these days, but a bad marriage will not deter many people from trying again, and it shouldn't. The rewards are worth the risk."

A woman from Atlanta put her reaction this way: "With satisfaction, I listened to you talk of your mixed marriage. We are a blending of Protestant and Judaism and have spent the last thirty years explaining to others how it is possible to succeed without anyone losing something. In many ways I believe we have a more meaningful faith." We agree. But just so we wouldn't feel too smug our correspondent added: "I seldom agree with your political views, but I do respect your sense of family and traditions."

One of Steve's former students, a Protestant, assigned the book to her Jewish boyfriend: "After that, I'll pass it on to my parents, so we'll all have a base to start from. It was interesting to read your story because it reflected so many of the things my parents have told me about their marriage and life, but it's different to hear it from someone else. Kind of like you say at the end—it's nice to have older friends who aren't your parents." By the way, it's nice to have younger friends who are not your children. Months after the first note we got a second one: the couple is now engaged! Perhaps we should send them the e-mail we got from the older brother of another student, five weeks after his wedding to a woman of another faith. We'd urged him to plan the ceremony "with a sense of inclusion not exclusion," and he wanted us to know how well things had gone: "Your message about 'inclusion' hit home, and as we all found out, it is truly the best way to go!"

Inclusion is almost always "the best way to go," but some

situations are more stressful than others. Take the friend of Steve's who wrote, "My son is getting married and is planning a wedding ceremony. He is half Jewish and half Protestant. His wife's family lives in the United Arab Emirates. Her father is Syrian-Jordanian; her mother is Palestinian. My wife and I had them at our house for a long lunch. They are nice people but hate Israel. This should be an interesting wedding to plan." It sure should. Maybe afterward they can hire out as Middle East peace negotiators.

A nun from Baton Rouge, Louisiana, told us that a priest had cancelled out on a Jewish-Catholic wedding only three weeks before the ceremony. So she had stepped in as a replacement: "Rabbi Weinstein and I stood together with the couple under the *chuppah*. I stood toe-to-toe with the groom and was very grateful that his aim when he smashed the glass was right on target. Comments from the wedding party and their guests were very positive about the inclusion, not only of both religious traditions but also of both genders. As far as I know it was a first, at least in conservative Baton Rouge." That's a shrewd comment. Including both genders in any ceremony can be as useful as including both religions. And bravo on the groom's aim. A relative of ours once kicked the glass across the floor trying to smash it.

A woman from Dublin, Ohio, gave a copy of our book to her daughter just before her wedding, but then went one better. "We chose five couples from our guest list who exemplify in their marriages the qualities, virtues, and 'seasoning' that you write about," she said. "To these five couples we sent a copy of *From This Day Forward* with a cover letter thanking them for their admirable marriages and honorable role modeling for our daughter." At the ceremony she was planning to get all five couples together with the bride and groom for a photograph. "We hope this little fraternity will be a source of support and encouragement to the newly-weds," she wrote. What a great idea. It embodies something we believe strongly: marriage is a communal act, not just a private one. In the middle of a storm, older friends and relatives can hold an umbrella over a young family and help keep them dry.

A new neighbor of ours in Bethesda said that moving here from Savannah, Georgia, was made easier by our story. "My twelve-year-old has moved ten times," she wrote. "Needless to say all the 'conversations' on moving, emotions of children, settling, and uprooting really hit home. Ha! We are again unsettled but knowing someone else went through it too is a comfort." Our own move to Bethesda happened long ago, in 1977, and Cokie's family originally bought our house forty-eight years ago. But our children, now living in London and San Francisco, are going through those same decisions about "settling and uprooting," so we know what she's talking about.

A "thirty-nine-year-old Jewish female attorney" living on the East Coast wrote about falling in love with a "thirty-four-year-old Mexican American from Southern California who lives in the Grand Canyon" as a park ranger. She admits to being "very gun-shy about seriously giving this relationship the chance it deserves." But reading our book, she says, "has inspired me at least to try and I am certain that many of the lessons you passed along will surely help." We're reluctant to give advice, because every relationship is so different. But she's right about one thing: the relationship does deserve a chance. We admire her courage and wish her luck.

A woman in Michigan said she listened to the book on tape and then gave it to her lesbian partner. They were particularly interested in our story about inviting a gay couple to our annual Chanukah party: "I believe it is important for you, as two professionals who make a living analyzing and shaping public policy and culture, to hear that both of your books are relevant to same-sex couples and their families." We're pleased to hear that. While we're uncomfortable with gay marriage we strongly support the sort of "civil union" adopted by Vermont earlier this year. As we wrote in our newspaper column: "Conservatives say civil union reflects the 'moral rot' in society but the very reverse is true. In our own circle of friends and family, we've known a number of gay couples who simply want what every heterosexual couple wants—intimacy, understanding, constancy. Partners who want to make a life together should be shored up not shut out, respected not rejected."

To all our readers, a grateful thank you. To those of you reading this book for the first time, we hope some of you will share your own thoughts and stories with us.

Suggested Reading

Akers, Charles W. *Abigail Adams: An American Woman.* Boston: Little Brown & Co., 1980.

Andrews, William L., and Henry Louis Gates Jr. *The Civitas Anthology of African American Slave Narratives.* Washington, DC: Civitas/Counterpoint, 1999.

Antin, Mary. *The Promised Land: The Autobiography of a Russian Immigrant.* Princeton, NJ: Princeton University Press, 1911.

Baskin, Judith R., editor. *Jewish Women: Historical Perspective.* Detroit: Wayne State University Press, 1991.

Battle, Kemp. *Hearts of Fire: Great Women of American Lore and Legend.* New York: Harmony Books, 1997.

Bennett Jr., Lerone. *Before the Mayflower: The History of Black America.* New York: Penguin Books, 1961.

Berlin, Ira. *Many Thousands Gone: The First Two Centuries of Slavery in North America.* Cambridge, MA: Belknap Press of Harvard University Press, 1998.

Blassingame, John W. *Slave Testimony: Two Centuries of Letters, Speeches, Interviews and Autobiographies.* Baton Rouge, LA: Louisiana State University Press, 1977.

Burrows, Edwin G., and Mike Wallace. *Gotham: A History of New York City to 1898.* New York: Oxford University Press, 1999.

Butterfield, L. H., Marc Friedlaender, and Mary-Jo Kline, editors. *The Book of Abigail and John: Selected Letters of the Adams Family 1762–1784*. Cambridge, MA: Harvard University Press, 1975.

Coan, Peter Morton. *Ellis Island: Interviews in Their Own Words*. New York: Checkmark Books, 1997.

Crichton, Judy. *America 1900: The Turning Point*. New York: Henry Holt & Co., 1998.

Daniels, Roger. *Coming to America: A History of Immigration and Ethnicity in American Life*. New York: HarperCollins Publishers, 1990.

Faragher, John Mark. *Women and Men on the Overland Trail*. New Haven, CT: Yale University Press, 1979.

Fox-Genovese, Elizabeth. *Within the Plantation Household: Black and White Women of the Old South*. Chapel Hill, NC: University of North Carolina Press, 1988.

Franklin, John Hope, and Loren Schweninger. *Runaway Slaves: Rebels on the Plantation*. New York: Oxford University Press, 1999.

Gates Jr., Henry Louis, and William L. Andrews. *The Pioneers of the Black Atlantic: Five Slave Narratives from the Enlightenment, 1772–1815*. Washington, DC: Civitas/Counterpoint, 1998.

Goldberg, Michael. *Breaking New Ground: American Women 1800–1848*. New York: Oxford University Press, 1998.

Hine, Darlene Clark, and Kathleen Thompson. *A Shining Thread of Hope: History of Black Women in America*. New York: Broadway Books, 1998.

Holmes, Kenneth L., editor. *Covered Wagon Women: Diaries and Letters from the Western Trails*. Omaha, NE: University of Nebraska Press, 1989.

Horowitz, Joy. *Tessie and Pearlie: A Granddaughter's Story*. New York: Simon & Schuster, 1996.

Howe, Irving. *World of Our Fathers: The Journey of the East European Jews to America and the Life They Found and Made*. New York: Schocken Books, 1976.

Johnson, Charles, and Patricia Smith, WGBH Series Research Team. *Africans in America: America's Journey Through Slavery*. New York: Harcourt Brace & Co., 1998.

Joselit, Jenna Weissman. *The Wonders of America: Reinventing Jewish Culture 1880–1950*. New York: Hill & Wang, 1994.

Karp, Abraham J. *A History of Jews in America*. Northvale, NJ: Jason Aronson, Inc., 1997.

Kass, Leon R. "The End of Courtship." *The Public Interest*, Winter 1997.

Kazin, Alfred. *A Walker in the City*. New York: Harcourt Brace & Co., 1951.

Kivisto, Peter, and Dag Blanck. *American Immigrants and Their Generations: Studies and Commentaries of the Hansen Thesis After Fifty Years*. Champaign, IL: University of Illinois Press, 1990.

Levin, Phyllis Lee. *Abigail Adams: A Biography*. New York: St. Martin's Press, 1987.

Luchetti, Cathy, and Carol Olwell. *Women of the West*. New York: Three Rivers Press, 1982.

Nagel, Paul C. *The Adams Women: Abigail and Louisa Adams, Their Sisters and Daughters*. Cambridge, MA: Harvard University Press, 1987.

———. *Descent from Glory: Four Generations of the John Adams Family*. Cambridge, MA: Harvard University Press, 1983.

Norton, Mary Beth. *Liberty's Daughters: The Revolutionary Experience of American Women 1750–1800*. Ithaca, NY: Cornell University Press, 1996.

Patterson, Orlando. *Rituals of Blood: Consequences of Slavery in Two American Centuries*. Washington, DC: Civitas/Counterpoint, 1998.

Popenoe, David, and Barbara DaFoe Whitehead. *The State of Our Unions*. National Marriage Project, Rutgers University, 1999.

Rowbotham, Sheila. *A Century of Women: The History of Women in Britain and the United States*. New York: Viking, 1997.

Schlissel, Lillian. *Women's Diaries of the Westward Journey*. New York: Schocken Books, 1982.

Simon, Kate. *Bronx Primitive: Portraits in a Childhood*. New York: Penguin Books, 1982.

Simons, Henry. *Jewish Times: Voices of the American Jewish Experience*. Boston: Houghton Mifflin Co., 1988.

Sorin, Gerald. *The Jewish People in America: A Time for Building—the Third Migration 1880–1920*. Baltimore: The Johns Hopkins University Press, 1992.

Stampp, Kenneth M. *The Peculiar Institution: Slavery in the Ante-Bellum South*. New York: Vintage Books, 1956.

Stratton, Joanna L. *Pioneer Women: Voices from the Kansas Frontier*. New York: Touchstone Books, 1981.

Takai, Ronald. *A Different Mirror: A History of Multicultural America*. Boston: Little Brown & Co., 1993.

Umansky, Ellen M., and Diane Ashton, editors. *Four Centuries of Jewish Women's Spirituality—A Sourcebook*. Boston: Beacon Press, 1992.

Withey, Lynne. *Dearest Friend: A Life of Abigail Adams*. New York: The Free Press, 1981.

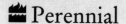 Perennial

Books by Cokie Roberts:

WE ARE OUR MOTHERS' DAUGHTERS
ISBN 0-688-16967-8

Sensitive, straightforward, and perceptive, *We Are Our Mothers' Daughters* celebrates the diversity of choices and perspectives available to women today, and affirms the female bond — a vital, powerful interconnection among all women, whatever their background.

"This book is a celebration of women in their various roles: mother, sister, civil rights advocate, consumer advocate, first-class mechanic, politician . . . . [It is a] paean to feminism and the solidarity of womankind."
—*The Washington Post*

FROM THIS DAY FORWARD
By Cokie and Steve Roberts
ISBN 0-06-095954-1

Roberts presents an in-depth look at the institution of marriage, American-style. Part chronicle of their own courtship, marriage and family life, and part social/historical examination of marriage as an institution, *From This Day Forward* uses the Roberts' personal stories as a springboard for discussing larger issues of love and marriage, work and family, parents and children.

"More thoughtful than the usual celebrity autobiography."
—*Library Journal*

Available wherever books are sold, or call 1-800-331-3761 to order.